D.C. Hopkins

True Cause of All Contention, Strife and Civil War in Christian Communities

D.C. Hopkins

True Cause of All Contention, Strife and Civil War in Christian Communities

ISBN/EAN: 9783337410766

Printed in Europe, USA, Canada, Australia, Japan

Cover: Foto ©Lupo / pixelio.de

More available books at **www.hansebooks.com**

OF

ALL CONTENTION, STRIFE,

AND

CIVIL WAR

IN CHRISTIAN COMMUNITIES.

A BOOK FOR ALL CHRISTIAN TEACHERS AND CHRISTIAN PROFESSORS OF ALL SECTS, NAMES AND CONDITIONS; AND FOR ALL PERSONS WHO DESIRE TO DO THEIR OWN THINKING.

BY

REV. D. C. HOPKINS, A. M.

NEW YORK:
PUBLISHED BY M. W. DODD, 506 BROADWAY,
OPPOSITE THE ST. NICHOLAS HOTEL.
1862.

CONTENTS.

I.

ANTHROPOLOGY: OR, THE IMAGE OF GOD IN WHICH MAN WAS CREATED.—INTRODUCTION............................ 7

II.

TRINITY OF PERSONS IN THE GODHEAD. INCARNATION OF DEITY.. 73

III.

THE LAW OF SIN AND DEATH.—INTRODUCTION................ 131

CHAPTER I.—SIN—HOW ORIGINATED—ITS NATURE.............. 133

CHAPTER II.—THE LAW OF SIN AND DEATH DEFINED............ 140

CHAPTER III.—THE INFLUENCE OF HABIT—HOW CONTRACTED....... 145

CHAPTER IV.—ORIGINAL SIN, ETC., THE TRUE SOURCE OF ERROR..... 147

CHAPTER V.—THE LAW OF SIN LOCATED IN THE FLESH—RELATION OF ADAM'S SIN TO THE CHARACTER OF HIS POSTERITY............ 155

CHAPTER VI.—THE NECESSITY OF DISTINGUISHING BETWEEN THE MORAL AND PHYSICAL SPHERES.................................... 158

CHAPTER VII.—THE DIFFERENCE BETWEEN THE MORAL AND PHYSICAL—THE CONSEQUENCES OF CONFOUNDING THEM................ 163

CHAPTER VIII.—LIMITATION OF THE LAW OF SIN AND DEATH........ 178

CHAPTER IX.—CONCLUSION—A SUMMARY OF RESULTS............... 180

IV.

THE LAW OF THE SPIRIT OF LIFE IN CHRIST JESUS: OR, THE TRUE THEORY OF MORAL RENOVATION.—INTRODUCTION.. 191

CHAPTER I.—THE NATURE OF THE CHANGE—WHAT IS CHANGED?—IN WHAT DOES IT CONSIST?—WHERE IS IT LOCATED?.............. 193

CHAPTER II.—NECESSITY OF THIS CHANGE......................... 200

CHAPTER III.—THE AUTHORSHIP OF THE CHANGE................... 205

PAGE

CHAPTER IV.—THE INSTRUMENT, CAUSE, OR INFLUENCE THAT PRODUCES THE CHANGE.. 222

CHAPTER V.—THE CONVERSION OF NICODEMUS...................... 247

CHAPTER VI.—SUMMARY OF RESULTS........... 259

CONCLUSION.. 270

I.

INTRODUCTION.

We often hear, even at this late period of the Christian era, and in this age of Christian revivals, reformations, and missionary enterprise, the lamentation of the evangelic Prophet; or inquiries quite equivalent. "Who hath believed our report? and to whom is the arm of the Lord revealed?" Isa. liii. 1. If the gospel of Christ is the power of God unto salvation, why has not the world been saved, from the dominion of sin and misery, ages ago? If the law of the Lord be perfect, converting the soul, why are there so many millions of unconverted sinners, in every part of the world; and especially in this Christian land, where the Bible is placed in every house, or offered at the door of every habitation, and where provision is made for teaching every child to read and understand the same? If God our Saviour has, by his word and Spirit, revealed to men for their salvation, his whole will, "in all things concerning their edification and salvation," why do ignorance of his will, transgression of the same, and the consequent sin and misery, constitute the general character and condition of the great mass of mankind, even in the most enlightened and Christian nations of the earth? Why, in every Christian city, community, and country, do the catalogues of crime, against the law of God, the law of nature, the laws of men, and the peace and happiness of human society, exceed, by many fold, the number of Christian conversions in the same communities? Why does not the preaching of the gospel, which has become the exclusive profession, office, business, and livelihood, of a large and very important class of men, sustained at great expense, in all Christian nations, exhibit its legitimate influences, and produce its natural fruits?

On the day of Pentecost, about three thousand were converted, under the first gospel sermon ever preached. And from that day, for two or three centuries, the progress of Christianity through the world was onward and rapid. Wherever the gospel was preached, the immediate results proved it to be the power of God unto salvation. The powers of the world, both church and state, were arrayed against the new religion. The converts were exposed to persecution, exile, and death. But they that were scattered abroad went every where preaching the word; and wherever the story of the cross was told, converts were multiplied, by scores, hundreds, and thousands daily. And Christian associations, or churches, were formed in pagan cities and heathen countries; often before a commissioned teacher had set foot in that country or city. Such are the legitimate influences and natural fruits of preaching the gospel of Christ; preordained and promised by God our Saviour, the divine Author of the gospel; foretold by his prophets from the beginning; witnessed and recorded by his inspired apostles, who received their commission and instructions from his own lips. Such are still its legitimate results, occasionally witnessed and acknowledged, by all Christians, to be the genuine effects of "the law of the spirit of life in Christ Jesus," making sinners "free from the law of sin and death." And such are, and always must be, the results whenever the pure, unadulterated gospel of Christ is addressed to human agents, who have been told, and really know and believe, that they have sinned and are guilty.

But somewhere about the third or fourth century of the Christian era, a very great change took place, in relation to the influence of the gospel on human society. From that time to the beginning of the sixteenth century, the progress of Christianity, in the world, was retrograde. In all that long period, the gospel of Christ seems to have lost its moral influence for meliorating the condition of human society in general, or for saving the world from sin and misery. And even to the present day a vast proportion of the preaching of the gospel, so called, appears to be entirely destitute of any moral or saving influence. Though to every generation have been given glorious and convicting illustrations of the power of the gospel to save souls, families and nations too, from the bondage of corruption, sin, and misery, yet these illustrations have been very limited, and generally of short duration. Even the great reformation of the sixteenth century was scarcely an exception. And whether the present revived missionary enterprise, and multiplied facilities and machinery for spreading the gospel through the world, will result in any very considerable improvement of the general character and condition of the human race, is rendered extremely uncertain, by the present divided and conflicting state of the Church and its theological creeds. Whatever number and variety of influences may be supposed to have concurred in preventing the promised and legitimate fruits of a preached gospel; when " All the ends of the world shall remember and turn unto the Lord: and all the kindreds of the nations shall worship before him:" Ps. xxii. 27, still one thing is certain and obvious, viz: that some primary, efficient, adequate, and widely diffused cause has, for ages, and does still, prevent the evangelizing of the world, and defeat the desired, the predicted and divinely appointed end of sending the gospel into the world.

What is this cause?

It is not of God, in any sense whatever. Resolving it into the divine sovereignty, or purpose, or providence, or permission of God, is not, therefore, a satisfactory solution of the difficulty. God's sovereign will and pleasure, in the premises, is that all men " should be saved, and come to the knowledge of the truth." The will of God, which Christ, the divine Mediator, reveals to men for their salvation, is a perfect remedial provision of law, " converting the soul." It has never yet failed of converting and saving the soul with which it was brought into contact. " The gospel of Christ is the power of God unto salvation, to every one that believeth." " It is able to save your souls." Embodied in human language as in the Bible, it is an essential constituent of that divine personality, the Holy Ghost, whose peculiar office and work it is to regenerate and to perfect the entire work of moral renova tion, in which the salvation of the sinner consists. This cause of failure can not, therefore, be found with God, the Author of the gospel, nor in the nature of the gospel. Nor can it be found in the nature of man, the subject of the desired and promised change. Human nature, the nature of man, as a subject of divine government,—that nature which constitutes him an accountable being, a subject of moral change and of moral retribution,—is the same now as on the day of Pentecost, when the gospel produced its legitimate fruits, and converts were multiplied by thousands daily. It is the same living soul it was in Adam the day that God breathed into his nostrils the breath of life, and man became a living soul; with the same moral endowments, abilities, or susceptibilities, which constituted Adam's human nature. Human nature is the same in all men to-day that it was in Jesus of Nazareth, while God manifested himself in his flesh as the divine Mediator and Redeemer, in the second person of the Godhead. " God sent his own Son in the likeness of sinful flesh, and for sin condemned sin in the flesh." Rom. viii. 3. " For verily he took not on him the nature of angels; but he took on him the seed of Abraham." Heb. ii. 16. He took on him the very nature of those for whom he gave himself a ransom, with all the infirmities and innocent liabilities contracted by four thousand years' bondage under the law of sin and death. But he committed no sin. " Himself took our infirmities, and bore our sicknesses." Matt. viii. 17. " But was in all points tempted like as we are, yet without sin." Heb. iv. 15. And human nature, consisting as it does exclusively in that image and likeness of God in which man was originally created, must for ever remain the same, as unchangeable, and as essential to the existence of man, while he does exist, as the same endowments are to the being of God, while he exists.

But this primary, fundamental, and Bible fact, respecting human nature, is denied, contradicted, controverted, and denounced as damnable heresy. And in the denials and inexplicable dogmas with which this plain historic fact is controverted, the original and only adequate cause of the great failure of the gospel begins to be developed. The general substitute for this gospel truth is designated as the doctrine of original sin. But the forms of language in which it is expressed are as various and as discordant as the sects who claim to be the only orthodox professors of Christianity. One sect or school will tell you that Adam, the first sinner, instead of begetting "a son in his own likeness, after his image," as God commanded him to do, and as the Bible affirms that he did, transmitted, by natural generation, the whole sin and guilt of his eating the forbidden fruit, to each of his posterity. In consequence, they are all born with sinful, guilty natures, under condemnation to eternal punishment. (See Westminster Con. and Cat.) One learned and pious expositor of the Bible tells us that this sinful nature, which he calls "a form of death," and "of all evils the essence and sum," is by God inflicted on each individual of the race, in the first moment of his existence, as the righteous judicial penalty for Adam's eating the forbidden fruit. (See Hodge on Rom. v. 12–21.) Another eminent professor and teacher of theology informs us that human nature is pure sin in the abstract, which each individual of the race created or contracted for himself, by his own agency, in the garden of Eden, at the time Adam ate the forbidden fruit, long before his own existence commenced. (Shedd's Essay.) "Sin a nature, and that nature guilt." And still another celebrated doctor of divinity assures us that God, by his immediate agency, creates every sinful emotion, volition, or exercise of the human soul. Therefore all the sin that exists is agreeable to the eternal purpose and will of God, and can never exceed what he sees to be best on the whole, (all things considered,) and necessary for the glory of God, and greatest happiness of the universe. (See Emmons' Works.)

By these, and a whole category of similar inexplicable dogmas, absurdities, and contradictions, this God-revealed fact, and ultimate antecedent of all knowledge relating to human nature, is wrapped up in profound obscurity, darkness, and mysticism; and totally divested of all motive influence for any moral change or improvement. And every other important or essential doctrine of the Bible is wrapped up in a similar shroud of mysticism. So that the greater part of what is called preaching the gospel, or teaching Christianity, at the present day, and for ages past, has been merely wrapping up the sword of the Spirit in impenetrable folds of mysticism and obscurity; thus divesting the word of God, the gospel of Christ, of all motive influence and saving power; or shielding the hearers against all such influences. And to cap the climax of solecism, absurdity, and contradiction, the teachers and defenders of these dogmas, while they constantly affirm that they are profound and awful mysteries, absolutely inexplicable by human agents, and entirely above, beyond, and out of the sphere of human intellect to know, understand, or comprehend, still at the same time affirm that they are revealed truth; fundamental and essential doctrines of the gospel of Christ; that God himself has revealed them to men for their salvation; and that men are therefore under the strongest obligations to believe them, on pain of eternal punishment.

Now, if a greater absurdity, or a plainer or a more obvious contradiction than this was ever constructed in human language, I have not seen or heard of it. Every person, who knows any thing, knows that to reveal is to make known, to discover, to make manifest, so that those to whom the revelation is made may, if willing to bestow the necessary thought and attention, know, understand, and comprehend, intellectually and clearly, so as practically to believe, whatever is revealed. But what is above and beyond the capacity of human intellect to know or comprehend, is not, and can not be, revealed to man, *not even by infinite wisdom, power, and goodness.*

Here, then, we have the true reason why the world has not been evangelized ages ago, and an adequate cause of all the failures of the gospel to produce its legitimate fruits, and the true, because the moral and primary cause, of all the controversies, conflicts, and civil wars which have distracted and rent the Church into factions, and desolated vast provinces of Christendom, for fifteen centuries past; and which still operates powerfully and extensively, retarding the work of evangelization, and multiplying divisions, conflicts, crime and misery, instead of producing "Glory to God in the highest, and on earth peace, good will to men."

Now, the design of this little book is, if possible, to divest the gospel of Christ of some of these inexplicable dogmas of mysticism; or to show, for the benefit of persons of only common sense and common education, that the system of truth, which God has revealed to men for their salvation, is not, as we are constantly told, a system of profound and inexplicable mystery, but of plain common sense truth, perfectly within the comprehension of every sinner of the race. I hope to show to the satisfaction of every candid reader, whose mind or opinions are not wholly shaped by the conventional influences of creed, sect, or social relations, that every doctrine, truth, or fact, that goes to constitute the entire gospel of Christ, with a single exception, is intuitively and necessarily made known to every sinner; so that he can not be ignorant of it, but by voluntarily, (that is,) wilfully excluding the light of truth from his intellectual and moral susceptibilities. The single exception is the fact that God has given his only begotten Son to be the propitiation for the sins of the whole world. Jno. iii. 16.

The four essays comprised in this volume are a part of a more extended work, prepared for the press several years since, but never published, (except the essay on the Law of Sin and Death.) These four topics are selected, because they are fundamental and essential doctrines of the gospel. The first, as necessarily antecedent to any knowledge or conception of moral government over human animals. The second, as presenting the only Author, or adequate cause, or qualified Sovereign, of a perfect moral government. The third, as naturally incidental to a government over free agents. The fourth, as the only result, perfectly explaining and harmonizing the relations of the preceding. And also because a correct presentation of Bible truth on these topics will furnish a key to divest the entire system of Christianity of every dogma of mysticism.

But the special motive for publishing these essays at this time, is the fact that the unnatural, the savage, and exterminating war, which the slaveocracy of the South is now waging against the government of the United States, presents a perfect demonstration, and an extended illustration, to the civilized world, of the truth of the leading sentiment of this whole volume, viz: that no inexplicable dogma, or incomprehensible mystery is, or can be, a part of the gospel of Christ which God revealed to men for their salvation.

The following inexplicable dogma has been taught, professed, reiterated and defended, for ages, in this land and throughout Christendom, as a fundamental and essential doctrine of Christian theology, viz: That God, in his eternal purpose, according to the counsel of his will, for his own glory, hath, by an unchangeable decree, foreordained whatever comes to pass. And all who teach or profess this dogma as gospel truth, declare that it is a profound mystery of godliness, utterly beyond and above the ability of human intellect to explain, understand, or comprehend. Says the slaveocrat, whatever this holy God of infinite wisdom, power, and goodness, chooses and unchangeably foreordains, must necessarily and continually exist, and must be a righteous, just, and beneficent divine institution. Our domestic institution of chattel slavery has been, for ages, among the comings to pass; and must therefore be a divine institution, right, just, and beneficent: an inalienable, Godgiven right of every slave-owner. This inference of the slaveocrat is perfectly logical and incontrovertible; and if the dogma of universal predestination be Bible truth, it is as evangelical as it is logical. But this dogma is not truth at all, but a falsehood, an absurdity, involving a positive contradiction, and a blasphemous slander of God, the moral Sovereign of the universe. For God, in the perfect exercise of his infinite wisdom, power, and goodness, has in every precept, every utterance and expression of his revealed will contained in the Bible, positively and peremptorily forbidden the commission of sin, in every relation that exists among the subjects of his moral government on earth. And in all the events of his gracious administration, wherever it is possible for him to indicate his purpose, will, or desire, in this behalf, to human intellect, he has manifested his infinite antagonism to all sin, and all its consequent misery. And common sense, as well as the Bible, teaches every moral agent that perfect antagonism is the only relation that an infinitely wise and good moral Sovereign can sustain to sin and misery. Therefore the dogma which affirms or implies that God purposed, willed, foreordained, permits, or consents to the commission of sin, is a complete parallel, in moral character, magnitude, and tendency, to the affirmation of the old serpent to Eve, "Ye shall not surely die." Does the God of truth and grace use false pretenses? "God is light, and in him is no darkness at all."

Now the spirit, temper, means, manner, and avowed purpose of the South, in waging this war of slavery against civil and religious liberty, clearly exhibit and illustrate perfectly the moral influence of such incomprehensible mysticism, when constituting a part of the religious creed of sinful men. As their pretended divine institution and special rights are founded on falsehood, the only appropriate means, method, and aim in defending and propagating them, are lying, treachery, fraud, perjury, theft, assassination, murder, and utter extermination of every thing that obstructs their course, or even doubts the sustaining dogma. The most brutal and fiendish passions are the only moving inspiration of such warfares; and the most demoralizing and destructive results to the authors and their agents can alone be anticipated. Such have been the nature and consequences of all the conflicts, controversies, and wars that have been waged to sustain or defend inexplicable religious dogmas, or rights founded on them or defended by them, ever since they began to be mingled with Christian theology. And such must be the results, for aught we can conceive, till the pure light of truth shines again from the golden candlesticks. Such, from the beginning of the world, have been the results of receiving inexplicable mysticisms for religious truth.

Let any reader carefully examine the history of the Church, from the fourth century to the present time, comparing it with the civil history of the nations, states, and communities which have constituted what has been called Christendom, or the Christian world, in distinction from the pagan, and these general facts will be seen standing out prominent in every age and country of Christendom during that period: 1st. That the greatest part of the civil wars that have distracted, impoverished, depopulated, and ultimately extinguished those states or nations, were waged to support or propagate some unmeaning, inexplicable, and incomprehensible theological romance; or to establish and defend some special right, prerogative or temporal interest, distinction or dignity; supposed to be derived to the claimants from, or supported by these theological romances.

2. In conducting such civil wars, the same means, the same manner, and the same malignant spirit, have been generally exhibited, which the South have thus far exhibited in the present war. Especially have lying, perjury, fraud, treachery, secret assassination and murder, been the common means, methods, and influences in creating and conducting such wars; and such means and influences have been so long used and justified, by professors and teachers of Christianity, that for ages it has been an established principle, or law of moral action and practical piety among the most numerous Christian sect on earth; that no faith is to be kept with heretics, and that to convert or destroy a heretic by such means, is the most meritorious service, the faithful can render to God or his church.

3. The only and invariable influences and results of all such conflicts, as they are seen cropping out, in all subsequent history, are invariably demoralizing, unchristianizing, uncivilizing, dementating, depopulating, impoverishing and destructive. The present condition of Western Asia, and Northern Africa, compared with the same at the close of the fourth century, furnish a full and perfect illustration of this truth; if not, just look at the state and condition of society in the seceding states.

The civil war, in which this whole country is involved, is of this peculiar nature. A special right, prerogative, or exclusive privilege is claimed, as derived to the claimants from a theological romance; viz: The dogma of universal predestination. And the right of propagating and entailing the divine institution to all generations, is sustained by the other kindred dogmas, or romances, called original sin, or sin and guilt transmitted through a thousand generations and attached to the person, antecedent to all knowledge, volition or action of the subject. Chattel slavery, the divine hereditary right of converting human beings into brute animals, mere things totally divested of personality, or personal rights, is the only right claimed or controverted in this conflict. This is the only question to be resolved; the only interest to be secured by this infatuated rebellion. And the solution must depend on the truth or falsehood of these theological dogmas. If they are divine truth, slavery is a divine institution, and will exist while truth and men exist in this world. If they are fiction, romance and falsehood, slavery must be annihilated before the world is evangelized, or this country enjoys peace with civil and political freedom. I believe that these, and their cognate inexplicable dogmas of theological romance, are the sole, the moral, the true cause, and the primary antecedents of all the hereditary sovereignty, royalty, nobility and aristocracy, and all the special divine rights, honors, prerogatives and dignities, which men now claim, or have done for ages either in church or state. I know of no specialties in the administration of grace to sinful men. The free gift of complete salvation from sin and all its consequent miseries, through the redemption that is in Christ Jesus, is a gift to the whole world without exception, and is proffered alike to every sinner of the human race, on the same condition of believing in him. "Look unto me and be ye saved all the ends of the earth." "For he is the propitiation for our sins: and not for ours only, but also for the sins of the whole world." And I hope to show that there are no inexplicable dogmas, or incomprehensible mysteries in the gospel of Christ or the religion taught in the Bible. But as long as these theological fictions are everywhere taught as fundamental doctrines of Christianity, we must expect to see Christendom continue to rival heathendom in fiendlike strife and human bloodshed.

In the discussion of these topics I have endeavored to state the plain simple truth on each topic, just as taught in the

Bible, but divested as far as possible of inexplicable dogmatisms, and incomprehensible mysteries, and expressed in such plain language that every person of common sense and common education may, if willing to bestow the necessary thought and attention, understand, comprehend, and practically believe the whole truth of the gospel. But let every reader be apprised and remember that such is the peculiar nature, the exalted relations and infinite importance of these topics, that without special attention, deep interest, and intense, continuous thought, no human intellect can understand or believe practically any truth relating to these subjects.

Every attentive reader will readily perceive that these essays were composed before the present rebellion and civil war commenced, or was apprehended as probable in the present generation; and that the writer could, therefore, have had no reference to any political question, relation, or controversy. And it must be equally obvious that he could have had no special allusion to any particular sect, division, or denomination of the Christian Church; for he knows of no sect or denomination, who call themselves Christian, that do not profess to believe, propagate and defend, some more or less, theological or metaphysical fictions, as revealed and essential doctrines of the Christian system. The principal object in discussing these topics has been to solve the inquiry, "Why has not the world been evangelized ages ago?" And having arrived at a satisfactory solution in the fact that the gospel of Christ, the system of revealed religion taught in the Bible, has been corrupted, vitiated, and thus divested of its legitimate and true motive influence, by the addition of numerous inexplicable and incomprehensible dogmas of mysticisms; mere fictions of depraved human intellect; the only remaining desire was to aid in some degree the removal of these corrupting redundancies.

Perhaps some persons may not readily apprehend the causal relation between assenting to theological fictions as religious truths, and civil war in Christian communities. It may, therefore, not be amiss to say something here respecting the medium and process of such causal influence. Every one knows, who knows any thing at all about human animals, that God has endowed them, in common with all other animal organizations, with a perfect array of all the instincts, appetites, and passions necessary for their well being, and adapted to their particular sphere of animal existence. Among these, the most essential and most influential on the condition of the human animal in this life, are self-love and acquisitiveness, or, in Scripture language, pride, which is represented as the condemnation of the devil, and the love of money, which is the root of all evil. These are the crying sins of all civilized and Christian communities, and are regarded as the cause of most of the crime and misery of the world. But these animal endowments are in themselves perfectly innocent and absolutely necessary to the existence and propagation of human animals on the earth. The first is the prescribed measure of my love to my neighbor; and, therefore, as right and as innocent as loving my neighbor according to the law of God. The other is the first and indispensable duty of every moral agent that walks on this footstool, enforced by the penalty of starvation if neglected. Their exercise or indulgence becomes sinful only when intemperate, and it becomes transgression of the law of God.

But through the motive influence of the physical depravity of the animal organization, and of the social surroundings and examples of human society, and (I am sorry to say) through the motive influence of parental cultivation and instruction, these animal passions become controlling and governing influences of the entire human being, antecedent to the development of any moral susceptibilities of the living soul, or any capacity of giving moral character to his actions; so that the intemperate indulgence of these animal passions becomes the object of his strongest affections, and the principal source of his pleasures. And continuing thus when his moral susceptibilities are developed, this intemperate and unlawful indulgence becomes his supreme object of pursuit; his idol, his God, his sin and destruction. Through this medium, and in this method, the physical depravity consequent of Adam's fall, and descending from him by natural generation to all his posterity, presents motive influence to the living soul, to induce or tempt it to commit sin, and thus create moral evil, moral depravity or sin.

Every human agent of common sense who has read the Bible and thought on the subject, knows intuitively, and by the reiterated testimony of the Bible, that God has endowed the living soul, which he added to the human animal when he breathed into his nostrils the breath of life, with a perfect array of moral faculties, susceptibilities or powers, necessary and perfectly adapted to the well being of his immortal nature, and to the high sphere of glory and felicity for which he was created. Among these moral endowments is the ability of perceiving, appreciating, loving, admiring, enjoying, and adoring moral beauty, virtue, goodness, and thus participating in perfect happiness, felicity or bliss. These religious susceptibilities are among the strongest passions of the living soul, because they are the most essential to his well being and perfect felicity. In the right use and exercise of these endowments alone does the soul live and enjoy that eternal life which is the gift of God, through Jesus Christ our Lord.

Now, this living soul, with its moral and intellectual endowments, constitutes man's entire human nature, his entire manhood, his entire subjectibility to moral government, to obligation, to reward and punishment, in contradistinction from his animal nature and physical being. Every thing that pertains to the creature man, besides the living soul and its essential endowments, is mere animal and physical machinery, created for the temporal use and accommodation of the soul during its probation in this world. The moral endowments or susceptibilities of this living soul are that image and likeness of God in which man was originally created, and which constitute him a subject of moral government, and render him capable of obligation, reward and punishment. These moral susceptibilities of the living soul are the only thing in the creature man, as he came from the hand of the Creator, in which any image, likeness, similarity, or resemblance of the invisible God can be shown to or perceived by human intellect. God is capable of perceiving, appreciating, and delighting in the beauty, excellence, and utility of moral rectitude, virtue, holiness, and truth. Man also is capable of perceiving, appreciating, and delighting in the same beauty of holiness. In these endowments the living human soul presents a perfect image of God, as like to God as God is like to himself, with the single exception that in God they are infinite, in man they are finite.

There are two kinds of influence in the universe by which these moral susceptibilities of the living soul may be put in motion, or excited to action. One is the motive influence of truth. The other the motive influence of falsehood. The first is the influence which God uses to work in saints both to will and to do of his good pleasure. And it is the only influence which God ever uses to produce right action in any human agent, or to produce any moral change for the better in any sinning subject of his government over this world. The second is the only influence which the devil and wicked men ever use, or can use, to work in sinners to will and do evil, or commit sin. It is the only influence that ever did or can influence men to commit sin. By this influence alone the one man, and he the first man, was tempted to commit sin, and thus sin entered into the world. And sin has never been committed since, or existed in the moral character of any human agent, but as the author of it has been excited by the motive influence of falsehood to transgress law. "And the serpent said unto the woman, Ye shall not surely die." But of God it is written, "Of his own will begat he us with the word of truth, which is able to save your souls." "Sanctify them through thy truth; thy word is truth." No intelligent human agent ever acts without motive. When the motive influence of truth is obeyed, the action is right, good, or holy. When the motive influence of falsehood is obeyed, the action is wrong, bad, or sinful. The agent gives moral character to his action by choosing which to obey. When, therefore, the moral susceptibilities of the living soul begin to be developed, so that the agent is capable of giving character to his actions, if then fiction, romance, mysticism, error, or falsehoods in any form be assented to as religious truths, or adopted as essential and fundamental parts of the gospel, all the religious emotions, affections, passions, and volitions of the living soul, are put under the motive influence of falsehood. The agent is deceived, or tempted, or enticed by his own animal lusts, viewed in the mirror of falsehood, to commit sin, and thus put himself voluntarily under the law of sin and death. The pious mother, the religious teacher, and the learned, the holy, ordained ambassador of Christ, iterates and reiterates from the pulpit the inexplicable dogmas of mysticism, affirming them to be cardinal doctrines of the Bible, and essential truths of the gospel of salvation, and the undeveloped moral agent assents to them as such, often before his moral endowments are sufficiently developed to distinguish between right and wrong, sin and holiness. Thus the habit of assenting to theological fictions has become a second nature, and is practiced without thought or reflection. Their truth and certainty are taken for granted, just as his own existence, or the existence of matter, is; such, for example, as the dogmas of original sin, universal predestination, imputation or transfer of moral character from one agent to another, God existing in three persons, eternal generation, eternal sonship, and such like. As all such dogmas, being inexplicable and incomprehensible by human intellect, are necessarily undefinable in human language, and will therefore readily, and with very little mental effort, take any form in the depraved and perverted human imagination, (where they were generated,) or assume any relation, and adapt themselves to any association, interest, or habit, which the depraved animal appetites and passions may have adopted as their supreme idol, thus every inexplicable or incomprehensible religious dogma, romance, or mysticism thus received as gospel truth, furnishes a very convenient and most powerful array of motive influences to confirm, sustain, strengthen and justify a transgressor in the grossest, most destructive and damning sins which the devil or sensual lust can conceive. Because the only influence of falsehood, received or adopted, or assented to as religious truth, must necessarily be to unite the entire moral force of all the religious susceptibilities of the living soul with the depraved and perverted instincts, appetites, and passions of the flesh in the production of sin and misery. Thus the whole agent, with all his endowments, both physical and moral, animal and spiritual, is religiously, devoutly, and piously engaged in doing evil and producing misery, under the delusion of falsehood that he is doing good, serving God and his country.

Now for an illustration. Says the advocate of slavery, "God hath foreordained whatsoever comes to pass." What God ordains is right, good, just, and beneficent. Chattel slavery has always been found among the comings-to-pass. It is, therefore, a divine ordinance; a good, wise, just, and beneficent institution. God imputes the guilt of eating the forbidden fruit to all the posterity of Adam, and the guilt of Ham to Canaan and his posterity, thus constituting a new and different race of human beings, adapted only to a state of slavery. "Cursed be Canaan; a servant of servants shall he be unto his brethren." And thus entailing slavery on all his posterity, to the end of time.

But Mormon polygamy, Mohammedan unitarianism, and Nicene trinitarianism are, and have been among the comings-to-pass, and the causes of endless contention, strife, war, and misery. The dogma of "One God existing in three persons; universal predestination; original sin; and imputation or transfer of moral character, guilt, and merit;" with their concomitant mysticisms and falsehoods, have, by their motive influences, produced more contention, war, bloodshed, and misery in Christendom, since the third century, than all other causes. Whether slavery, or some other physical or sensual interest, may have been the proximate cause or not, nothing but the motive influence of falsehood, received and assented to as religious truth, could ever bring all the religious and moral susceptibilities of the living soul, with all the intellectual and physical forces of a rational being, to unite in such fiend-like strife as now distracts this Christian nation. Such is the causal relation between assenting to falsehood and civil war. Nothing can result from the motive influence of falsehood, according to the law of nature and of nature's God, but sin and misery.

ANTHROPOLOGY:

OR,

THE IMAGE OF GOD IN WHICH MAN WAS CREATED.

"So God created man in his own image, in the image of God created he him; male and female created he them."—Gen. i. 27.

This history of the creation was written some five and twenty centuries after the events had transpired. It is here recorded by Moses as an introduction to the Bible. The Bible is acknowledged by Christians in general, and by all Protestants in particular, to be a revelation of the will of God to men, as a rule of faith and practice in all their moral relations during their probation in the flesh. It was therefore proper to contract this account of the creation of the material world, or the physical system of the earth, into the shortest compass consistent with this design, and to include in it only those facts which are necessary in order to understand the nature, the relations, the obligations, duties and destinies of men as subjects of moral government.

The first fact affirmed in this account of creation is, that God is the Author, the Creator, the original and proximate cause of the existence of the material world. "In the beginning God created the heaven and the earth." The next fact to be noticed is, that the whole process of the organization of the physical system of the world consisted in loco-motion of the ultimate atoms of which its various substances are composed. "And God said, Let there be light." "And God divided the light from the darkness." "And God said, Let the waters bring forth abundantly the moving creature that hath life." "And God said, Let the earth bring forth the living creature after his kind—and it was so." Another important fact worthy to be noticed in this place is, that God, by his own immediate and direct agency, created man, both soul and body, and gave him all his natural endowments, susceptibilities, faculties, or powers. "And God said, Let us make man." "So God created man." "And the Lord God formed man of the dust of the ground, and breathed into his nostrils the breath of life; and man became a living soul." Gen. ii. 7.

Two additional facts are affirmed in the text; first, that God created man in his own image; second, that God endowed man with the capacity of multiplying and perpetuating his own nature. "So God created man in his own image, in the image of God created he him; male and female created he them."

As these two facts are cotemporaneous, first in the order of nature, first in the order of time, first in the book of revelation, first in the intuitive perception of human intellect, and inclusive of all that God has ever revealed to us concerning man's substantive being, it is obvious that all our anthropology, or correct knowledge of human nature, that is, our real knowledge of ourselves, our relations, our obligations, duties and destinies, must grow out of these facts, as first principles, and must be connected with, depend upon, or re-result from these facts, as the tree depends upon and grows out of its root or germ. It is, therefore, of the utmost importance that we should attain clear and correct conceptions of these primary facts. A mistake with respect to such fundamental truths may involve our whole scheme of anthropology in error, mysticism, and absurdity. This image of God in which man was created must include the highest, most perfect, and useful or valuable endowments of human animals. It must also constitute the nearest, the highest, and most important relations between God and men. For what can be higher, more important and valuable, than that which is so like God as to constitute his very image? Or what in man can be nearer to God, or higher and more important in relationship, than to bear the image of the infinite God?

But all the knowledge we may acquire, or that God may condescend to bestow upon us, concerning himself, his attributes, his will, his government, law and administration, during our probation in the flesh, must be perceived by us, or acquired, conceived, inferred or received, in the exercise or by the use of those endowments which God conferred on man in this original act of creation, and which go to constitute this image of God. For example, if God bestows on us the knowledge that he is the moral Governor of the world, our conception of that truth must necessarily consist of our intuitive consciousness of the obligation of obedience, resulting from the relation of creatures, which we sustain to God the Creator, extended in thought to the whole race, and abstracted from all limitation and imperfection. And we possess the knowledge of that fundamental truth in theology, in, by, and through the exercise or action of that moral endowment or susceptibility which God gave us and made essential to our nature, in the act of creation mentioned in the text whereby we became a living soul. It must, therefore, be obvious that a mistake in relation to this image of God in which man was created may involve our whole system of theology in error, contradiction, and absurdity. If we conceive, affirm and believe, that this image of God consisted in something in which it did not consist, we of course conceive a fiction, we affirm a falsehood, we believe a lie. Our theology, our professed knowledge of God, is mingled with falsehood and mysticism.

It becomes us, therefore, to approach this subject divested of all conventional, sectarian, and secular influences; moved only by the love of God and benevolence for lost men. And may that light of truth which constitutes the infinite wisdom and moral omnipotence of God direct us in all our investigations.

The text presents two subjects of inquiry to be solved.

I. What constitutes this image and likeness of God in which man was created?

II. What are we taught by the phrase, "Male and female created he them?"

I. This image and likeness of God in which man was created must have consisted in something that would distinguish him from and raise him above all the other species of organic beings belonging to this material system. It must have been something that would qualify and render him fit and worthy to be invested with the possession of and dominion over all the earth, and all its contents. This is the declared design of the divine counsel in giving man this image and likeness of his Maker. "Let us make man in our image, and let them have dominion over the fish, the fowl, the cattle, and over all the earth, and over every creeping thing that creepeth upon the earth." And as soon as man was created, God invested him with these high prerogatives and privileges. "And God blessed them, and God said unto them, Be fruitful and multiply, and replenish the earth and subdue it: and have dominion over the fish, the fowl, and over every living thing that moveth upon the earth." No other reason, motive or design is mentioned, or can be conceived, for man's being endowed with this image while in the flesh, but to distinguish him from and qualify him to exercise dominion over the animal tribes of the earth. It must, therefore, have consisted in something of which no likeness can be found in any other species of animal organization. For if the likeness of it may be found in any animal organization, it could not be an image of God, for God is a pure Spirit. The supposition would degrade the Deity to the likeness of a brute animal. But the Scripture saith, "Thou madest him a little lower than the angels; thou crownedst him with glory and honor, and didst set him over the works of thy hands." Heb. ii. 7.

2d. The image of God, in which man was created, must have consisted in something essential, both to the divine and human nature. Something without which, God neither could nor would be God; and something without which man neither could nor would be man. Because, whatsoever is only incidental or contingent with God, can not constitute or amount to any image or likeness of God. And the same holds true in the case of man. For in that case God might exist for a time without the existence of his own image or likeness; which is an absurdity. And man, also, in that case, may be truly and perfectly a man, though entirely destitute of his own likeness or the image of God, which involves a contradiction and a very gross absurdity. Besides, whatever was produced in man, by the creating act of God, must also be an essential constituent of his nature. Without it he must cease to be a man, cease to exist as a man, or cease to be at all. Hence the image of God, in which man was created, is an essential part or constituent of his nature. Without it he would not, can not be, and is not the creature of whom God said, Let us make man in our image. Therefore God affirms in his word that man, irrespective of his character, condition, and every thing incidental to him, "Is the image and glory of God." 1 Cor. xi. 7. And all human beings, who develop manhood in the flesh, whatever their character, condition, or circumstances, whether believers or infidels, Christians or pagans, heathen idolaters or worshippers of the true God; whether good or bad, sinful or holy, are in the Bible; in all history, in the providence of God, and in the administration of his grace, perfectly identified, as the individuals whom God created on the sixth day. Therefore, every individual of the race when he commences actual existence, commences it in the image of God; and as long as he exists he must sustain that image, for the moment he ceases to sustain that image, he ceases to be one of that race; because that image of God is the distinctive trait of that species of animal called man. The child that is born to-day, and dies to-morrow, is born in the image of God, as truly as Adam was created in that image. If not, he must be a mere brute animal, not one of the human race. But he is not of any mere animal or inferior species of organic matter. He is one of those identical individuals whom God created on the sixth day, whom he fitted to exercise dominion over all the earth, and every living thing that moveth upon the earth: and whom he blessed and said unto them, Be fruitful, and multiply and replenish the earth, and subdue it, and of whom he declared the kingdom of God consists. Luke xviii. 16. Hence,

3d. This image of God in which man was created, could not have consisted in any attribute, endowment, susceptibility or faculty belonging to his physical nature or his mere animal organization, nor in anything he possessed in common with brute animals or inorganic matter. Because the very design of this image and likeness of God, as expressed in the context, and clearly taught in other scriptures, was to distinguish man from, and raise him above the whole material system of this earth, and qualify him to exercise dominion over all the living, sensitive beings that move on the earth: and also to qualify him for the still more exalted and sublime employment, and ultimate end, of glorifying God and enjoying him for ever. "For of him, and through him, and to him, are all things: to whom be glory for ever. Amen." Rom. xi. 36. "Whether therefore ye eat or drink, or whatsoever ye do, do all to the glory of God." 1 Cor. x. 31. As this material world was created for the glory of God, and as man was created to rule over, to dispose of, and use it for his own benefit, so as thereby to glorify God and ultimately to enjoy him for ever: man was necessarily related to both God and the material world around him. It was proper, therefore, and necessary that his endowments should capacitate him to perform all the duties, and discharge all the obligations resulting from these relations. But his physical endowments, including all the susceptibilities and faculties which he possesses in common with brute animals, or inorganic matter, do not capacitate him, or give him ability to perform, or even conceive, feel, or understand any duty or obligation resulting from his higher relation to God. No mere animal, as far as we know, is capable of forming any conception of a God, or of moral obligation. And certainly there is no similitude, resemblance, or likeness between God, the infinite Spirit, and material substances, however perfectly and skilfully organized. Therefore the whole physical universe, with all its material furniture, with all the animal endowments of man himself, are necessarily and totally excluded from constituting any part of this image and likeness of God in which man was created.

4th. It did not consist in any thing pertaining to his mere

intellectual endowments, or his susceptibilities of receiving knowledge, of understanding, of reasoning, and judging of material things; nor did it consist of anything pertaining to the faculty of willing, or of originating locomotion or physical change. For all these endowments to man possesses in common with the inferior species of animal organization, differing only in extent, according as the spheres of their action and well-being differ from each other. "The ox knoweth his owner and the ass his master's crib: but Israel doth not know, my people doth not consider." Isa. i. 3. "Yea, the stork in the heaven knoweth her appointed times; and the turtle and the crane and the swallow observe the time of their coming: but my people know not the judgment of the Lord." Jer. viii. 7. These prophets ascribe to both birds and beasts intellectual emdowments, or susceptibilities of knowledge, of understanding, of judging, willing and doing, or of originating physical change. And the contrast which they make between the use of these endowments by the brutes and birds, and by God's professing people, is perfect proof that these endowments are of the same nature in man as in the brutes and birds. Otherwise the charge of blame which God makes against Israel, and which he sustains and illustrates by this contrast, are false and slanderous, and they can justify themselves from blame against all such proof by pleading the difference, if indeed there be any essential difference in these natural endowments, as they exist in men, and in other inferior animals. But this can not be, because "the judgments of the Lord are truth and righteous altogether." Ps. xix. 9. Therefore, nothing that pertains to any of these endowments distinguishes man from other species of animals, or raises him above them in any respect whatever.

As far as we are acquainted with the intellectual physiology of brute animals, they generally exhibit these capabilities, within their own proper sphere of action, where their well-being lies in a more perfect condition for right action, or in a superior degree to what man has ever exhibited in the flesh. But as these capabilities are all endowments of physical organizations, that is, of mere animal substance, therefore, there must still be an infinite dissimilarity between them and God the infinite Spirit. As they exist in these animals they constitute no image or likeness of God; neither can they as they exist in man.

5th. The image of God, in which man was created, could not have consisted in mere knowledge of things material; for if the endowments which rendered him capable of acquiring knowledge, did not constitute any image or likeness of God, as we have just shown, of course the knowledge acquired by the exercise or use of those endowments could not have constituted any such image or likeness. We can not expect the consequent will exceed the power of the antecedent, or exist preceding the antecedent. If the susceptibility of knowledge may be a mere physical endowment, as every person of common sense knows it may be, and is and must be in relation to all the knowledge of mere brute animals, then the knowledge acquired through that susceptibility may be the acquisition of mere physical being. There may, indeed, be knowledge of a superior kind, which indicates the existence of a superior endowment, or a divine image and likeness of God. As all moral science in man proves that men possess some moral endowments or susceptibilities in common with God. But even this knowledge of moral subjects and distinctions can constitute no part of the image of God in which man was created; for all the knowledge of finite created beings is necessarily finite also, and, therefore, must have had a beginning, and must have been acquired or received by the possessor, or the knowing agent. And every knowing agent on the earth knows intuitively that the very idea of knowledge necessarily involves the conception of a preëxistent intelligent agent, who receives or acquires the knowledge, and in whom the knowledge exists. Man must therefore have existed without knowledge, but with a capacity of receiving or acquiring knowlege antecedent to his first perception, or first mental feeling, which constituted the beginning of his knowledge. But the image of God mentioned in the text, in which man was created, was something produced or brought into existence by the original creative act of God, antecedent to all acquisitions of the creature. He must, therefore, have existed without knowledge before the acquisition of knowledge commenced, or was possible. "God created man in his own image." The image was in the thing created; but the receiver must exist before the reception can commence. The vessel must be finished before it can be filled. The image was in man, the vessel that receives the knowledge. Hence the supposition that the image of God, in which man was created, consisted in knowledge, involves a contradiction, an absurdity. It confounds and utterly destroys the distinction of antecedent and consequent, that is, of cause and effect, by making them cotemporaneous. It was physically impossible that Adam should have known any thing, even so much as the first perception or consciousness of his own existence at the time, or cotemporaneously with his creation. For all the knowledge of creatures is a consequence, or at least subsequent of their creation, or of their actual existence. Their creation, or actual existence, bears the relation of antecedent to the very first idea that constitutes knowledge in the mind. And the antecedent must necessarily precede the consequent. They can not be cotemporaneous in their beginning or creation.

We believe in the omnipotence of God; and that God can put himself in the relation of antecedent or cause to any change or event which does not involve a contradiction. But any supposed change which involves a contradiction or absurdity, is just as impossible for the omnipotent God as it is for the God of truth to lie. The Bible assures us that it is impossible for God to lie; Heb. vi. 18. But why can not God lie? Because infinite goodness is an essential attribute of his nature, and an essential trait of his character; and infinite goodness necessarily includes unchangeable truth. To suppose or affirm that this God of unchangeable truth can lie, involves a flat contradiction, and, therefore, an impossibility. The antecedence and consequence of cause and effect are a law of nature established by this same God of truth; as unchangeable and universal as his own omnipresence. Every proposition, therefore, that makes the antecedent and consequent cotemporaneous, involves a contradiction, and is therefore an absurdity, a falsehood. *A physical impossibility even to Omnipotence.*

Again, it is also certain that knowledge can constitute no part of this image of God in which man was created, for that knowledge in the abstract has no substantive existence in itself. It can exist only as an accident, circumstance, relation or quality of some intelligent substantive agent. All human knowledge must, therefore, exist as an accident, circumstance, relation or quality of a human agent. But knowledge is not an essential quality of a human agent; because men do exist without the knowledge of many things. And if man can exist without the knowledge of one thing, he may also exist without the knowledge of another, and of all things. And there is but one conceivable method in which it is possible, even for Almighty God, to communicate knowledge to a human intellect while in the flesh; and that is, by bringing the subjects of knowledge to act upon the animal organs of sensation. The locomotions produced in these organs convey corresponding feelings or sensations to the mind, or the intellectual endowments or susceptibilities. These mental feelings or ideas, thus acquired, furnish the materials of all the knowledge of all men as long as they continue in the flesh. By combining, abstracting, comparing, and inferring all the knowledge that men ever attain in this world, or that they ever could have attained in the flesh, had they never sinned, is communicated to them or acquired by them in this method, and through this medium. Even all their knowledge of their own existence, and of their own intellectual and moral endowments, their knowledge of God, their knowledge of moral distinctions, of right and wrong, of sin and holiness, with all their intuitive conceptions and imaginary creations, must be acquired in this method. And all the knowledge which God has ever revealed to man, either by dreams, by visions, by oral language or articulate sounds, or by inward suggestion, must of absolute necessity have been communicated in this method and through this medium alone, because no other medium existed, or can exist, while man lives in the flesh.

I may here be taunted with the declaration that all this is

vain philosophy, or "babblings and oppositions of science, falsely so called." But truth is truth, whether revealed by God or acquired by human intellect, prompted by the love of knowledge. If, however, I have been able to read the Bible correctly, after fifty years of continuous effort to do so, the history of Adam before the fall, and of the whole race since, as far as contained in that book, teaches as plainly as can be taught in human language, that all the knowledge God ever communicated to Adam, or to any of the race, was communicated in this method, and acquired through this medium. We are told that "The Lord God formed man of the dust of the ground, and breathed into his nostrils the breath of life; and man became a living soul." Gen. ii. 7. In this passage are narrated several circumstances of man's creation not mentioned in the text or preceding chapter. These circumstances are related here to teach us some important and essential truths necessary for us to know, in order to understand the nature of our own moral endowments, relations, and obligations: or this passage of Scripture is a vain, childish repetition of insignificant circumstances, entirely useless in an introduction to the higher law. I adopt the first alternative. But what does this passage teach us?

1st. It teaches us that the human animal man was from the beginning a creature of vastly superior importance to all other species of physical organization. That he was created for an infinitely superior destiny. That his animal organization was designed and created for the residence of an immortal spirit during its probation, and to furnish the necessary physical machinery for the development and cultivation of his intellectual and moral susceptibilities. Therefore, God with his own hand, or direct, immediate agency, formed his physical organization. Whereas the earth, by the physical laws of matter, brought forth all the inferior species of animals. "And God said, Let the earth bring forth the living creatures, and it was so." But the Lord God formed man.

2d. We are taught in this passage that man was created with endowments infinitely superior to any that mere animals ever possessed, or could possess or attain: endowments of which there is no likeness, nor the least shadow of similarity or resemblance, in all the physical creation besides. "And breathed into his nostrils the breath of life; and man became a living soul." What are the essential and distinguishing attributes of a living human soul? First, immortality, or a susceptibility, or a capability in himself of continuous existence. That is, no created power in the universe; neither his own will, nor any other finite being can cause this living soul to cease existence. Second, this living soul is endowed with a moral sense, or a capacity or susceptibility of perceiving and understanding the nature and requirements of law, the relations between law and voluntary action, or the distinction between right and wrong, holiness and sin, good and evil, in the high and moral sense of these terms, and of feeling obligation, suffering penal infliction, and enjoying reward of merit; in short, the ability to contract a moral character, and to discern the relations between that character and his future destiny. These are some of the essential attributes of a living soul. Without these attributes of immortality and moral susceptibilities, man never could have become a living soul at all; but must have ranked with the brutes among mere physical organizations, whose spirit, or life, when the body dies, goes down to the dust whence it originated. Now, however, by these endowments he is exalted in his nature far above the entire physical universe; and is fully introduced into the moral sphere, constituted a subject of God's moral kingdom, and endowed with a natural right to all the privileges and immunities of God's moral subjects; and subject to all the responsibilities of the same. This living soul of man, endowed with immortality, when the body dies, ascends to God who gave it. These high, immortal, essential, and, therefore, unchangeable endowments of man, were the immediate consequents of this inflation of the breath of life, immediately from God, into the creature man. Now, the normal intuitions of all human intellect, the dictates of common sense, this text, and the entire scope and meaning of the whole Bible, direct us to look for the image and likeness of God, in which man was created, in the essential and distinguishing endowments of this living soul, which exalt man above the whole material creation, and place him in the sphere of God's moral kingdom. Here, then, in these moral endowments of the living soul we have the entire and sole image and likeness of God in which man was created. And in this moral sense alone consists the only likeness or resemblance to his Maker which can be found in his original nature, attributes, or endowments.

A third truth taught in the passage last quoted is, that a point of time succeeded after man's creation, in which he existed without the knowledge necessary to commence a moral existence or moral agency. The phrase, "Man became a living soul," describes a process or change subsequent to and consequential of God's act of breathing into his nostrils the breath of life. Man, as to his animal organization, existed previous to and during this change, for he was the subject of the change. He had been formed; he had nostrils. He was endowed with the physical susceptibility of animal life. He, therefore, existed necessarily a living creature, actually having animal life. But he had no soul. He was only susceptible of being a living creature like other mere animals. But this divine inflatus commenced a process by which he became a living soul. Not a living creature merely. This process or change added to his nature an immaterial, spiritual, and substantive existence, the essential attributes of which were immortality and moral susceptibilities. Without this process, without this spiritual substance, and without these high moral attributes, the first conception or knowledge of a God, of moral law, moral obligation, moral government, accountability, or any moral distinction whatever, could never have been attained by the human animal. But how did God communicate knowledge to the man Adam, and how did he acquire knowledge?

Some time after he became a living soul, "The Lord God took the man and put him into the garden of Eden to dress it and to keep it." Ch. ii. 15, 16, 17. Here we have the whole process of instruction and acquisition of knowledge minutely and definitely described. And the whole process, method, medium and instrumentality, are identically the same by which human agents at the present day acquire knowledge. The subjects of knowledge were brought into contact with, or near enough to produce loco-motion in the animal organs of sensation. The ideas thus conveyed to the mind furnished the whole material of human knowledge. These were wrought up by combination, abstraction, comparison, and inference. When moral science was to be added, the same material was used. The ideas of material objects were associated with such physical changes as had been witnessed and felt, both pleasurable and painful to physical sense, and from these the nature of law, obligation, and the consequences of voluntary action under motive influence of law, were inferred and illustrated; and man was put on probation to learn the infinite wisdom, power and goodness of God, and the absolute perfection of his law, by a series of experiments. The trees of the garden, and their relations to the animal instincts, appetites, and passions of man, furnished most instructive examples, and were used to convey to the living soul the ideas of the moral consequences of voluntary actions under motive influence of law. Articulate sounds were associated with the ideas or images of the objects of sense, and of their relations and differences; and thus language, the medium of social intercourse, was taught. Every beast of the field, and every fowl of the air, was brought unto Adam to see what he would call them, because he had no knowledge of their existence, nor could have had till they were brought within the ken of his animal senses. But the beasts and fowls existed long before man was created. And the rib also, which the Lord God had taken from man and made a woman, was brought unto the man, because he had no knowledge of her, nor could have had till she came under the inspection of his senses.

But if Adam had been created in knowledge, or with knowledge, or if knowledge constituted any part of the image and likeness of God in which he was created, or if knowledge, in any way or manner, had been the immediate consequence of the creating act of his Maker, then all this description of the process of instruction and acquisition of knowledge is not merely an idle, useless, and childish repetition of insignificant circumstances, but is necessarily and absolutely false. For these primary facts relating to the food necessary to his animal life and comfort, and the nature and relations of his fellow creatures, must have constituted the first knowledge that existed in his intellect. But if this knowledge was created in him, or constituted the image and likeness in which he was created, then this description, which represents God communicating and Adam acquiring this identical knowledge subsequent to the period of time which separated his antecedent creation from his subsequent existence as a living soul, must be false. And it matters not whether that period consisted of a single moment or a thousand years. A single moment marks as perfectly the distinction between antecedent and consequent, as a thousand years. But this description is not false. Every word of it is Bible truth. Is God's truth: and, therefore, eternal, unchangeable, and infallible truth. And the assertion that the image and likeness of God, in which man was created, consisted in knowledge, is not truth, but is a gross error, because it plainly and distinctly contradicts the word of God. Man must know his own existence before he knows any thing else: and he must exist before it is possible for him to have the first conception of his existence. All his knowledge, therefore, is a subsequent matter; and its acquisition entirely an after concern.

In relation to knowledge, we may observe that the knowledge of God is infinite, eternal, unchangeable, self-existent, an essential attribute or constituent of his nature, independent, universal, comprehending all beings, and all relations, events, and circumstances of all things—past, present, and future—and is infinitely perfect in relation to all things, both possible and impossible. But all possible knowledge of created or finite beings, even of the highest archangel in glory, though he may have bowed before the throne of God for myriads of ages, and have contemplated, admired, and studied the nature, attributes, and character of God, and witnessed all his works of creation, providence, and grace, and all the illustrations of his infinite wisdom, power, and goodness, through all those ages, still all the knowledge he can have attained must necessarily be finite, temporary, changeable, incidental, perfectly dependent, limited to a comparatively few particular things and events, and very imperfect, partial, and limited in relation to every thing knowable. Here, then, we have an infinite diversity, dissimilarity and unlikeness, between the knowledge of God and all possible knowledge of finite creatures. And in whatever aspect you may contemplate the knowledge of God, or compare it with the knowledge of creatures, though you may perceive no contrariety, though it may be as truly knowledge in man, as far as it goes, as in God, still this infinite dissimilarity and unlikeness will be obvious and unavoidable. Whosoever, therefore, affirms that knowledge in any creature constitutes any image or likeness of God, greatly errs, and illustrates the influence of the law of sin and death, in retarding the development of his natural endowments.

Another class of facts confirm and illustrate our position in relation to the acquisition of human knowledge. It is a fact, well established by scores and hundreds of experiments, both accidental and designed, that the nervous organs of animal sensation may be totally paralyzed for a time, and yet the living soul continue to live in the flesh, constituting the same identical agent, man, as before. It is also a fact, established by the same experiments, that during this paralysis of the animal organs of sensation, all action of the intellectual endowments of the man, and all use of his capabilities of knowledge, of reasoning, perceiving or thinking, are perfectly suspended: so that the living soul called man is, for the time being, just as incapable of receiving or acquiring knowledge, or of using knowledge previously acquired, as a dead corpse or a block of marble. We infer from these facts that the moral endowments of man, which constitute the living soul, are perfectly dependent on the physical organs of animal sensation, as the only medium through which he may or can receive knowledge during his connection with the flesh, and that the soul may exist independent of and separate from the body; and, therefore, that he may have existed for a time, without knowing any thing at all; and that he did exist subsequent to his becoming a living soul, and antecedent to his first acquisition of knowledge: and, of course, that he was not created in knowledge, or with knowledge.

6th. The image and likeness of God, in which man was created, could not have consisted in righteousness, or true holiness, or in any thing else pertaining to moral character; because all moral character is the consequence of the voluntary action of the subject, acting under the motive influence of the law of God, the only standard of moral rectitude, of right and wrong, of holiness and sin, in the universe. Righteousness, when predicated of a moral agent, like man, signifies the conformity of his voluntary actions to the law of God, including in the word actions, all the emotions, feelings and affections of the soul, which he willingly indulges, together with all his overt actions. When his actions conform to the requirements of the law they are right. They go thus far to constitute right moral character, or the personal rightness of the agent. Holiness when predicated of a finite moral agent, a subject of moral government, like man, signifies precisely the same thing. When predicated of mere things, and their relations, holiness has a more general application, and a more indefinite signification. Its relation to the law of God is more remote and indirect, coming through the agency of some real subject, of moral obligation. In such cases holiness does not signify real moral purity, but only a kind of metaphorical purity, or consecration to a holy use, or service. As when a thing, a place, a person, or animal is consecrated to the worship of God, it is called holy. Not because any moral purity or moral quality is added to it, but because it now sustains a secondary relation to persons and things where moral rectitude is enjoined by law, and expected by the Law-giver. But whenever holiness is applied to man as a subject of God's moral government, it can mean nothing else, more or less, than the perfect conformity of his voluntary actions to the law of God, or the perfect conformity of his moral character to the only standard of moral rectitude and purity.

Therefore we infer, that neither righteousness, nor holiness, nor any thing else that constitutes moral character, when predicated of man, has any substantive existence in themselves. They never did exist, and never can exist, but as the mere quality of a relation. And the relation, which they qualify, is not the relation of a substantive existence, but only the relation of the voluntary action of a substantive being of a peculiar nature, that is of a nature possessing moral endowments, and acting in peculiar circumstances, that is, acting under the motive influence of the law of God. The same is true of all moral character, and of every thing that goes to constitute moral character; it never had any existence and never can exist, but in the relations of the voluntary actions of moral agents to the law of God. Every thing of the kind, right or wrong, holiness or sin, necessarily depends for existence on the relations it qualifies. It never does, nor can exist in the abstract, or separate from the relations it qualifies. For no quality can exist antecedent to or separate from the subject or relation which it qualifies. And no relation can exist antecedent to the subject which sustains that relation. And no action can exist or be performed, or change take place, antecedent to the author of that act or change. So teacheth the Holy Ghost in the word of God. "Whosoever committeth sin transgresseth also the laws, for sin is the transgression of the law." 1 Jno. iii. 4. "Little children, let no man deceive you: he that doth righteousness is righteous, even as he is righteous." v. 7. That is even as God is righteous. But how does God constitute and perpetuate his perfectly holy and righteous character? God creates and maintains a holy or righteous character by always doing righteousness. His volitions and actions are always necessarily in perfect conformity to the law; because his perfect law, the only standard of moral rectitude, consists solely and exclusively in the expression of his own holy will in human language. God's holiness then consists, or is found in the relation of his voluntary action to his own perfect law of moral rectitude. Holiness in man is the same identical quality, produced in the same manner as in God; that is by doing righteousness, or always acting in perfect conformity to the higher law, the only rule of righteousness, or the only line of distinction between right and wrong, between holiness and sin.

Righteousness and true holiness are predicated of Adam. No doubt he was a holy man, perfectly righteous, as far as his character was formed, antecedent to his eating the forbidden fruit. But the question occurs, when and how did Adam acquire these traits of moral character? You say that God gave them to him in the process of his original creation, or that God created him righteous and holy. But God himself says, in the two passages already quoted from 1 Jno. iii. 4 and 7, that every trait of moral character, good or bad, right or wrong, holiness or sin, is created by the voluntary action of the subject, and is found only in the relation, which the action of the subject, sustains to the law of love. That this is the true meaning and intention of the Holy Ghost in these quotations, is confirmed and illustrated by the whole context. By the two great and primary laws of biblical criticism, (the *locus loquendi*, and the *usus loquendi*,) every other interpretation or meaning is excluded. The subject and main obvious design of the Apostle, throughout the chapter, is to state distinctly and illustrate clearly, to the weakest apprehension, the difference between the character of the adopted children of God by grace, and of those who have no claim to such adoption. "Behold, what manner of love the Father hath bestowed upon us, that we should be called the sons of God." "And every man that hath this hope in him purifieth himself, even as he (God) is pure." He then directs the attention of the reader to the ultimate analysis of moral character, and in plain, positive language affirms that all wrong character or sin is the result of actual transgression of the law. Whosoever committeth sin transgresseth also the law, etc. The assertion that sin, in any degree or manner, or any trait of moral pollution exists in the character, nature, heart or mind of a human being, antecedent to his actual transgression of the law of God, contradicts the testimony of the Holy Ghost in this text: and is, therefore, a falsehood. With respect to right moral character, or righteousness and holiness, he, in the seventh verse, affirms that every trait of right moral character, even the first and last, is the result of voluntary action. "He that doeth righteousness, even as he (God) is righteous." He is a child of God, by grace. That renovation of character which assimilates him to God, in character, is begun. The first generic act of the will, in conformity to the requirements of the higher law, constitutes the first holy trait in the character of the regenerate soul. And this first trait of right character, and every subsequent trait, till it rises to perfect holiness, is affirmed in this verse to be the result of right doing. "He that doeth righteousness is righteous." And, therefore, no trait of rightness or holiness can exist or be imparted by God himself antecedent to the right doing of the subject. For he declares in the tenth verse, "In this the children of God are manifest, and the children of the devil: Whosoever doeth not righteousness is not of God, neither he that loveth not his brother." Nothing but right doing, or voluntary action, can constitute a child of God, or give a human agent a single trait of right, moral character. For the Apostle goes on to confirm and illustrate his meaning, and says, verse seventeenth, "But whoso hath this world's good, and seeth his brother have need, and shutteth up his bowels of compassion from him, how dwelleth the love of God in him?" Just as if he had said, that the supposition, that righteousness, or holiness, or any thing else that pertains to right, moral character, can be imparted to, or exist in a human agent, antecedent to his voluntary action under the motive influence of the law of love, is a deceitful and real delusion of the devil: as absurd and as contradictory as to say a man may hate his brother and murder him, as Cain did, and yet be a holy, loving child of God.

Now, no human intellect can conceive how either God or man can put human language together, so as to express more definitely, clearly and strongly, the impossibility of imparting to a human agent the least trait, shade or item of moral character, good or bad, holy or sinful, right or wrong, antecedent to his voluntary action under motive influence of the law of God. This truth is repeated several times, in plain, simple, laconic sentences, in both the positive and negative form, in relation to both good and bad, holy and sinful character.

And the meaning of each sentence is illustrated by examples of the most prominent and conspicuous facts that ever transpired within the sphere of human knowledge. The first, by the most glorious display of infinite love and moral purity ever made in the universe: God manifested in the flesh to take away the sin and guilt of men and destroy the works of the devil, vs. 5 and 8. The other, by the first premeditated murder that ever stained his footstool with human blood, v. 12. And with this positive testimony of the Holy Ghost by John, agrees the whole word of God contained in the Bible. There is not a sentence in the whole book, alluding to the subject, but what represents moral character as consequential of voluntary action under motive influence of the law of God. And Adam's righteousness and holiness, and every thing that constituted his perfect character before he ate the forbidden fruit, was the result of his right-doing under the motive influence of the law. But he had never done righteousness, nor ever had a right voluntary emotion of love towards God or his brother, antecedent to his creation in the image and likeness of God. He must have existed and acted under the law, to acquire the first trait or shade of moral character. But before he could act under influence of law he must have learned what law meant, and what the law required, and must have felt the obligations imposed by the law. But before he could do this, he must have acquired some correct knowledge of the relations whence the obligations and duties imposed by the law are derived; for no duty or obligation is imposed by the law of God, but such as result from the natural or voluntarily assumed relations of sensitive beings. The law of the Lord is also the law of nature, imposed by the God of nature; and is, therefore, perfectly adapted to the natural relations of things. But before Adam could attain any adequate knowledge of these relations, he must have known the existence of the subjects who sustained these relations, and must have acquired some good degree of knowledge of their natures and their susceptibilities of good and evil, pleasure and pain. For example, he must have acquired some knowledge of God, of his attributes and perfection, before he could have any correct conception of the relations of Creator and creature, or could have felt any obligation resulting from those relations, to love and obey his Creator. So of his fellow-creature, he must have known him and understood the relation he sustained and his susceptibility of pleasure and pain, before he could feel any moral emotion towards him, either right or wrong, love or hate.

Here then we have a lengthy chain of sequences, or series of antecedent and consequent changes which Adam must have passed through before he could give any moral quality to his volitions or actions, either right or wrong. But every step in this series must necessarily have occupied time. Because the living soul, Adam, at the time existed in a physical organization, and acted through the medium of the organs of animal sensation and motion. And all change in the physical system consists of locomotion; and loco-motion occupies both time and space. Even the thoughts of the living soul, while in the flesh, must occupy time, because they are finite; they had a beginning, they are successive, and each thought necessarily involves the locomotion of some physical organ.

I believe that Adam was created a perfect living soul, and a perfect human animal, and was perfectly adapted in all his endowments by infinite wisdom, power and goodness, to the sphere he was designed to occupy, and, therefore, capable of acquiring knowledge and performing duty as rapidly as possible for any human animal. But acting in the flesh, every breath of the body, and every thought of the soul, must have occupied time. Therefore, days and weeks, if not months and years, must have elapsed, before he could have acquired sufficient knowledge to act under motive influence of law or begin to acquire moral character. At least, he must have been created in the image and likeness of God, and must have existed in that image before he could begin to do righteousness, or have any holy emotions of love to God or his brother. Therefore, it was absolutely and physically impossible that righteousness or holiness should have constituted any part of the image and likeness in which he was created. Because it is impossible that the consequent should precede the antecedent, or that an effect should exist before the cause that produced it.

But admitting the thing were possible, and that God did create Adam perfectly righteous and holy, his righteousness and holiness could have constituted no image or likeness of God. Because all the righteousness and holiness, and all the right moral character of created agents, during probation, is incidental, changeable, contingent, or uncertain as to duration. Such was all the moral character that Adam possessed before his fall. But God in all his endowments is unchangeable; and contingency cannot be predicated of an infinite being. And the image of God in which man was created, as hath been shown, must have consisted in something essential both to the nature of God and of man, and, therefore, unchangeable. But neither righteousness nor holiness is essential to human nature. For thousands exist without either, as truly men, as the most holy.

Again, the image of God in which Adam was created was the effect of the divine agency in the creating act exclusively, and without the knowledge, concurrence or agency of Adam. But all righteousness and holiness, and every thing included in moral character, as we have proved by the testimony of God, reiterated throughout the whole Bible, is exclusively and wholly resulting from the action of the subject, and is found only in the relation his actions sustain to the law of God. And therefore nothing that belonged to Adam's moral character could have constituted any part of the image of God in which he was created.

7. We, therefore, adopt with the utmost assurance the only remaining alternative, viz: that the image and likeness of God in which man was created, consisted in his moral endowments, or those susceptibilities which constitute his moral sense, and which are generally denominated natural conscience. Or, in other words, it consisted in those endowments or capabilities which enable man to act under the motive influence of law, freely choosing his own course, doing right or wrong, contracting righteousness and holiness, or sin and guilt at his pleasure, and thus constituting a moral character and creating

or deciding his future destiny. These endowments alone place man within the moral sphere of created existence. They alone constitute him a moral agent. They only make him a subject of God's moral government. As soon as these endowments are developed by the necessary knowledge, they render man capable of holy emotions, of right-doings, and of acquiring moral character. But without these endowments, the prohibition of the tree of knowledge, and the consequences of eating of it addressed to Adam, would have been as senseless and destitute of meaning as if addressed to a stone or a block of wood. Without these endowments the thing which God formed of the dust of the earth could never have become a living soul, or a moral agent, or a subject of moral government, or capable of moral obligation, or of doing right or wrong, or of acquiring moral character, or of possessing it by gift of God. And if these endowments were not the identical thing which God imparted to his nature when he breathed into his nostrils the breath of life, and which constituted the image of God in which he was created, then the animal man must have eternally remained a mere brute animal, as destitute and as incapable of the first conception of moral distinction, or quality, of right or wrong, of holiness or sin, as any oyster.

But these endowments were in man and of his nature, before it was possible that he could do righteousness, or have a holy emotion, or possess or reflect the least shade of moral quality. And they do constitute in the very nature of man, the most perfect image and likeness of God that can be conceived in the finite. An image or endowments in the nature of man just as essential to, and as permanent in his nature, as his continuous or immortal existence. And these endowments are just as essential to the divine nature as they are to the human nature. This image of God thus constituted in man, is just as like to God as God is like himself, with the exception of one single trait or circumstance. In man these endowments are finite; in God they are infinite. But man in his finite, appropriate sphere of action, where all his duties, interests and happiness lie, was as God created him, just as capable of knowing and fulfilling his duty and securing all his interests and happiness, as God was of knowing his obligations, and securing his honor, glory and blessedness in the infinite sphere.

Now this is the obvious and the only conceivable meaning (if they had any meaning at all) of the Westminster Assembly, in their larger catechism, when they affirm, with respect to this identical creation of man in the image of God, "Having the law of God written in their hearts, and power to fulfil it." But, whatever they may have meant, the Holy Ghost, by Paul, whom they quote as proof of their affirmation, did undoubtedly intend to teach that man was created with perfect ability to know and perform his whole duty, even as God knows and performs his duty. Rom. ii. 14, 15. "For when the Gentiles, which have not the law, do by nature the things contained in the law, are a law unto themselves: which show the work of the law written in their hearts, their consciences also bearing witness, and their thoughts the meanwhile accusing or else excusing one another." And Solomon also, whom they quote, meant the same thing. Eccl. vii. 29. "God hath made man upright" (or right). His entire nature, with all its endowments and tendencies, was perfectly adapted and fully competent to fill his intended sphere of action with righteous doing, holy character, and perfect happiness.

We can not charitably suppose that the Assembly of Divines intended to commit any solecism, or teach any absurdity, or contradict themselves or the word of God. But we have very good reason to believe that the greatest and best of men, since the fall, may err. This truth we often see illustrated and confirmed in the pulpit, in books, and in public assemblies; when the most learned, pious, and orthodox divines of the land publicly affirm that all the sin in the universe, and especially the sin of kidnapping human beings and selling them into perpetual slavery, treating them like brute animals, is a holy institution of God, unchangeably established from eternity by the counsel of his will, for his own glory and the good of his nature. The Assembly do most truly and correctly affirm the truth, and the whole truth on the subject, in the words we have quoted; and prove by their quotations from Rom. and Eccl. that the image of God, in which man was created, did consist in the moral endowments of his nature, and in nothing else. For if the law of God was written in their hearts, it was absolutely impossible for them not to know intuitively and immediately, on the first conception or knowledge of any relation involving duty, every obligation which the law of God can impose in connection with such relation. This endowment, with power to fulfil the law of God, certainly must constitute the highest, most extensive and perfect moral endowment which Almighty God can confer on any created, intelligent, human, angelic, or super angelic; and the most exact and perfect image of God which created intelligence can conceive. But in the preceding affirmation, that the image of God in which man was created consisted in knowledge, righteousness, and holiness, they say much more than the truth, and actually get a little the start of the Creator himself. God teaches, as we have shown, that righteousness and holiness are the consequents of duty both known and actually performed, or of actually doing righteousness, and loving his neighbor in deeds that may be seen, felt, or tasted, or relieve some need of a brother. But it certainly looks a little solecistic to see Adam performing the works of a moral agent, before he had the endowments that constitute a moral agent, or to see him exhibiting traits of character which belong only to tried living moral agents, before it was possible for him to have known a single relation from which duty could result, or to have felt the least obligation or holy emotion. If they do not contradict themselves in ascribing moral character to Adam before his voluntary action under motive influence of law, they certainly contradict the plain, positive testimony of God, and all the intuitions of common sense. They place the consequent before the antecedent. They affirm the effect as actually in being before the cause existed. Knowledge, righteousness, and holiness must, therefore, be expunged from the image of God in which man was created, and appropriated to his moral character, which was necessarily an after concern both with God and man.

But the Assembly quote Scripture to sustain their assertion that knowledge, righteousness, and holiness constituted the image of God in which man was originally created. With respect to knowledge they quote Col. iii. 10: "And have put on the new man, which is renewed in knowledge after the image of him that created him." And to prove righteousness and holiness as constituents of that image, they quote Eph. iv. 24: "And that ye put on the new man, which after God is created in righteousness and true holiness." These two passages are very nearly parallels. They are by the same author, Paul: addressed to the same class of persons, to saints and faithful brethren in Christ, at Colosse and Ephesus: they both treat of the same subject, the moral characters of professors in Christ: they both employ the same metaphors to express the same things, taken from the history of the original creation of man in our text: and they both teach the same important and fundamental truth. The characters of these saints are expressed by the metaphors of the old man and the new man. The old man represented their former characters as pagans, or unregenerate sinners. The new man represented their renovated characters as faithful believers. To the Colossians the perfect moral character of God is presented under the metaphor of the image of him that created him, as the model after which they were to shape their characters. To the Ephesians the same pattern is presented in a somewhat varied metaphor. The important and fundamental truth taught in both these quotations is, that righteousness and holiness, and every thing else pertaining to right moral character in man, is created, brought into existence, and acquired by the voluntary action of the subject acting under the motive influence of the law of God. "Seeing that ye have put off the old man with his deeds; and have put on the new man, which is renewed in knowledge," etc. Here this truth is affirmed as a positive fact of their past history. "And that ye put on the new man, which after God is created," &c. Here the same truth is affirmed as an indispensable duty. The method by which they put off the old man, and put on the new, was by ceasing to lie, steal, and commit fornication, etc.; that is, by ceasing to do evil, or ceasing to transgress the law. And they put on the new man by speaking truth, working with the hands the thing which is good, or by obeying the law, after the example of Christ. Now, this fundamental truth of all moral government, obligation, and accountability, involves a positive contradiction to the proposition that righteousness and holiness constitute the image of God in which man was created. For the latter proposition affirms that moral character in man is created by the immediate agency of God, without the knowledge, concurrence, or agency of man. And the other, the truth taught in these quotations, affirms that moral character in man is created by his own voluntary agency, under motive influence of the law of God.

So far from giving any support, countenance, or proof of the dogma of original righteousness, these quotations teach the falsehood of that and every other dogma that imputes moral character, good or bad, holy or sinful, to any human agent antecedent to his voluntary action under motive influence of law. In this they harmonize perfectly with all truth, revealed, intuitive, or by rational induction. God creates man in his own image by endowing his nature with the susceptibilities, or capabilities, or faculty of perceiving, understanding, and performing all the duties resulting from all the relations which he sustains; thus bringing him under the motive influence of the higher law, and adapting all the tendencies of his nature to right moral action, or obedience to that law. This is the utmost extent of all that the Almighty God has done, or can do, in relation to the production of moral character in human agents. All the rest is the result of the voluntary action of the human subject. These moral endowments or susceptibilities constitute the only image of God which omnipotence can impart to a finite created being, or of which a created being can be the recipient, or can form any definite conception. If afterwards there exists a similarity or likeness of moral character, that is created by the voluntary action of the subject himself; and depends solely and exclusively on his action.

II. The phrase male and female created he them, teaches this important and essential truth of God's moral system, viz. That man was created with perfect ability to transmit this image of God to his posterity, from one generation to another, to the end of time. This was absolutely necessary for the continuance of God's moral government over this world, and for the perpetuity of the human race, or the existence of mankind beyond the first generation. As the image of God was essential to the nature of man, and was also that peculiar, distinguishing and characteristic endowment, which constituted him a man, in distinction from mere animal existence, which made him a moral agent, and a subject of moral government, if Adam might have lost that image, or might have failed to transmit it to his posterity, or if any subsequent generation of the race might have failed to transmit it, their posterity must necessarily have ceased to be men, or human agents, or moral agents, or accountable beings, or capable of moral government at all, in any way, sense or manner. They must have degenerated into mere brute animals, or creeping things. And God's moral kingdom in this world must have become extinct.

But when God had created Adam in his own image, he "Blessed them, and said unto them, Be fruitful, and multiply and replenish the earth, and subdue it: and have dominion over the fish of the sea, and over the fowl of the air, and over every living thing that moveth upon the earth." Here is a plain, positive declaration, and assurance, of the perpetuity of that image of God, which qualified man to have dominion over the earth, and which constituted him a man, in distinction from brutes as long as man existed, and wherever man should exist, and in whatever state, character or condition man may exist. This truth is confirmed by the entire history, experience and consciousness of the whole race to the present day. If any seeming exception occurs, as of moral idiocy or intellectual imbecility, it is always ascribed, by universal consent, to some physical defect, malformation, disease or viciosity of the animal organs. Therefore, when Adam begat children, he begat them in his own likeness. "And Adam lived an hundred and thirty years, and begat a son in his own likeness, after his image."—Gen. v. 3. And every generation since, have done the same, and transmitted the same moral nature and endowments, or susceptibilities to their posterity.

Now the declaration, by which this testimony of God has been falsified and perverted, viz: that this image and likeness of Adam, in his son, consisted in a sinful nature, or sinful inclination, or innate moral depravity, or original sin, transmitted by natural generation, is plainly a falsehood. It is a falsehood because it contradicts the whole testimony of God on the subject, as has been fully shown. It is false because it contradicts the entire history of the human race. No man was ever born with a sinful nature, or sinful inclination, or innate moral depravity, or original sin; the thing is a physical impossibility, as has been demonstrated, because it involves a contradiction. But all men are born with moral susceptibilities. It is false because it contradicts all human consciousness. Every human being, that ever lived on the earth to develop manhood, was conscious of obligation to do right and avoid the wrong. But no man on earth was ever conscious of obligation, or ever could be, antecedent to his knowledge of law. "For by the law is the knowledge of sin." And also of holiness. "For where no law is there is no transgression." And no obedience likewise. Therefore, any consciousness of moral obligation, moral distinction, or moral quality antecedent to the knowledge of law, is just as impossible, as seeing is, where there are no eyes and nothing to be seen. But without this image of God, consisting in these moral endowments or susceptibilities of creating his own moral character, the two-legged animal called man, would be just as incapable of perceiving any moral quality or distinction of actions or persons, or of feeling moral obligation, or sustaining moral character, as any creeping thing, that ever moved upon the earth.

Finally, the word man, as used in the text, is a generic term, including the whole human race and every individual of the human race. This is perfectly obvious from the use of the plural pronoun in the text, and in the preceding and following verses, and also from the grammatical connections of the context. God said, "Let us make man; and let *them* have dominion." "So God created man in his own image—male and female created he *them*." "And God blessed *them*, and said unto *them*, Be fruitful and multiply and replenish the earth and subdue it." If the word man is not used in the text as a generic term, meaning the whole human race, and if the whole human race and every individual of the human race was not created at that time and by that act and in that image of God, this language of Moses is not truth, but is solecism, absurdity, contradiction, and impossibility. For Eve, not being then formed, it was impossible for Adam to be fruitful and multiply or replenish the earth. It is perfect absurdity and nonsense to talk of a single individual's subduing the earth, and having dominion over every living thing that moveth upon the earth. But a vast number, sufficient to replenish the earth and subdue it were addressed, and spoken of as then created in the image of God. If, therefore, Adam's posterity since the fall, or any part of them, have come into existence destitute of the image of God in which he was created, this passage of the history is false and contradictory. We are, therefore, compelled, in order to reconcile the connections of this context, and avoid absurdity and contradiction, to adopt as the final conclusion that the image of God, in which man was created, consisted exclusively in his moral endowments or susceptibilities, and in nothing else. And that this image of God is an essential constituent of his nature, without which he cannot exist at all. And, therefore, that every individual of the human race commences existence in this image of God just as Adam did, and necessarily retains it perfect and entire, whatever his character and condition may be, as long as he continues to exist.

1st. From this discussion we learn that all moral character, that is, all holiness, all righteousness, all personal rightness of character, all moral character, all moral virtue, all moral purity, and all sin, all moral depravity, moral pollution and guilt, and every thing that pertains to moral character, either good or bad, right or wrong, is found only in, and exists no where else, and is exclusively dependent upon the relation, which the voluntary action of the subject sustains to the law of God. This is true of every moral agent and of every thing, of which moral character or quality can be truly predicated, both in the infinite and the finite. This is truth, because the true God, the God of truth, of whom it is written that "It is impossible for him to lie," hath affirmed it in plain terms. "He that doeth righteousness is righteous." "Whosoever doeth not righteousness is not of God, neither he that loveth not his brother." 1 Jno. iii. 7 and 10. "Whosoever committeth sin transgresseth also the law: for sin is the transgression of the law." 1 John iii. 4, and Eze. i. 5–9. It is impossible, therefore, for righteousness or holiness to exist, but in that relation to the law, which is called obedience or doing righteousness, or for sin to exist, but in that relation to the law which is called transgression. With this agrees the entire teaching of the Bible throughout. The word is not found in that book that intimates the possibility of moral character or quality existing any where else but in the relation of the voluntary action of the subject to the higher law. Every thing that goes to constitute moral character or moral quality, right or wrong, sinful or holy, is represented in the Bible as resultant of the voluntary action of the subject under motive influence of law, or under conscious obligation imposed by law.

I know and believe this teaching of the Bible to be the truth of God, because all the intuitions of those intellectual and moral susceptibilities or endowments which God gave me in the act of my creation, confirm this truth, and perfectly concur with the word of God in compelling me to believe it as divine truth. I mean those intuitions of the human intellect and conscience which are involuntary, necessary and unavoidable by any human agent, when their antecedents are presented to the mind. For example: when a man fulfils a conscious obligation imposed on him by the law of God, he can not avoid feeling justified in the performance of that act. And when he violates an obligation, which he is conscious the law of God imposes upon him, he can not avoid feeling conscious guilt or ill desert for doing it. Again, if moral action or crime is ascribed to any human agent, which he never performed, nor consented to, or had any knowledge of till long after it was performed, he can not avoid knowing and feeling that he is perfectly innocent, unaccountable and irresponsible in relation to that act or crime. He cannot repent of, nor avoid feeling self-complacency for doing the same. These unavoidable intuitions I know and believe, and I can not avoid knowing and believing them to be the first, the highest, the most infallible and unmistakable revelation that God ever made, or can make to any human intellect existing in the flesh. I believe this truth also, because I know, by continuous experiment, for more than sixty years, that it is absolutely impossible for a human intellect, in the flesh, to attain, acquire, or receive even from God, the least perception, or to form the least conception of moral character, quality or distinction, but as resultant of voluntary action, under motive influence of the law of God. This higher law of the Lord is the only thing in the universe which marks the line of distinction between right and wrong, holiness and sin. It runs through every relation that exists, or that can exist among moral agents, finite and infinite, from the throne of Jehovah down to the lowest creature ever endowed with moral susceptibilities. By placing his own act, volition, emotion, or affection in contact, and comparing it with this law of the Lord, the human agent acquires a conception of moral distinction. And by no other way, means or method, and by no other medium or influence, can he attain any perception of moral distinction or quality. By abstracting all limitation and imperfection from this perception of righteousness thus acquired, he obtains a conception of the infinite holiness or moral character of God; and in no other way. Therefore, every supposition of moral character, either holiness or sin, antecedent to voluntary action, under motive influence of law, necessarily involves a contradiction, an impossibility, a falsehood.

2d. We learn from this discussion that the dogmas of original righteousness and original sin, and every other dogma, doctrine, proposition, or affirmation, that predicates moral character of a human agent antecedent to, or separate from his voluntary action, under motive influence of law, are mere fictions of the depraved human imagination, without foundation, without cause, and without existence, either in the nature, relations or accidents of things existent; because all moral character, right or wrong, sin or holiness, exists only in the relation of voluntary action to law, and is impossible in every other place and relation. And yet these fictitious dogmas have been the subjects of long and bitter conflicts and contentions in the Church for ages, producing divisions, persecutions and bloodshed. And they are still a prominent subject of theological conflict, as recently announced in the declaration of war by the Calvinistic allies of New England and New York, against the whole host of Armenian recusants of the United States. See the "American Theological Review, the Introduction." And yet not a single dogma of this whole category has any real connection with or relation to Christianity, or can in any way promote the end of the Christian system. Christianity is a remedial scheme of grace, for the recovery of human agents, from the consequents of a bad character, by an entire moral renovation of the same. But every dogma of this class removes the case of the sinner entirely out of the moral sphere of the universe, and places him and his depraved condition as perfectly in the physical system as any distempered horse or sheep. Such dogmas can only tend to befog, obscure and scandalize the Christian doctrines of the Bible, and hide revealed truth from the light of common sense and human experience. But the Christian system of theology, when divested of such dogmas of mysticism, is a plain, simple, harmonious connection of divine truth, perfectly natural, and easily understood by every human agent of common sense, who is willing and wishes to understand it. And it never fails when the story of the cross is told in plain, common sense language, to exhibit its convicting and saving influence on every guilty soul that listens to it. But this same gospel of Christ, which is the power of God unto salvation, when wrapt up in the fog and mysticism of these theological fictions, may be and is often preached to large congregations of very civilized and cultivated sinners by learned, pious and zealous theologians, in eloquent and interesting sermons, for months and years, without pricking a single heart, or disturbing a human conscience, or converting a sinner from the error of his way. And this has been the case ever since these dogmas were introduced into the Christian theology in the fourth century, because their only tendency ever has been, and must be, to obscure the Christian doctrines, and destroy their moral influence, for the conversion of sinners.

3d. From this disscussion we infer, that a total repudiation, and expunging of all such dogmas from Christian theology, is the only method of saving the character of God, the moral Sovereign, from the blasphemous scandal of creating moral agents and placing them on probation under a government of law, but without ability to form a right moral character, and secure a happy futurity. This scandal is the natural and necessary inference from the affirmation that God created man in righteousness and holiness; or that man needed special upholding grace in his primitive state of rectitude, or that he needs any supernatural power of God, for his salvation, since Christ has made perfect provision for the pardon of all sins past, and for the perfect moral renovation of every believing sinner; especially where the gospel of Christ, which is the power of God unto salvation, is in the hands of the sinner, enforced by ten thousand most powerful motives. And this scandal is also the necessary and unavoidable inference from the declaration that God inflicts a sinful nature or innate moral depravity, involving total inability, for right moral action, upon infants of the human race, in punishment for Adam's sin. Indeed, it is a necessary inference from every dogma that imputes human character to any other cause, influence or antecedent, than the voluntary action of the subject under motive influence of law. The idea that God creates, or causes, or in any way determines or fixes the character of a subject of his government to be, what it ought not to be, and then punishes the subject for its being so, is not only preposterous and absurd, but blasphemous, ascribing to God the very conduct of the adversary. And these scandals drive many honest, sincere inquirers from orthodox places of worship to seek instruction where the true doctrines of the gospel are ignorantly repudiated, in order to avoid these scandalous dogmas. And thus multitudes in this Christian land are induced to embrace universalism, deism, unitarianism, destructionism, and similar delusions, to avoid these scandals which common sense can not believe, and human intellect will not assent to. And such delusions will and must continue to increase, and their deluded followers multiply, with the increase of popular education, so long as such dogmas are inculcated as Christian doctrines.

4th. We learn from this discussion, that man is not that imbecile, nonefficient, physical, intellectual or moral machine, which is often described by the advocates of these inexplicable dogmas. A mere physical intellect, like other material animals, from which God may, by operating the machine with his own direct, immediate agency, and putting on the whole influence of his supernatural omnipotence, force out a small portion of moral virtue, or right moral action, to the praise of his own glory. But which, the moment God shuts off his supernatural power, the devil may occupy, and sit to the tune of moral evil, and pour out a tremendous, overwhelming flood of sin and misery, in spite of the subject and his Maker too.

But when these fictions of mysticism are brushed out of the Christian theology, man stands forth in the light of truth, a living, immortal soul, with intellectual endowments, as far above all mere animal organization as the moral sphere of existence is superior to materialism; and with moral susceptibilities as like his divine Creator as God is like himself, the limitation of finite extent only excepted. By these high endowments man is rendered perfectly able to fill up the entire sphere of agency, for which he was created, with right moral action and pleasurable emotion; thus constituting for himself a right moral character and perfect blessedness; or to fill up his sphere of action with trangression, and involve himself in sin and misery. Thus endowed, we behold him on probation, and the entire responsibility of deciding the contingency of his character and destiny imposed upon his own free voluntary choice. First under an administration of perfect law; and as soon as he had transgressed that law, under the administration of the gracious provision of the same law, which provision constitutes its crowning perfection; but still under the same solemn responsibility of deciding his own character and destiny by the free action of his own will.

This image of God, and this perfect ability in man which it constitutes, are as essential endowments in the human nature of man while he exists, as any attribute of Deity is in the divine nature while God exists. The loss of this image, and the perfect ability it constitutes, by any human agent, must, therefore, constitute the loss of existence or annihilation of that man; for this image of God is the thing which constitutes the two-legged human animal a man and a moral agent, in distinction from brute animals. Therefore, the moment he is divested of this image, he ceases to be the creature man, of whom it is written, "So God created man in his own image, in the image of God created he him." Divested of this image, and its consequent moral ability, he necessarily ceases to be accountable, and is totally incapable of being rewarded or punished.

The law of the Lord, under which every moral agent exists and passes his probationary trial in the flesh, is an absolutely perfect law or system of moral government. The perfection of this law necessarily includes three traits of divine excellence above all other systems, actual or conceivable. 1st. It secures to every obedient subject perfect freedom of choice; so that the emotions, desires, and actions of the subject can never be determined or necessitated by any influence *ab extra* to his own will. 2d. It carries its penal sanction in its own absolute perfection, and executes the same by its own motive influence, independent of all other influences, powers, or causality in the universe. 3d. It contains ample, adequate, and perfect provision for every possible contingency of a perfect moral government. Any system of moral government lacking either of these divine perfections must be exceedingly defective, and totally inadequate for an everlasting dominion. Among the contingencies of such a moral government is the introduction of sin by transgression. The adequate and perfect provision for this contingency is the gracious scheme of salvation, by the atoning sacrifice of a divine Mediator in human flesh, as exhibited in the gospel of Christ. Therefore, immediately on the occurrence of this contingency, God presented himself in the likeness of a human person, and proposed this scheme of salvation to the agents by whom sin entered into this world. They concurred in it, accepted it, performed the conditions of it, repented of their sins, and believed in the promised seed of the woman, the divine Mediator. Their sins were pardoned, their guilt was removed, and they for ever absolved from liability of penal infliction for sins past.

But the physical effects of their transgression on their animal organization could not be removed without the dissolution of the flesh; and this could not be effected without defeating the gracious provision of the law for the salvation of transgressors, till their probation should be ended. For the seed of the woman was the only capable person to give the ransom. Therefore, this physical depravity or viciosity of the animal organization remains, and is transmitted by natural generation to every individual of the race. But this image of God, the moral endowments with which man was created, and the perfect ability which they constitute to fulfil all obligation imposed by law, still remain in every human agent just as they were in Adam on the day in which he was created; and must necessarily so remain as long as that agent exists a moral agent, a man, a subject of moral government, or an accountable creature in any sense whatever. For this image alone constitutes him an agent, a man, a subject of moral government. But in consequence of the physical depravity of the animal organization, these moral susceptibilities are retarded, or wholly prevented in their development; and hence, in a large proportion of the race, they never begin to be developed, and the subjects never begin to contract a moral character in the present life, merely for want of the physical machine necessary for the intellectual being to commence action. But they die in infancy, in idiocy, or in ignorance of a moral Sovereign and a moral government, and are removed to a more wholesome moral atmosphere, for the development of their intellectual and moral susceptibilities; while all who live in the flesh, to develop manhood and moral agency, and begin to form moral character, are still on probation, under the same perfect law of the Lord which converts the soul; but under an administration of pure grace, with perfect ability, both physical and moral, to perform every duty, and fulfil every obligation, which this perfect law may, or can, impose upon them, or which may result from any relation they may sustain while in the flesh.

Thus, in the light of truth, the character and condition of human agents are divested of all those inexplicable dogmas and unmeaning mysticisms which contradict the word of God and common sense, and are often read in books and heard from the pulpit. Such, for example, as that all the human race are suffering from their birth, a sinful nature, total innate moral depravity, guilt, and a complicated load of misery, inflicted by God in punishment of Adam's sin, committed ages before they existed. Or, that the whole human race are now on probation, under the most solemn obligations to fulfil all righteousness, and at the same time totally destitute of moral ability to put forth a single right emotion or act of moral character. But every human agent of mature age and common sense may know and understand, if he wishes to know and is willing to see, the whole subject of his character, condition, duty, interest and destiny, as a subject of God's moral government. Nay, he can not avoid knowing and understanding the whole, without constant effort to exclude the light of truth from his intellectual and moral susceptibilities; for it is all matter of conscious, practical experiment with him in all his intercourse with human society.

5th. We learn from this discussion the true reason why the world has not been evangelized ages ago, and the whole earth now occupied with Christian churches, walking in the peace and fellowship of the gospel. For two centuries after the day of Pentecost the progress of the gospel was such that, if continued without interruption, the whole world must have been evangelized eight or ten centuries ago. At the close of the third century the geographical bounds of Christendom were greater than at the present time; and the comparative number of Christians on earth, and the influence of Christian truth in converting human agents, was apparently greater than at any period since. In the beginning of the Christian era, the gospel could be preached in any place, by any person who had heard and believed it, without any long or expensive preparation. Illiterate, uneducated persons, common laborers, travelling journeymen, and even women, could publish the good news; and wherever the story of the cross was told, converts were multiplied daily, and scores, hundreds, and thousands added to the Church. But as soon as Christian doctors began to assume authority, and impose their own theological fictions on the Church, as Christian doctrines, the influence of Christianity began to decline. The Church was rent into sections, contending and fighting for the dogmas of different schools and teachers.

From sometime in the fourth century to the fifteenth, the movement of Christianity in the world was retrograde. Vast countries, which in the fourth century were occupied with Christian churches and millions of pious believers, were, in the beginning of the fifteenth, perfect moral desolations, without a church or a Christian, and almost without human inhabitant. Pure Christianity could only be found in a few obscure locations, such as the mountains of Switzerland, Scotland and Wales, the farther India, and perhaps some remote province of China or Persia. In the same period, millions of human agents had been slain in the wars and persecutions waged for the defence of human dogmas as foreign from Christianity, and as false as any pretended measurement of a mountain on the back side of the moon. And since the great reformation in the sixteenth century, in Western Europe, the influence of Christianity has been, on the whole, rather retrograde in all those countries most favored at that period. And the present increased efforts and success in diffusing the knowledge of the gospel among pagan nations, give very little promise of soon evangelizing the world; while the assimilation of the Church to the world continues to be quite as rapid as the conversion of pagans to Christian morality. As long as so great a portion of the best talents, agencies and means of the Church are wasted in creating, propagating and defending such inexplicable human dogmas, theological fictions, and sectarian distinctions; and as long as a system of ever so highly refined transcendental materialism is substituted as a preached gospel, instead of the great Bible facts, that every fallen creature is the sole author of his own sins, and that the perfect, all-sufficient and infinite provision of the higher law, in the person and work of Jesus Christ, when practically believed, must necessarily and naturally constitute the salvation of every sinner that believes; that is, as long as the present supernatural materialism, or physical force, is the fashionable substitute for the simple power of God which Paul preached without fear or shame, we may expect the world to continue as it was, and generally has been for fourteen centuries past. And that the true Church and simple gospel of Christ will be driven from the wealthy seats of human power, civilization and refinement by the conventional influences and ecclesiastical tyranny of corrupted Christianity, as the pilgrim fathers were driven across the Atlantic, to seek shelter in this recently savage wilderness.

6th. We may also infer from the truths presented in this discussion, another important fact, which must, more or less, qualify all the theological knowledge attainable by man while in the flesh. It is the fact, that all our theology or knowledge of God is subsequent to, derived from, and dependent upon, our previous anthropology, or knowledge of our own human nature, its endowments and acquisitions. The moral endowments, susceptibilities, or attributes, which constitute the image of God, in which man was created, and which also constitute the entire and only real manhood of the human animal, we have in perfect personal unity, with a physical organization, or animal nature. And this living soul, with all its God-given moral susceptibilities, and spiritual endowments, is perfectly dependent upon the locomotion of the animal organs of sensation for every mental feeling, emotion, sensation, or impression; that is, dependent for all the materials of knowledge which the soul ever does, or can attain in the present life. The knowledge of himself, of his own existence and endowments, in the case of every intellect, must necessarily precede all possible knowledge of any thing else. He must exist and must be conscious of his own existence as an individual being, distinct from all other beings; and his intellectual endowments, or susceptibility of acquiring and receiving knowledge, must have begun to be developed before it is possible for him to know the existence or the qualities, relations or endowments of any other substantive existence. This knowledge of self-existence, and of self-endowments, is acquired by every human intellect intuitively; but only as the immediate consequence of the contact, of his physical organs of sensation with some other substantive being. Consciousness of self-existence is the first perception, in the order of nature, of every perceptive being. Knowledge of the existence of some other substantive being, in contradistinction from himself, must be the next.

The knowledge of God as a universal, first cause, or Creator of all things, must, therefore, necessarily be preceded by a practical knowledge of his own causality, or his ability to produce changes, acquired by actual experiment in confirmation of the intuitive axiom, that every change must be preceded by an adequate cause. This perception, or consciousness of ability to produce changes, or of being himself endowed with actual causality, as an essential constituent of his own nature, is the germ or ovary in every human intellect, of all his knowledge of a universal first cause or Creator. By multiplying and extending this notion of causality, thus acquired, to every conceivable change, and every finite existence, and by abstracting from it all limitation and imperfection we attain our only conception and knowledge of the supreme Creator of all things; a Being of infinite physical power, ability, or causality. In the same manner, by extending his own intuitive perception of his ability to acquire and create knowledge, man acquires the conception of an omniscient Being or an intelligent Spirit of infinite wisdom. The ideas of omniscience, and of infinite wisdom, necessarily involve each other. But before any human intellect can form any conception of a supreme moral Governor of the universe, his own moral susceptibilities, which constitute the image of God, in which he was created, must have begun to be developed, and he must have acquired the knowledge of the distinction between right and wrong, sin and holiness, by actual experiment, in the inferior relations that he sustains towards his fellow-creatures. This consciousness of personal rightness of moral character, thus previously acquired, when extended to all the relations between Creator and creatures, enlarged and divested of all limitation and imperfection, constitutes the only human conception of infinite goodness, holiness, or moral rectitude ever acquired by human agent in the flesh. Thus, every conception of the supreme Being, or of an infinite, self-existent Spirit, or of an almighty, infinitely wise and omniscient Creator, or of an infinitely good, holy and beneficent moral Sovereign of the universe, or of any of his attributes, acquired by any human intellect in this life, is created out of, and is derived from, and consists of the combinations and modifications of those sensations conveyed to the mind by the locomotions of the physical organs of animal sensation; that is, all our theology or knowledge of God is dependent upon, derived from, and consists of previously acquired Anthropology, modified by multiplication and abstraction. This is necessarily true, because the living soul, this knowing human agent, now exists in an absolutely perfect, personal identity, with this physical organization of animal sensation. And no other medium of communication or access to the human soul has been created, revealed, or discovered. When God created man a living soul, he did it by breathing into his nostrils, into his organs of sensation, the breath of life. And he taught him knowledge by presenting the subjects to his organs of sensation.

But all human beings are created finite, limited agents. Their acquisitions of knowledge, their conceptions of things, must, therefore, necessarily be finite, limited, and imperfect. Even their highest, most extensive, most exalted and perfect conceptions of the infinite God, and of any of his essential attributes, perfections and purposes, must be infinitely inadequate, imperfect, and defective. When, therefore, young theologians make dogmatical affirmations concerning the divine essence, the divine nature, or substantive existence of God, or concerning the attributes, the perfections and purposes of God, and then undertake to reason and construct theories from these dogmas, they are very liable to err, and to fall into gross absurdities and contradictions. And, generally, they thus err, by carrying the axioms of physical science into their theological and moral reasoning; or by predicating the accidents of material, finite, created beings, of the spiritual, the infinite and self-existent Being. A very clear and instructive illustration of this kind of error we have in the affirmation which we often hear and read, and sometimes find in the symbols of faith, of Christian churches, "That the living and true God exists in three persons." Here numerical distinction and personality are predicated of the divine essence, or of the substantive existence of the Deity. But numerical distinction is an accident of finite, created substances only. An infinite, eternal Spirit, essence or substance, is a perfect unity, an absolute identity, an indivisibility. All the numerical distinctions in the world can not convey to a human intellect the least conception of any distinction or variety in an infinite, eternal Spirit. And personality never qualifies substantive being of any kind; and never expresses or conveys any meaning when predicated of a substantive being, either finite or infinite, material or spiritual. It is a contrivance, or variation of human language, to express or distinguish varieties among the relations of moral agents, both human and divine. Yet out of this theological fiction have grown all the errors, absurdities, contradictions, controversies and contention about the trinity, which have disturbed the Church and the world for ages.

A similar illustration is given in the dogma "That God hath preordained whatsoever comes to pass." But there can be no before nor after to an eternal purpose. The fore and aft, when used in reference to the divine purpose, will or mind, are intended only to describe the method in which we are obliged to conceive of it, and the order in which we are obliged to arrange or think of its relations. But God's eternal purpose is an eternal and unchangeable unity. Among the comings-to-pass are a great many sins, and a great deal of consequent misery. But for an infinitely good, holy or righteous Sovereign to decree, will or purpose the existence of sin, or its consequent misery, involves a positive and plain contradiction, an obvious absurdity, and an infinite falsehood. An infinitely holy being can sustain but one relation to sin and its consequent misery: that is the relation of infinite opposition, or infinite antagonism, both to the existence of sin and of all its malignant consequences. And this infinite antagonism to the existence of sin and all its influences, is the grand theme of all the revelations of God to man since he created him a living soul. His positive decree, forbidding the existence of sin in any form whatever, is repeated a thousand times in the volume of revelation. Yet, from this romance of the imagination originates the subject, and all the militant machinery, of the conflict of ages, between Calvinists and Armenians.

7th. In the light of this subject we may form some correct, though very inadequate, conceptions of the retributions of God's moral government over the children of men. That is, of the rewards of obedience, and the punishments of disobedience, which human agents may expect in the future state of retribution. This is a subject concerning which a variety of conflicting opinions are entertained in the world and in the Church, and even among religious teachers; and not a little materialism is often mingled in the descriptions, both of the future rewards of the righteous and punishments of the wicked. It is highly important, therefore, that correct views on this topic should be propagated.

We have endeavored to show, in this discussion, that those moral susceptibilities which constitute the image of God in which man was created, and the real manhood of human agents, are as indestructible and as imperishable as the immortal soul itself. Among these immortal endowments is the susceptibility of perceiving, appreciating, and perfectly enjoying the moral beauty, excellence, and utility of infinite goodness, holiness, or conformity to the law of moral rectitude: and also the ability of perceiving, appreciating, hating, abhorring, and loathing the moral deformity, ugliness, and degradation of sin or transgression. When, therefore, the living soul of the believer is divested of the physical organization of the depraved, sickly animal body, and is furnished with, or clothed upon, with that incorruptible, spiritual machinery or building for the further employment and development of his immortal endowments, which, saith the apostle, we know is prepared of God for us, when our earthly house of this tabernacle is dissolved, then the perfectly renovated believer will be a pure spiritual being, perfect in holiness, and capable of enjoying the infinite blessedness resulting from the favor, the love and the fullness of God, and the friendship, esteem and relationship of all good and holy beings of every order; and also capable of enjoying all the happiness resulting from the sure consciousness of perfect moral beauty, loveliness, and worthiness in his own person, of the esteem and friendship of all holy beings. Thus the rewards of the redeemed, their future bliss and their perfect happiness, will consist of moral enjoyments, of spiritual peace, pleasure, and felicity, constituting fullness of joy and pleasure at the right hand (that is, in the perfect favor) of God for ever more.

Such is the gift of God, the eternal life, through Jesus Christ our Lord. All materialism, all physical pleasure, all animal enjoyment, all sensual gratification, are necessarily excluded; because there will be no physical organs to be excited, no material organs of sensitive pleasure, no animal instincts, appetites or passions to be gratified. The subject of reward will be a pure spirit, in his entire nature, person, endowments and susceptibilities. The ground, the primary reason or proximate cause of his felicity, will be seen in his perfect moral character, which is formed by doing the truth. For though his blessedness will be all of grace, his redemption, sanctification, perfect moral character and entire salvation, will be the fruit of God's infinite mercy and free gift in Jesus Christ; and though no saint in glory will ever be able to cease ascribing his whole salvation and happiness to grace alone, yet every redeemed soul in heaven will possess in his own personal character, contracted by his own voluntary agency, a perfect merit of congruity, rendering it right, just and equitable for God the moral Governor thus to reward the believer in his son Jesus Christ.

Nor will the happiness of the redeemed consist at all in mere indolent, passive enjoyment, or reception of good from other beings; but, being perfectly qualified and capacitated to become ministering spirits, as the angels of light now are, they will be for ever employed, in perfect obedience to the will of God, the higher law, in doing good, creating and diffusing happiness to other sentient beings. Their happiness will, therefore, be divine, holy enjoyment, because, like the infinite blessedness of God, it will consist very much in the pleasure of doing good and imparting happiness to others. Their own agency will be included in the cause of their own felicity. "And in keeping of them," the statutes or judgments of the Lord, "there is great reward." Ps. xix. 11.

With respect to those who die in their sins, impenitent, unreconciled to God and his perfect law, being divested of all material substance, and still retaining the image of God in which they were created, they also will not only be able to see, understand, appreciate and sympathise with, but it will be an unchangeable and unavoidable necessity of their immortal nature, to see in the light of eternal truth their own sinful character, in all its moral deformity, odiousness and degradation, and to hate, abhor, and despise themselves for contracting such a character. They will also be under an unavoidable necessity of seeing and understanding perfectly their own natures, endowments and susceptibilities; that they have always existed in the image of God, constituting in their very natures a perfect ability to do all that the law of God ever required of them. That is, to contract a right moral character, and secure their own happiness; or, after having sinned, to repent, believe, make a new heart, and do all that the gospel of Christ requires, to secure their salvation from sin and misery; that they have always exercised perfect liberty and freedom of choice; that their entire moral character and consequent destiny are both alike, of their own choosing and creating; that neither their character nor destiny are, in any sense, the consequence of God's purpose, volition, permission, consent or agency, but entirely of their own procuring. "Oh Israel, thou hast destroyed thyself, but in me is thy help." Hos. xiii. 9.

"The law of the Lord is perfect, converting the soul." It executes its penal sanction by its own omnipotent moral influence, employing no agency or influence but the moral endowments of the transgressor himself, which constitute the image of God in which he was created. God has never put forth the least degree of his physical power to punish an impenitent soul in the future state, and never will. The subjects of moral government, in the state of retribution, are spiritual beings exclusively. No influence can affect them, for weal or woe, but the moral influence of truth or falsehood. The light of eternal truth, beaming from the character of God, illustrated in the higher law, will be the proximate cause, the efficient instrumentality, both of the happiness of the redeemed and the torments of the wicked. And this fact will for ever illustrate the absolute perfection, the infinite glory and sublime beauty of God's moral government, above all that human intellect in the flesh can conceive.

II.

TRINITY OF PERSONS IN THE GODHEAD. INCARNATION OF DEITY.

THE doctrine of a trinity of persons in the Godhead appears to be one of the earliest and most universally diffused and acknowledged religious dogmas of the human family. It seems to have been an article of belief in every system of religion of which we have any authentic or credible history. Every system of paganism, idolatry, or superstition, which has been adopted or practiced by any considerable portion of mankind, has included among its credenda, or things to be believed, a triad of personal agents or relations, constituting a monad, or one identical being, which they worshipped and honored as the supreme Sovereign or first cause, or as the Deity, the best and highest of all beings. The probable reason of this universal belief of a trinity of persons in a Godhead is, that it has been found impossible to conceive or describe intelligibly any method by which a righteous and beneficent moral governor can save a rebellious subject from the consequences of his rebellion, without introducing a second and third person into the transaction. It is for this cause that the Christian, or true system of religion for fallen men, has necessarily from the beginning, or first entrance of sin into the world, included the doctrine of a trinity of persons in the Godhead; and all sincere worshippers of the one only living and true God find it necessary, in performing public social worship to the one God, to introduce three personalities into their service, and ascribe divine attributes and pay divine honor to three distinct persons. From this universal necessity, even the modern unitarians, of the most liberal and improved description, have not been able entirely to free themselves. But notwithstanding the universal reception of the doctrine in one shape or another, perhaps no religious dogma, true or false, has ever been the subject of more controversy, or been the occasion of more bitter, inveterate and bloody conflicts among civilized and Christian communities. The cause of this is most probably the fact that this doctrine of the trinity is fundamental and absolutely essential to Christianity. So much so, that when this doctrine is repudiated or expunged from the system, not a vestige of Christianity remains; and all the moral and religious teaching of Jesus Christ, and his apostles and prophets, is converted into a collection of absurdity, contradiction and mysticism; and all knowledge and hope of salvation from sin and its consequences are obliterated and extinguished. No wonder that Christians should contend earnestly, and even to blood, for the privilege of cherishing the belief of this essential doctrine.

The present condition, character, and constant fluctuations of opinions of every sect or community who have undertaken to controvert this doctrine, fully illustrate and confirm the truth of this cause of contention, and show that this is an essential and fundamental doctrine of Christianity.

But my object in introducing the subject here is not to enter into any controversy for or against any opinion in relation to the doctrine of the trinity. I shall not even attempt to prove the truth of the doctrine; because no person of common sense can receive and read the Bible, as a revelation from God, and doubt it. The Bible is the Christian's infallible authority and rule of faith. And the doctrine of the trinity of persons in the Godhead is a doctrine of pure revelation; and the proof of it has been so often collated and expounded by able and more learned intellects, that for me to attempt any improvement or addition would be vain and superfluous.

But my sole object is, to divest the subject of those absurd dogmas of mysticism, which the theological speculators have cast around it, so as to leave the plain, simple Bible truth of the doctrine, open to the perceptions and understanding of all common sense persons who wish to understand it, and who are willing to bestow the necessary attention and thought for that purpose. I believe that the principal cause of doubt, uncertainty and infidelity in relation to the subject, among common people, is the fog of mysticism, which their learned teachers and controversialists have cast over the doctrine. Those teachers who believe and defend the doctrine, when they have stated what they suppose we are bound to believe, as the revealed truth in relation to it, proceed to tell us that this subject is a profound mystery of the divine nature, which of course can not be explained or understood by any human intellect, because it is entirely above and beyond the sphere of human conception or intellect. Those teachers and writers, who disbelieve and ridicule the doctrine, after perverting and distorting the opinions of the orthodox, (so called,) tell us that the whole doctrine of a trinity of persons in the Godhead, is a perfect absurdity, a contradiction, and a ridiculous superstition. The plain common sense, unlearned hearer naturally retires from the teaching of either class, with the impression that it is perfectly useless for him to think or inquire on the subject. He very naturally and correctly infers, that any intelligent or practical faith on the question is, in his condition, utterly impossible. He either dismisses the subject wholly, as a topic utterly above his conception, and out of his reach; or, he concurs with one class of teachers, by assenting to the doctrine, with a blind know-nothing and do-nothing faith; or, with the other class, he dismisses the subject with contempt as unworthy of occupying his superior intellect.

But, if the doctrine be true, and if it be a fundamental article of the Christian system, as it must necessarily be, if true, then it can not be an inexplicable mystery, but a plainly revealed truth. It must be a truth made plain and intelligible to the understanding of those to whom and for whose benefit and salvation it has been revealed. Any other supposition involves a contradiction. If the doctrine of a trinity of persons in the Godhead be not a truth, it certainly furnishes no occasion for ridicule, or perversion and distortion of opinions. Error, on so important and grave a subject, is too solemn to be trifled with, and too dangerous to risk the perversion of opinions. If, however, the subject be carefully analyzed and divested of extraneous matter, of mere human invention or inference, I apprehend there will be found no great difficulty for those who are willing to do their own thinking on the subject, to understand and believe this great mystery of Godliness.

But in order to clear away the human interpolations from the subject, it will be necessary,

1st. To ascertain the true meaning of the term Godhead.
2d. To define precisely the nature and extent of personality.
3d. To show in what manner and for what purpose personality is predicated of the Godhead; and what is the extent of its meaning when so predicated.

1st. What is the true meaning of the term Godhead? By many writers this word has been understood and used as synonymous with Deity. They have used it as the proper name of the Supreme Being, and as including in its meaning not merely the substantive existence of such a Being, but also the numerical quality of that Being. They use the term Godhead when they mean to express or convey the same idea as when they use the word God in its highest sense, or as when they use the word Deity or Supreme Being; meaning the infinite omniscient, omnipresent, self-existent, first Cause. But I apprehend that this is an improper use of the term. There is in every cultivated language a certain class of words which are used only to express relations, or the circumstances and accidents of relations, but never to express things that have substantive or independent existence. But the relations which this class of words express, instantly and necessarily suggest the existence of the subjects which sustain these relations. Loose and inaccurate thinkers sometimes include the subject of a relation in the meaning of the word, which, when properly used, signifies only a certain relation. And afterward using the word in this extended sense, they may involve themselves in solecisms and absurdities, and be led into gross errors and useless controversy. For example, the word parent is always used, when correctly used, to express a certain definite relation, and never to express a real substantive existence. The term offspring is equally definite, and limited in signification to the corelative of parent. But if a speaker or writer should in his mind include the subjects of this relation in the meaning of these relative words, and then begin to reason with these terms, affirming that wherever this relation exists, certain duties and obligations necessarily result, and the subjects of the relation are very sinful and guilty, and deserve punishment, if they neglect these duties, and do not fulfil these obligations. This affirmation is a very solemn and important truth in relation to human parents and offspring, because they are moral agents and subjects of moral government. But the same relation of parent and offspring is common with every species of animal organization, as truly as with human parents and offspring of the genus man. It would, however, seem rather singular and out of place to hear a grave divine arguing the duties and obligations of a horse, an ass, and a mule from this relation, as it sometimes exists among them; or charging them with sin and guilt for neglecting their duty. The fact is, that using words in a loose, undefined signification, exposes a speaker to commit great absurdities in reasoning.

But the sustaining of one relation by any individual does not exclude that individual from sustaining other and entirely different relations to the same, or to different substantive beings. The being which sustains the relation of father may at the same time sustain a variety of very different relations to the same, or any number of different beings. He may be a supreme magistrate, a teacher, a physician, a merchant; and the being, or beings, which sustain the corelations of sons, may also sustain the corelations of subject, of pupil, of patient, etc.; and the ascription of these different corelations to the beings between which they exist, implies no difference or variety in the substance of either subject of these relations, nor of the manner of their subsistence. Nor does it involve any reference to their substantive identities, or to the unity or plurality of the parties of these relations. We never dream of any impropriety, inconsistency or absurdity, in using the words which signify these different relations, and their various circumstances, when speaking of the same identical being.

These relative terms have no reference to substantive being, or to numerical difference of substantive being; but they properly and exclusively refer to relations of things, and the various circumstances of such relations. A single individual may sustain a number of different personal relations, and half a dozen or more individual persons may be united in sustaining the same identical personal relation.

Therefore, in determining the signification and precise extent of meaning and appropriate use of the term Godhead, we must be governed by the same principles of interpretation which limit the signification of all the same class of words exclusively to the relations of things. Of this class of words are such terms as governorship, captaincy, presidency, conductorship, superintendency, dictatorship, maidenhood, Lordship, and Godhead. Now, we may use or understand any of these words as expressing a variety of personal relations to any number of other individuals; but we can not properly, or intelligibly, use them to describe the mode of existence of the beings who sustain these relations. Nor will it vary the signification of the term, or involve any impropriety, though we should represent two or five personal relations, or personal individuals, as sustaining the same identical relation. The judgeship may be invested in one, two, three, or more individuals. The superintendency may include the agency and labors of a number of individuals. Or a single individual may act in a variety of different personal relations, in performing the duties of a single general relation. Thus the father of a family, in performing the duties of that relation, may find it convenient and necessary to assume the relation of physician, teacher, guardian or agent, and to perform the personal duties pertaining to these relations in his own person. Perhaps he may find it necessary to take another agent into personal unity with himself, to enable him legally and rightly to perform some of the personal duties of these subordinate relations. In like manner the one living and true God may sustain the various different relations of Creator, supreme moral Governor, Preserver, Saviour, Mediator, Redeemer, Sanctifier, Judge and Benefactor, to myriads of different subjects of his moral kingdom, without involving any denial of his perfect unity and identity. And this one God may find it necessary, or judge it expedient, to take into personal unity with himself another agent of a different nature, in order to perform in the most perfect manner some of the duties resulting from these relations, without implying any plurality in his being, or any variety in the manner of his subsistence. Now, the word Godhead is a very convenient term to express, collectively, all these relations of God to fallen men, without reference to any other circumstance of his existence. We may presume, therefore, that the word was framed for that very purpose: and that when applied to any other purpose, or its meaning extended to the substantive existence of the Deity, or to any circumstance of his existence, besides these relations, it is improperly used, and constitutes a solecism.

2d. We may, therefore, proceed to the next topic of discussion, viz: The nature and extent of personality; of what subjects may it be predicated, and how does it qualify such subjects? Human language must sometimes vary in signification, according to the varying natures and circumstances of things which it is used to describe. Human language is finite, and words are limited in number, but things and their relations, circumstances and accidents, are infinite. When we describe things and their relations and accidents, we are necessarily obliged often to use the same word in a variety of different shades of meaning. These varying shades of signification are sometimes indicated by varying the form of the word, and are sometimes left to be inferred from the circumstances of the subject spoken of at the time.

The word person, or personality, in its various grammatical forms, as noun, adjective, verb, participle and adverb, has a variety of shades of meaning, according with these various forms, and also a similar variety, resulting from the nature and circumstances of the subject. When we say of any particular man, he is the person, we predicate personality of that man. We use the word in its substantive form, and its most common and primary signification. But in what does the personality of the man consist, or what constitutes him a person? Not his substantive existence. For rocks, mountains, rivers and oceans have substantive existence, but they have not personality. Nor does his fearful and wonderful organization, curiously wrought by infinite wisdom, constitute him a person. The tree, the plant, the flower, the horse, the butterfly, the oyster, and ten thousand other curious organizations display the wisdom of the divine Architect, but have no personality. Nor does his vitality as a living, active and intelligent being, his capability of originating motion, acquiring knowledge, or causing change, give him personality. The elephant, the ox, the ass, the beaver, the ant, and a thousand other animal species, are intelligent, acquire knowledge, originate changes, and are, in their own limited spheres, real causes, as truly as God is, in the infinite sphere. Many of them, in their own sphere, show far quicker perception, superior knowledge and more skill than human animals, in the flesh, ever attain. "The ox knoweth his owner, and the ass his master's crib: but Israel doth not know, my people doth not consider." Yet none of all these animated organizations are ever invested with personality, or are called persons, either by God in his word, or by men in any of the relations of civilized human society.

We must, therefore, ascend to the ultimate and highest endowment of human nature; that endowment, which allied man at first with his maker, and which constituted the image and likeness of God in which man was originally created. "So God created man in his own image, in the image of God created he him; male and female created he them." To find the personality of the man, we must rise to the moral sense: we must look to the moral susceptibilities, which liken him to God his Maker, and constitute him a subject of moral government. Man, by his moral endowments, is distinguished from and raised, in the scale of existence, above the mere animal and intellectual beings, and stands next to the angels; being with them a pure, mortal, indestructible spirit. While at the same time, in his physical or material part, he is on a level with all sensitive animal existence.

By these moral endowments he is related to God, to the higher law, or law of God, to God's moral kingdom, and to the interests and retributions of that kingdom. His personality is therefore found, only in these relations, which as a moral agent and subject of moral government, he sustains to God, to the law of God, and to his fellow subjects, of God's universal kingdom. Now, the variety of relations which God sustains towards the myriads of subjects of his government, and which his subjects sustain towards each other, and the things around them, are innumerable. And the duties and obligations resulting from these relations are also innumerable, and as various as they are numerous. The personalities, likewise, which may be predicated of the subjects of these relations, are just as numerous and as various as the relations from which they result. For example: take the first and most important relation ever existing in the human family, constituted by God himself, and made the basis and pattern of all other relations of human society. After the institution of the marriage relation Adam sustained a personality, in that relation, totally different and diverse from what was possible antecedent to that institution. The personal duties and obligations, the personal benefits and enjoyments resulting from the relation were new and different; and antecedent to that relation were absolutely impossible; and but for the institution of that relation, had for ever remained impossible. Yet the personality created by this relation involved two individual substantive beings, who in all other relations were two distinct persons. The personal duties and obligations could neither exist or be fulfilled, but by a perfect unity of two individual moral agents, who in other relations were two distinct persons. Each agent, in other relations, may have a separate personal individuality, while the two, in this particular relation, constitute an individual personality, which could not exist, but by a perfect personal union, both moral and physical of the two individuals. "They shall be one flesh." That is, one individual person, in this relation, as long as the relation exists.

When we say of a particular man, this is the person who

wrote that book, we predicate personality of that man. The personality which we mention is found in the relation of authorship which the man sustains to that book. His agency in making the book, created, or brought into existence his personal relationship to it; and being the sole author, the whole responsibility in the case attaches to his personal relation to the book. If it was a good and useful book, the whole merit of its production belongs to him. If it was a bad book, or libel against his neighbor, injurious to the morals, or wealth, or health of the community, he is alone responsible for the damage: because his personal relation to it is a unity, a single individuality.

But here is another book, the authorship of which he shared with two or five other writers; they each contributing an equal share in the work, and being perfectly agreed and united in the production. Here, then, we have a single personal relationship constituted by the unity of several agents in the production of the same results. In that one relation they constitute a single personality. And yet in other relations each retains his own distinct individuality. No one of these individuals was author of that book, or sustained that relationship to it, and yet all of them as an aggregate sustained that relation to it. This was a personal relation, because it involved personal obligation; the action that created it was either right or wrong, the production was either good or bad; each individual was responsible for the production, but the responsibility was a joint responsibility. The personality predicable in this case, was therefore in one aspect of the case, a single personality, in an other aspect, it was plural. In reference to one subject of the corelation, the personality may be a single individuality; in reference to the other subject of the relation, it may be a plurality.

An individual substantive being, or moral agent may sustain in different relations a variety of personalities; and a large number of agents may sustain a single personality, which could never exist in the case of an individual. Every business firm, of two or more human agents, every joint stock association for any purpose, every corporate body constituted by human laws, or instituted by divine appointment, as the family, and the Church, every court constituted of more than one magistrate, every legislative body, every legally organized civil association of accountable beings, as a town, city, state, or nation, is a person in the literal and primary meaning of the term. Each corporate or associated body, whether consisting of two individual agents, or of two hundred, or of millions, is described in the word of God, and treated in the providential government of God over this world, as an individual personality, in all the relations, duties, obligations and responsibilities involved in the association. In all human languages the various grammatical forms of all words implying, or suggesting personality, are applied to these corporate bodies in the singular number. In all legal transactions they are regarded and spoken of as single individual persons. In all the moral relations and judicial or criminal proceedings, and in all commercial transactions of human society, these corporations, in the numerous relations they sustain to other persons and things, are regarded and spoken of as individual persons. The proper names, by which they are severally designated, are used in the singular number, just as the proper names of single men and women are. And the various actions, interests, gains and losses of these persons of multitude are described, as those of individuals in the singular number. Many of the most important relations that exist among human agents in this life are created by these voluntary associations. Many of the most important duties and obligations that rest upon human agents, in this state of probation and mutual dependence, result from these associations and the personal relations created thereby: which duties and obligations never could exist or be fulfilled but for the creation of these artificial personalities. The most important, difficult and delicate duties which men ever perform to their fellow men, the most solemn and responsible obligations ever imposed on human beings, involving the highest, most important and dearest interests of individuals and communities are created by and depend on these artificial personalities. Take for example the institution of trial by a jury of his peers, which every man in this favored land boasts of as his personal right and highest civil privilege. When such a jury is constituted a most responsible, efficient and useful individual personality is created. But antecedent to the perfect organization of the jury, and the legal qualification of every member of it, not one of the duties, obligations, or responsibilities incident to, and most solemnly binding on that organized personal agent, have any existence at all. Not one individual, nor all the individuals collectively, who compose the jury, though ever so willing and desirous to do so, can perform the least act or fulfil the least duty or obligation of this personal agent before their perfect organization. Should any or all of them attempt to do any such thing, their action would be a perfect nullity in relation to every party and thing interested in the case. If this organization be broken by the loss of a single member, the personality ceases to exist, and all the personal relations, duties, obligations and responsibilities coexisting with it are annihilated.

We perceive, therefore, that personality is not essential to, and does not necessarily belong to substantive existence, and is not identical with actual being or existence. Personality in itself has no independent substantive being, any where, or in any case. It is a mere accident of a certain genus of substantive existences, viz., of that genus of substantive beings which we call moral agents, including the moral Sovereign of the universe, and all the subjects of his moral government. Personality is found only in the relations of such substantive beings as have permanent or continuous existence in themselves; who to their substantive being and their intellectual endowments have added a moral sense, or a susceptibility of distinguishing between right and wrong, in the high and moral sense, of acting under the motive influence of the higher law, and of thus forming a moral character. Only in the relations of such moral beings as involve obligations, can we conceive of personality; and to such relations exclusively can we ascribe personality in the literal sense. Divest a human agent of those relations and susceptibilities, which involve moral obligations and accountability, and you have divested him completely of personality, and of every thing that distinguishes him from mere irrational brute animals, or that can constitute any reason or furnish any ground for calling him a person rather than calling any mule a person. I know that illiterate, careless thinkers and talkers, who never analyze their thoughts, are in the habit of confounding personality with substantive existence, or with sensitive intellectual being. But such persons, in every such case, practice an illusion on their own intellectual perceptions, just as children do when they imagine that color is some material substance, or some thing, or at least that it adheres in, and is, therefore, essential to material substances. But a very little common sense observation and reflection, on what passes before their eyes daily, teaches them that color has no material existence at all, but is found alone in the animal sensations produced through the organs of sight, by the varying relations which material light assumes to these organs as its motions and positions are varied. Exclude all material light from material substances and they are as destitute of color, as if color had never been conceived of in the universe. Deprive the most sprightly intellectual being of the organs of sight, and to him color ceases to exist. If he never had the use of the organs of sight, all the human intelligence, learning, and skill in the world cannot give him the least conception of the nature of color. And in like manner, abstract from your conception of any intellectual being the idea of moral susceptibilities, obligations, and accountability, and you have divested that being of all personality.

We may, indeed, by a figure of rhetoric, and the help of imagination, clothe the whole material system, animal, vegetable, and inorganic, with personality. But to do this, we must first imagine them endowed with the moral sense and rationality of accountable agents, and ascribe to them the appropriate motions and actions of moral agents. The rhetorical figures of personification and prosopopœia are often used by the inspired writers, and constitute the chief beauty and sublimity of sacred poetry. But the use of them always furnishes full confirmation of the fact, that all personality necessarily implies the pre-existence of moral susceptibilities, relations, and obligations as the subject or basis of personality, without which personality can not exist. Thus the Psalmist invests the whole material system of things with personality, and organizes them into an enrapt choir of worshipers praising God. "The heavens declare the glory of God, and the firmament showeth his handy-work. Day unto day uttereth speech, and night unto night showeth knowledge, etc."—Ps. xix. 1-6. And again, "Praise the Lord from the earth ye dragons, and all ye deeps; Fire and hail; snow and vapors; stormy wind fulfilling his word; Mountains and all hills; fruitful trees and all cedars; Beasts and all cattle; creeping things and flying fowl; Kings of the earth and all people; princes and all judges of the earth, etc." —Ps. cxlviii. 7-13.

But all these mere things, in order to personify them or invest them with imaginary personality, must be animated with intellectual life and moral relations, endowments, emotions, and obligations. They must, in imagination, be supposed capable of understanding and appreciating the high moral motives which are presented to excite them to praise the Lord. "For his name alone is excellent, his glory is above the earth and heavens. He also exalteth the horn of his people, the praise of all his saints."—v. 14.

Nothing is personified, even in imagination, till it is invested with the susceptibilities, relations and emotions proper and peculiar to moral agents. The necessary and unavoidable inference is, that the personality of God, angels, and men, pertains exclusively to the relations which they mutually sustain to each other and to other things in general, as the sovereign and supreme Administrator and the subjects of a vast moral system. And as these relations are innumerable and of countless varieties, the personalities of moral agents are innumerable and infinitely various. One individual agent may sustain a number of various personalities, just as numerous and as different from each other as the different personal relations he sustains, which involve moral obligation. And any number of individual agents, even millions, may sustain one individual personality, and in that relation constitute a single person;

which person or personality no individual of the number can sustain, and which cannot exist at all but by the association or combination of that number of individual agents. But human language is finite and very limited. It is, therefore, impossible to furnish words to designate the infinite variety of personalities which moral agents sustain. Nor is there any necessity for it. A few general distinctions are sufficient to answer the general purposes of human intercourse. The grammatical use of personality in the construction of language is sufficiently accommodated by three distinctions, called the first, second, and third persons. These three distinctions are used both in the singular and plural numbers. One class of personalities is distinguished by the name of the relations to which they pertain; as the person of the wife, the husband, the parent, the child. In another class they are distinguished by the business of the agents to which the personal relations belong; as the person of the physician, the inventor, the mechanic, etc. In another, by the designation of the office with which they are associated; as the person of the president, the emperor, the queen, the bishop, the judge, the general, etc. In histrionic representation, the various personalities which the actor attempts to exhibit are generally designated by the names of the originals. But in the greatest number of cases no words are necessary to indicate the personal relations, duties, and obligations of the parties concerned. They are intuitively and necessarily conceived on the bare mention or thought of the subjects. Take a single phrase of Paul before the court of Areopagus, on Mars Hill, and the learned Athenian, and the pagan strangers there congregated: "God that made the world and all things therein." No human intelligent of common sense, on this footstool, can think consecutively or speak intelligibly, for five minutes, on the subjects presented in that phrase, without conceiving in his own mind, or suggesting to his attentive, thoughtful hearers, a variety of personal relations, obligations, duties, and actions which this Creator sustains, owes, and performs to the creatures of his power; that is, a variety of personalities sustained and acted out in absolute perfection, by the one living and true God, and a like variety of personalities pertaining to the relations of every individual subject of his moral government in this world. And all these personalities, both of the Creator and his moral subjects, are as distinct from each other as the persons of any two or more individuals are distinct personalities, and as various as the relations, characters, conditions, and circumstances of the subjects.

3d. We are now prepared to show in what manner and for what purpose personality is predicated of the Godhead, and what is the extent of its meaning when so predicated. I affirm that there are three persons in the Godhead. I believe this proposition as truly and as firmly as I believe my own existence. I receive the knowledge of this truth in the same manner that I receive the knowledge of my own existence; that is, intuitively and necessarily. I can not avoid knowing it and believing it, any more than I can avoid knowing my own existence. The process of acquisition may be a few steps longer, but it is the same process in the same direction. I am conscious of existing. I am conscious that I can not exist without an adequate cause. The only adequate cause I can conceive of is a God of infinite wisdom, power and goodness. I have sinned by transgressing the higher law; the law of this infinite Creator and Lord of all. I am as necessarily conscious of sin and guilt as I am of existence. I know intuitively and necessarily, from my own consciousness, that this God who made me now sustains various new and different relations to me, from those he sustained antecedent to my transgression. I can not avoid the consciousness of this, more than of my own existence. I am intuitively conscious that these new and varied relations are moral relations; that is, relations from which moral obligations and duties result, and that personality exclusively belongs to, and can be truly predicated only of such relations, duties and obligations, and of nothing else. These relations, involving personality, personal obligations, duties and actions, I collectively designate by the title Godhead. Such is the process by which I come to the knowledge and belief of this proposition. But this is not the only means of knowing, or the only evidence on which to believe this important truth. I find it clearly and abundantly taught in the Bible, which is the word of God; and I see a thousand facts transpiring in the providential government of the world to confirm the word of God and the intuitions of human intellect. But the single fact that the normal intuitions of all human intellect, and the word of God, as recorded in the Bible, perfectly agree and harmonize on this and every other topic relating to the nature and character of God and his moral government, is sufficient confirmation and evidence of the truth of any proposition.

When, therefore, I affirm that there are three persons in the Godhead, I mean to express the notion, or convey the idea, that as God sustains a variety of different relations to fallen, sinful men, in fulfilling the duties and obligations resulting from these relations, he in these relations sustains a variety of personalities, or that he acts out a variety of personalities in the beneficent works he performs toward sinful men, and for their benefit. I make no reference, in this affirmation, to God as a substantive existence. I neither mention nor suggest any numerical distinction of God, the Creator and moral Governor of the universe, nor affirm any other fact, circumstance or accident of his being, except the single fact that he sustains a variety of different relations to sinful men. The hearer of my affirmation must immediately infer the existence of God, because no relation can exist till subsequent to the existence of its subject, and the corelative of that subject. God can not sustain the relation of Creator till some thing is created, nor till the creature, as subject of the corelation, exists. When I speak of the relations which God sustains towards men, under the title of Godhead, what I affirm I affirm of these relations, and not of God the antecedent subject of them. I know that in this affirmation I impute no numerical distinction to God my Creator; because I know that when I use the word Godhead, I mean the relations in the concrete which God sustains towards sinful men in the flesh. I do not use the word Godhead as a concrete term in the logical sense, including the relations God sustains to men, and God the subject of these relations, but I use it in the philosophical sense, as including, in its meaning, nothing but these relations in the concrete, and abstractly from the substantive being or essence of the Deity. I know and believe, just as surely and in the same manner (described above) that I know my own existence, that the Deity—the infinite, omnipresent, unchangeable, self-existent and eternal God—is a perfect unity, an unvarying identity, of whom numerical distinction can not be predicated but falsely. At the same time I infer, intuitively and necessarily, that neither personality nor obligation can be predicated of Deity, abstractly from the relations which he sustains to other beings. When, therefore, I predicate personality of God, I must use the word God as a concrete term, including in its meaning both the Deity and the various relations which he sustains toward lost men. But I know, and I can not help knowing intuitively, for the Bible, common sense, and the universal testimony of all the intelligent beings with whom I am acquainted confirm my intuitions, that the relations which God sustains are a thing as different from God as the garments a man wears are different from the man. God is a substantive existence; a self-existence; an independent existence. The relations which God sustains towards men have no substantive existence at all. They only exist in the conception of moral intelligence. They are mere accidents of moral agents. They had no existence antecedent to the creation of man, or to his actual existence; because it is a flat contradiction to say or suppose that God sustains any relation to a thing that does not exist. It is uttering a simple falsehood. But the relations which God sustains towards man since the fall, as his Saviour, his Mediator, his Redeemer, his Sanctifier and Comforter, had no existence antecedent to that event. They came into existence as consequents of that catastrophe. They are, therefore, new, in comparison with all the relations existing between God and man antecedent to that rebellion. As the subjects of these relations, on the part of sinning men, are totally different in moral character, in condition, in circumstances, wants and necessities, so the personalities, the duties, obligations and actions resulting from these relations, are new, totally various and different, and as numerous as the varying characters, conditions, circumstances and wants of the subjects of the corelations.

Now, in affirming three persons in the Godhead, I do not intend to predicate personality of the Deity at all, in any sense. Personality, as I have already shown, exists in the relations of moral agents, from which result duties, obligations, and moral character. Personalities, therefore, can be imputed to God only as qualities, circumstances, or accidents of the relations he sustains as moral Governor of the universe. Antecedent to the creation of finite subjects of moral government, no personal relations, duties or obligations existed between God and men; and, therefore, nothing existed of which personality can be predicated, nothing to be called personal only an infinite substantive Being, the distinctive nature and qualities of which no human agent has yet been permitted to form the first conception. The relations he sustains to us and other things in general, constitute the utmost limit of our knowledge or conception of his actual existence. Indeed, all the knowledge or conception of his existence which we have, or which any human being ever attains in this world, is merely inference from the consciousness of our own being, and consists in a perception of a relation which he sustains towards us. We are so constituted that, whenever we perceive any thing existent, whether substantive being or mere change, we intuitively and necessarily infer a preëxisting adequate cause for that consequent. Thus all our knowledge and belief of the existence of God ultimately depends upon, and is only found in the relation between cause and effect which he sustains towards us. The same is true with respect to personality. It is found only, and exists only, in the relations he sustains to us as our moral Sovereign. Therefore, to avoid a gross solecism, confounding the infinite and eternal substance—the distinctive nature and qualities of which I have not the least conception—with the finite personal relations and obligations he sustains, and the works he performs towards sinful men, which must all vary and multiply as the characters, conditions, and necessities of their objects change, I avoid ascribing personality to the eternal, unchangeable, self-existent God.

I use the word Godhead, a term constructed for the very purpose, as I conceive, of expressing in the concrete all the various personal relations which God sustains towards sinful men. I make a triple distinction of these personal relations, by affirming three persons in the Godhead. I find it useful and necessary to make this numerical distinction, in order to attain for myself, or to convey to others, any definite or intelligible conception of these relations, their duties and obligations, and especially of the glorious works of grace, mercy and salvation, which God performs in these different relations. And the God of infinite wisdom, as I learn from his word, has also deemed it convenient and necessary to make the same numerical distinction in revealing his purposes of grace and salvation to fallen men. He teaches us, as distinctly and as plainly as can be taught in human language, that he himself, the one living and true God, in the perfect unity of his identical substantive being, does act in a variety of personal relations, as different and distinct as it is possible to conceive of any three human persons, and in these relations fulfilling a variety of personal obligations, and performing a variety of personal works for the preservation, comfort, and salvation of men. Though these personal relations are as various as the characters and conditions of the objects, yet a triple distinction of persons is sufficient to make the different personal relations and works intelligible.

In the first personal distinction, which we designate by the term Father, he sustains the various personal relations, and performs the various works of Creator, Preserver, Benefactor, and moral Sovereign. By his physical power, through the physical laws of matter, he brings this material world into the proper condition, preserves it in this condition, producing and directing its successive changes for the production, sustenance, and preservation of a succession of human agents, during their probation in the flesh. "For in him we live and move and have our being." "Seeing he giveth to all life and breath and all things." Acts xx. In the second person, which we call the Son, he performs the personal duties of Mediator, Redeemer, and Advocate, including the distinct personalities of Prophet, Priest, and King. In these personal relations he acts at one time, in one personality by physical power, in another by passive endurance in the flesh, in another by motive influence of truth. "For there is one God, and one mediator between God and men, the man Christ Jesus: who gave himself a ransom for all to be testified in in due time." In the third person, the Holy Ghost, he acts in the personal relations of a Comforter, Instructor, Sanctifier or Saviour from the law of sin and death. The appropriate works of this personality are all effected by the motive influence of truth, communicated to sinful men through the medium of their depraved animal senses and perverted intellect. "Sanctify them through thy truth: thy word is truth." Jesus Christ, Jno. xvii. 57.

Now personality, when applied to the agent who acts in these various personal relations, has no reference, implication or allusion, to numerical difference, either of unity or plurality; because the same identical being may sustain and act in each and all of these personal relations, and, as to the substance of his being and the mode of his existence, may continue to be the same identical unity. And the same identical unity of being may take into unity with himself, as to purpose, will, obligation and action, another, two, three, or any number of individuals, and thus constitute a new individual person in a particular relation, and perform new personal duties or actions, and effect new and most important results, which could never have existed or been effected but for the constitution of this new personality. Such are the facts that occur, exist and come to pass, whenever a legislative body is organized, a jury is empanelled, a court constituted, or any joint stock or partnership is formed. And these composite persons and their doings, in their proper relations, are, by good writers and correct speakers, put in the singular number, and their doings represented as the acts of an individual agent. And no solecism is committed; no impropriety of language is imputed; and no absurdity is charged. Because common sense, the word of God and general usage of all civilized society, teach all men that these artificial personalities are as truly single persons, in the particular relation for which they were constituted, as the personality of a single individual agent.

When, therefore, a trinity of persons is predicated of the Godhead, the words are used in their plain common sense signification, expressing a fact that is always present in the relations and doings of organized communities. It indeed involves a general truth, universally understood, acknowledged, and acted upon by all men, but involving no mysticism or inexplicable dogma : viz., the simple truth that a single agent may sustain and act in a variety of different personal relations towards other agents and objects, and retain his own unity and identity of being.

The relations which God sustained to man immediately after the fall, were such as to render it necessary for him to constitute a new and unique personality, that never existed in the universe before ; and to create, or bring into substantive existence, a person essentially different, in relations, endowments, and capabilities, from all antecedent existences. God, antecedent to the fall, sustained the relation of Creator, Father, and universal parent to all the human race, and subsequently to each human being, as they successively came into being, according to his will. This relation of universal Parent involves the obligation of providing, to the extent of his ability, for the highest moral perfection and greatest happiness of each and all of his intelligent, moral, sentient offspring. His ability is infinite in wisdom, power and goodness. In constituting the higher law, or that system of moral government by which he governs the human race, under which they form their moral characters, and by which they determine their final destinies, he made that provision. That provision is as perfect and adequate as infinite wisdom, power and goodness could conceive, prompt, and execute. It was infinitely perfect and adequate. Sin is incidental to a perfect moral system, under a perfect moral law. This we know by sad experience. "The law of the Lord is perfect, converting the soul." But we have sinned in transgressing that perfect law. The provision for the perfect rectitude and happiness of man, contained in the higher law, must, therefore, have included a complete, adequate, and perfect remedial provision for the salvation of every sinner of the human family. If the higher law does not contain such remedial provision for every possible contingency that may occur under its influence, it is a very imperfect, lame, and totally inadequate instrument of moral government. But the law is infinitely perfect; it contains such provision for every contingency. The paternal relation which God sustained to men, is not extinguished by such an incident. The obligations resulting from that relation were still binding. It was still possible for a sinning human agent to be saved from sin and its consequent misery. God is love, and in him is no darkness at all. Infinite benevolence could not but desire the salvation of every fallen creature. Parental love could not abandon his child for a single fault. There is hope till the privileges of probation are entirely exhausted. The obligation to develope the glorious remedy of grace, and give the sinner a new probation under grace, was felt by infinite love. "God so loved the world that he gave his only begotten Son, that whosoever believeth in him should not perish, but have everlasting life." But how could the remedy be applied in the case of sinful men in the flesh?

"The law of the Lord is perfect, converting the soul." The absolute perfection of this law involved these three important truths: 1st. This perfect law was adequate, in itself, to secure to every obedient subject, the highest moral perfection and greatest blessing or happiness his nature was capable of, by its own moral influence, independent of all other influences, agencies, or causality in the universe. Of course, therefore, it was the sole basis or foundation on which all the happiness and hope of created subjects of moral government must rest. 2d. This perfect law embodies, constitutes, or includes all the moral power, influence and causality, for right moral action and spiritual enjoyment, in the universe. It constitutes God's entire moral omnipotence. It is the law of truth; and God never put forth any other influence for the production of moral change or right action but truth. There is no other influence or causality for the production of right moral action in the universe. 3d. This perfect law carries its penal sanction in its own perfection, and executes the same by its own moral influence, independent of all other agency or causality. Hence there is no power in the universe that can save from this penalty, not even omnipotence, physical or moral, but on two indispensable conditions. First, a completely equivalent substitute for the punishment of the transgressor; and second, a perfect renovation of his moral character by perfect conformity and obedience to the law. To save a sinner of the human race these two conditions must be fully accomplished. The first as an absolutely necessary preliminary, and the second as the change, in which his salvation must consist.

The only equivalent substitute, for the punishment of the transgressor of the higher law, must consist in such an illustration of the perfection of the law as would be made by the execution of its penalty on the transgressor; so as to leave the moral influence of the law upon all subjects the same as if the penalty had been inflicted. Such an illustration is what in the Bible is called atonement or reconciliation. No being existing antecedent to the fall was competent to make such an atonement. None but a divine Mediator, uniting in the same individual personality the attributes, the dignity and the perfections of the Deity with the infirmities, susceptibilities, and emotions of man as he was, degenerated and debased by four thousand years' experiment under the law of sin and death. Such a divine Mediator was necessary, that he might comprehend the infinite interests to be secured by his mediation, and also to give dignity, importance and influence to his doings. Such a human mediator was necessary, to adapt his doings and endurings to the condition of those to be redeemed; "that he might be a merciful and faithful High Priest in things pertaining to God, to make reconciliation for the sins of the people." No human or finite being could, by obeying and suffering, honor and magnify the law so as to restore and sustain the motive influence of the same, and yet survive to rejoice in the triumphs of redemption. No divine being could know or sympathize with the sufferings of humanity in the flesh. A combination of Divinity and humanity, in one personal unity, could alone qualify for the office of Mediator, in this case, between God and man. Such was the infinite disparity of nature, and the perfect moral contrariety of will and affection, that it was both morally and physically impossible for the parties to meet on equal or equitable terms, and construct a reconciliation, or repair the evils, or counteract the consequences of sin.

As soon, therefore, as the contingency of sin occurred in the human family, God presented himself to our progenitors in a new and perfectly unique personality; a personality that never before existed, but in the divine purposes of grace to fallen men,—a personality that never existed in any other relation, and can never exist in any other relation. The relation itself, which called for this unique personality, never existed till that day, because the subjects of the co-relation never existed till then. There were no human agents that needed salvation antecedent to that transgression. But immediately on the occurrence of that event God presented himself in a human person, addressed the offenders in human language, made known his presence to them through the medium of the animal senses of the human body: "And they heard the voice of the Lord God walking in the garden in the cool of the day; and Adam and his wife hid themselves from the presence of the Lord God among the trees of the garden." Here were the two natures, the divine and the human, united in one single person, first exhibited on the earth. Here the God-man Mediator first spoke to the sinful agents, for whom "he gave himself a ransom to be testified in due time."

When he had convicted the offenders out of their own mouths, and pronounced sentence on the tempter, he then declared to them the promised Mediator of the woman's seed. "And I will put enmity between thee and the woman, and between thy seed and her seed; it shall bruise thy head, and thou shalt bruise his heel." He then and there preached the gospel of Christ, which "is the power of God unto salvation to every one that believeth." He undoubtedly explained to them the great mystery of godliness; God manifested in the flesh, and the whole doctrine of mediation, atonement, propitiation, redemption, and moral renovation. For they perfectly understood, and practically believed in the divine atoning Mediator, repented and received remission of their sins and absolution from guilt, and all liability to penal infliction for past sins, both of themselves and their posterity. So that for the sin of eating the forbidden fruit, and all their sins previous to that meeting in the garden of Eden, no penal suffering hath ever been inflicted on any human being, or ever can be, because it hath been all atoned for and absolved, and for ever annihilated. Only the physical consequences of that sin, which infinite wisdom, power and goodness can not move, till the probation of grace in the flesh is ended, continues to affect the human family. By that act of absolving our progenitors from the sin of the fall, God became the Saviour of all men, especially of them that believe. The whole subsequent race were saved from utter extinction on that very day that Adam transgressed the law, and incurred the penalty. "In the day thou eatest thereof, thou shalt surely die." But they did not die. They were saved by grace, "through the redemption that is in Christ Jesus:" and lived to have an innumerable posterity, to replenish the earth and subdue it.

Though the physical and intellectual organization, which afterwards constituted the man Jesus of Nazareth, did not come into substantive existence till four thousand years later; yet the person of the God-man Mediator was constituted, created, or brought into existence, and commenced the glorious work of saving a ruined race of created, intellectual, immortals, on the very day they incurred the ruin. "The Lord hath said unto me, Thou art my Son; this day have I begotten thee." Ps. ii. 7. He had no existence before that day. A son does not exist before he is begotten. But his passion was, that very day, accepted as the propitiation for the sins of the whole world; and the world being saved thereby, was put on a new probation under grace. And the whole administration of the same was committed to this one divine and human Mediator between God and man. From that day to the present, the whole work of Mediation and Redemption has been carried on by him, and will continue to progress under his hand, till he brings forth the key-stone thereof, "with shouting, crying grace, grace unto it." It was, and always must be competent, and perfectly within the ability of the omnipotent and omnipresent God to put himself into personal unity with human nature, or with any created existence, that occupies space, whenever he wills it, or chooses to act in such a personal unity. And since the day of the fall there has never been the least intercourse between God and sinful men, but through the agency, intercession and propitiation of this God-man Mediator, Jesus Christ. Nor has God ever abandoned, for a single moment, any sinning human agent, till his probation under grace was ended, and his character of moral evil was perfected and confirmed beyond hope of renovation. Such then is the second person in the adorable Trinity of the God-head. A perfect man without sin, but made in the likeness of sinful flesh, with its infirmities, as they were after four thousand years' bondage under the law of sin and death; and at the same time, in the same person, the infinitely perfect and unchangeable God. This infinitely glorious and unique Person was created or brought into being by a special act of divine sovereignty, and not by ordinary generation, as other human agents are; nor yet by eternal generation, as theological romancers have dreamed, but in time for the definite purpose of saving sinful men. "This day have I begotten thee."

In the constitution of the person of this divine Mediator there is no inexplicable mysticism. No dogma asserted that cannot be explained and made intelligible to any human agent of common sense, who wishes to understand it, and is willing to bestow the necessary thought and reflection. There is no proposition involved in this view of the subject but what is perfectly reconcilable with all truth, both moral and physical. We do not deny; we believe, we know, and understand the mystery of godliness. We know that the whole gracious provision of the higher law, the wonderful plan of saving sinful men, by a divine Mediator, voluntarily giving himself as a propitiatory sacrifice, in human flesh, for the redemption of the whole fallen race, is the most profound, the most sublime and glorious mystery ever conceived of by finite intellect. "Without controversy great is the mystery of godliness." This mystery and its results are the things which the angels desire to look into. It was hid in the secret counsels of the divine mind, till the contingency for which it was provided had occurred. And even after that it was hid from ages and generations by the influence of prevailing sin and aversion to the light of truth. But as soon as the contingency occurred, a full and clear revelation of the mystery was made to the transgressors; and the nature, design, conditions and results of the divine plan were so fully and adequately explained to our progenitors, that they clearly understood and practically believed, and were saved. And a significant typical illustration of the mystery was given them as an essential part of their weekly devotions, till the actual manifestation in the flesh should be perfected. God at that time instituted the sacrament of animal sacrifice, by shedding the blood of innocent subjects, and clothing the naked culprits with their skins.

But since the incarnation, and especially since the resurrection of the Saviour and the completion of the New Testament, it is very inconsistent for ministers of the gospel and doctors of divinity to tell poor, lost sinners that this subject is involved in profound mysteries, which they cannot explain and no human intellect can understand or comprehend. Every sinning agent must understand, comprehend, and practically believe this great mystery of godliness, or perish in his sins. The apostle tells us that "God was manifested in the flesh." It must have been in this relation and in this very person of Jesus Christ, in this very work of redemption, and in the very article of atoning for sins. No other manifestation in the flesh can be pretended. Whatever is manifested is made clear, plain, visible to the eye, obvious to the understanding, apparent to the conception, no longer obscure to the sight or understanding. Every thing that can be conceived as relating to this mystery, was done publicly before the eyes of thousands, has been explained by all the illustrations that infinite wisdom could devise and adopt to make it plain and understandable to sinners in the flesh; and all has been recorded in plain, common sense language. The apostle tells us the reason of this manifestation, or why it was necessary that such a personality should be constituted, and such a propitiatory sacrifice offered. That God might be "justified in the Spirit." The God of infinite wisdom, power, and goodness, the moral Sovereign of the universe, now sustained the relation of Saviour to sinful, rebellious man, and was absolving them from guilt, or delivering them from liability to suffer the penal consequences which his own law (that is, his own will, for his will and the higher law are identical) inflicts on the transgressor. It was necessary, to justify himself from manifest absurdity, self-contradiction, partiality, favouritism, injustice, cruelty, and barbarous tyranny to other subjects of his government, that he should develop and fully illustrate the crowning perfection of the higher law, to the view and comprehension of the whole moral universe. This consisted in the infinite provision of grace which the law included, or rather in what God himself, in personal unity with a sinless human agent, was under obligation to the law to do, and could and would do, for the salvation of sinners. " Being justified freely by his grace through the redemption that is in Christ Jesus; whom God hath set forth to be a propitiation through faith in his blood, to declare his righteousness, for the remission of sins that are past through the forbearance of God; To declare, I say, at this time, his righteousness: that he might be just, and the justifier of him which believeth in Jesus."—Rom. iii. 24-26.

This development and illustration of the perfection of the higher law, which was made in the flesh, "was seen of angels." They were interested subjects of the same moral kingdom. But being finite intellects, they had never before comprehended the infinite perfections of the higher law, nor the infinite goodness of God in the gracious provisions of that law. But their own perfection and blessedness, and, indeed, every interest of every obedient subject of moral government depended on the motive influence of that perfect law. If the law was not magnified and made honorable, or if its motive influence was not perfectly sustained, they were ruined, as well as sinful men. But they saw the God-man Mediator, of his own will, freely, of choice, bearing "our sins in his own body on the tree;" ("and the Lord hath laid on him the iniquity of us all," even of the whole human race;) not by suffering punishment or penal infliction of any sort, or in any sense whatever; but by voluntary endurance in the flesh, illustrating the infinite and crowning perfection of the law, and the infinite goodness and benevolence of the Lawgiver; thus establishing and confirming forever the motive influence of the law. In making this illustration, two important, evangelical, saving truths were revealed to the created moral universe, which previously had been unknown and inconceivable to all finite intelligence. First, that such is the nature and absolute perfection of the higher law, that it is just as impossible for Omnipotence to save a sinner from its penalty, without such an atonement, to be made only by a divine Mediator, and received in penitence and faith by the subject, as it is for imbecility itself, unaided, to create a universe. The second truth is, that now such an atonement being made, God can be just and the Justifier, the Saviour and Sanctifier of him which believeth in Jesus.

This same God, who was manifested in the flesh, was also "preached unto the Gentiles, even to all the human race," as the only Saviour of men, and this atoning sacrifice the only possible method of saving a sinning human agent. This was done to illustrate the infinite benevolence of God in making this propitiation, not for a part, not for a few, nor even a very great select number, "but also for the sins of the whole world." Even for the sins of every individual human agent that ever did or ever shall commit a sin during his probation in the flesh, and that thus every sinner may have an opportunity of saving himself from the consequence of his transgression, unless prevented by human agency.

This doctrine of atonement for the sins of men was believed on in the world before the Saviour was born, or the propitiatory illustration consummated. Even from the day it was first preached to Adam and Eve in the garden of Eden, to the present hour, it has constituted a fundamental article in the religious belief of the whole world, with very few if any exceptions, either among pagan Gentiles or in Christendom. The universal prevalence of propitiatory sacrifice of some sort or another, and in one shape or another, among all pagan nations and savage tribes of men, is demonstration perfect that the necessity of atonement, in order to obtain absolution from guilt and misery as the consequence of sin, is an intuitive truth to the human intellect, which the sinning human agent can no more evade or get rid of than he can get rid of his own existence. This conviction is an essential part of his character, just as soon as transgression constitutes his relationship to the higher law, and must continue so to be, and constitute a fruitful source of misery, till absolved by the blood of the "Lamb of God which taketh away the sins of the world."

The sinner must obtain reconciliation by some other person, or he must make atonement himself, because it is impossible for him to get rid of this conscious intuitive necessity. But neither conscience nor intuition can suggest any other means of atonement but voluntary personal suffering. Hence the thousands of self-tormentors among pagan devotees and Christian ascetics. And even among evangelical Christians, as the speculating theologians and pious romancers obscure the glorious doctrines of the Trinity, the incarnation and atonement, by their fogs of mysticism, personal austerity and exclusiveness, unnecessary self-denial and mortification, with self-sacrificing and painful and useless observances, are very apt to be multiplied, and often take the place of piety towards God and benevolence to our fellow sinners.

Finally, this incarnate Deity, this Son of God in human flesh, "When he had by himself purged our sins, was received up into glory, and sat down on the right hand of the Majesty on high." There, in the court of heaven, he is the resident advocate and representative of all who believe in him; and is "able also to save them to the uttermost that come unto God by him, seeing he ever liveth to make intercession for them."

The entire providential government of this world is committed to him, all things being put under his feet, or at his disposal, and he given to be the head over all things to the Church. "For he must reign till he hath put all enemies under his feet. The last enemy that shall be destroyed is death." God hath constituted him a king, and put every thing in this rebellious province of his dominion under his control, till he has perfectly quelled the rebellion, and brought the last sinner, that infinite wisdom, power and goodness can save, to the full enjoyment of the liberties of the adopted sons of God, to wit, the redemption of the body. "Then cometh the end, when he shall have delivered up the kingdom to God, even the Father; when he shall have put down all rule and all authority and power; then shall the Son also himself be subject unto him that did put all things under him, that God may be all in all." The work of saving lost men had a beginning, and we may be sure it will have an end, for God never leaves his work half accomplished, but always completes what he begins. Sinners must be saved in time, or perish for ever. The personal relations, the personalities and the personal doings, that have been constituted and employed in that work, must have an end. But this human agent, Jesus of Nazareth, who, in the second person of the Godhead, achieved the redemption of a world, "Being made so much better than the angels, as he hath by inheritance obtained a more excellent name than they," must of course be exalted in dignity, honor, and glory; "far above all principality, and power, and might, and dominion, and every name that is named, not only in this world, but also in that which is to come."

4th. But we have affirmed a third person in the Godhead. The necessity of a third personal distinction among the relations which God sustains towards men as the Saviour of sinners, arises out of the personal character and condition of men as transgressors of the higher law. By the first act of transgression the sinner puts himself under the law of sin and death. He becomes subject to that influence which Paul described as a law in his members warring against the law of his mind, and bringing him into captivity to the law of sin which was in his members. In another place, in analyzing the law of sin and death, I have shown that the immediate, the natural and necessary consequence of the first transgression of the law of God, is to close the intellectual vision of the transgressor against the light of truth as it shines in the higher law, and to beget an inveterate hatred and aversion to that light. "For every one that doeth evil hateth the light, neither cometh to the light, lest his deeds should be reproved."

But this light of truth in the perfect law of the Lord, which converts the soul, being the only influence, power, or causality in the universe for the production of right moral action, or any moral change for the better, it must be brought into contact with the intellectual perception, and the moral sense or conscience of the sinner, in order to begin his moral renovation. Notwithstanding all that the second person had done as Mediator, Redeemer and Intercessor, God could do nothing to save the sinner from sin and its consequent misery till a new method of access to his moral susceptibilities was devised and instituted. But this perfect law of the Lord executes its penal sanction by its own motive influence, independent of all other causality. The penalty in the case of the first transgression of man was, "In the day thou eatest thereof, thou shalt surely die." If the moral Sovereign had not graciously interfered, on that very day our progenitors must have died under the motive influence of the very law which is the only power in the universe that can save a sinning human agent. And they must also have died childless, and the whole race must have become extinct in the first couple. But God did interfere to save the race. This interference was by an act of his physical omnipotence, in the first person of the Godhead, shielding and sustaining the physical organization of Adam and Eve from dissolution, under the shock of their first sight of their new character and condition in the light of truth. Had the full light of eternal truth from the higher law shined into their moral susceptibility, and revealed to them their new character and condition in their whole extent, and in their relations to the future, they would not have survived a single day. And here we may observe a beam of the infinite wisdom and goodness of God, reflected from the law of sin and death. The immediate influence of the first transgression of the law of God is to beget aversion to the light of truth, and to array all the self-preservative instincts, appetites, and passions of the animal nature of man in opposition to, and avoidance of, the light of moral truth. Now, this hatred and aversion to the light of truth operated on Adam, and continues to operate on every sinning human agent, as a temporary shield and protection against the penal effect of that light on a guilty conscience. The unmitigated light of eternal truth on a guilty conscience, is the flaming sword of vindictive justice, instantly sundering every bond of union between soul and body, and sending the immortal part naked to the everlasting punishment of the guilty. But in the hand of mercy it turns every way to keep the way of the tree of life. For the same motive influence of the light of truth, reflected from the cross of the divine Mediator, and mitigated by the infinite love of God for a lost and ruined world, falls upon the same guilty conscience as the reviving water of life, healing the deadly wounds of the soul, and inspiring new moral life and saving hope into the trembling culprit. Or, as Paul describes the thing, it becomes "The law of the Spirit of life in Christ Jesus hath made (or making) me free from the law of sin and death." This application of the light of truth to the moral susceptibilities of the sinner, producing conviction, melting the affections into penitence, and persuading him to cease to do evil and learn to do well, is a spiritual, a moral influence, operation, or work. It lies totally without the sphere of all physical power, influence, force or causality. The effect produced is a moral change of the action, and, of course, in the moral character of the subject. It is the commencement of that moral change in which the salvation of the subject from sin and its consequent misery exclusively consists. It is the change technically called regeneration, or the new birth. It is that begetting with the word of truth which the Father of lights produces by a direct act of his own will.

The will of God and the higher law of eternal truth are identical. It is produced by moral influence alone and exclusively. The agency, therefore, which God puts forth to produce it, is totally different and distinct from all physical power. It is produced solely by the motive influence of truth, modified by reflection from the cross of Christ and the love of God to sinning human agents. The personal relation in which this agency is put forth, is totally different from any other relation which God sustains, or can sustain, towards men. It, therefore, constitutes a personality entirely different from what can exist in any other case or relation. The action or influence which God puts forth in the first personal relation, is often in direct contrariety, and apparent opposition, to that which he puts forth in the third person. By his physical power, in the first person, God sustains and protects the sinner from the just deserts of his conduct, shielding him, by the influence of falsehood under the law of sin and death, from the penal influence of the higher law, which would at once destroy his life, and send him to suffer the consequences of his rebellion; while at the same time, in the third person, he is using all appropriate and all possible means, agency and influence, to bring the light of that same law, modified indeed by reflection from the cross, to bear on his conscience and persuade him to right moral action. But this light of truth must come gradually, in such measure as the subject of renovation can bear and digest: a few plain simple facts about the character of that seed of the woman who should bruise the serpent's head; and then a plain visible illustration of the nature of the atonement; and then a few rays of light from the higher law, showing the exceeding great reward there is in keeping the commandments of the Lord. And all must be communicated through the depraved, viciated, and diseased animal senses of the sinner. And surely nothing short of infinite wisdom could so modify and balance and direct these apparently conflicting influences of truth, as to preserve the life and continue the probation of the sinner, in the flesh and under grace, till he shall have enjoyed a full, fair, and adequate opportunity of perfecting the renovation of his moral character, and thus securing the gracious gift of God, even eternal life by Jesus Christ our Lord.

This third personal relation of the one living and true God, to fallen men, is personified in the Bible, and by the Saviour himself, under the titles of "The Comforter, The Holy Ghost, The Spirit of truth, The Spirit of life in Christ Jesus." "I will pray the Father, and he shall give you another Comforter, that he may abide with you for ever; even the Spirit of truth." Jno. xiv. 16. "The Comforter, which is the Holy Ghost, whom the Father will send in my name, he shall teach you all things, and bring all things to your remembrance whatsoever I have said unto you." Verse 26. "But when the Comforter is come, whom I will send unto you from the Father, even the Spirit of truth which proceedeth from the Father, he shall testify of me." John xv. 26. "And when he is come he will reprove the world of sin, and of righteousness, and of judgment." Jno. xvi. 8. "He shall glorify me: for he shall receive of mine, and shall show it unto you. All things that the Father hath are mine: therefore said I that he shall take of mine and show it unto you." Jno. xvi. 14, 15.

In these quotations Jesus Christ speaks of three distinct persons, including himself, each of them at the same time performing actions, as distinct and as different from each other, as can be conceived; actions, which no agent in the universe, but the infinite, omniscient and omnipotent Spirit can perform. In the first quotation these three persons, the Father, Son and Holy Ghost are perfectly identified as one substantive Being, not in the same, but in three totally different relations. In relation to sinful men, and the gracious work of saving them from sin and its miserable consequences, the three persons and their actions in this gracious work, are as distinct and as different from each other as the persons and actions of any three different human agents acting at the same time on the three great continents of this globe. While in the relation of Proprietor of all things, they are a perfect unity; and in all other relations, as far as we know, God may be spoken of in a single personality. Or, if he chooses, he may speak of himself in as many varieties of personality as he sustains varieties of relation to his creatures. But that self-existent Being, whom we call God, Deity, and Creator, is always a perfect unity, a simple identity, though he may be acting in ten thousand different places, on millions of different subjects, by different influences, forces, or causalities, and in ten thousand different personalities or personal relations. Hence, whenever we predicate personality of the Godhead, we refer to and intend to qualify only the relations which God sustains towards fallen men, as their Creator, Preserver, and Saviour. We use the name Godhead as a concrete term to express only the relations which God sustains to fallen men, and personality to distinguish certain varieties qualifying these relations and the peculiar works of grace which belong to them. In the first person, God creates, sustains in the flesh, and protects the sinner from the penal influence of the higher law. In the second person he performs the entire works of Mediator, Redeemer, and Judge, including the offices of Prophet, Priest, and King. In executing these offices, and performing these relative duties, or works of grace, it was an absolutely necessary qualification of the personal agent, that he should unite in his personality, the divine and the human nature, the Creator and the creature, the spiritual and the material. It was necessary, on the one hand, to include the infinite in his personality, in order to sustain him in works infinitely beyond finite power or endurance, and to give dignity and motive value and importance to his doings, sufficient to magnify and honor the law, or to illustrate the righteousness of God in enacting such a law. That he might be just, and the justifier of him which believeth in Jesus." And also to show the impossibility of saving the sinner without atonement. On the other hand it was essential that he should include the material, or animal nature, in order to reach and influence the intellectual and moral susceptibilities of sinful men, through the medium of their viciated and perverted animal senses.

In the third person God begins, carries on, and perfects the moral renovation of the sinner, from his first conviction to the complete redemption of all his endowments from the law of sin and death. This is purely a moral change, effected by the moral influence of truth alone, to the exclusion of all physical force, power, or causality. But such is the condition of men in the flesh, and subject to the law of sin and death, that the truth, or will of God in the higher law, in order to gain access to his moral susceptibilities, must be embodied in personal unity, or identity with human language, either oral or written. Antecedent to the fall, the knowledge of moral truth, or of the will of God, on the higher law, which are an identity, was intuitive to human intellect and conscience. That is, as soon as any relation involving duty, and imposing obligation, was perceived by any human intellect, the duty involved was intuitively, necessarily and instantly conceived and understood, and the obligation felt in all its extent, and the human will perfectly concurred with the truth, or divine will. But since his transgression, the perceptive vision of the human intellect is voluntarily and habitually closed against the light of truth, for fear of reproof for his evil deeds. Not that he is unable to perceive, understand, and obey: for his ability is always and necessarily co-extensive with the obligation; but he hates the light, because it torments him, and would very soon extinguish his animal life. Therefore, God embodies his will, or the truth, as far as it relates to sinful human agents, in human language, that may affect the ear, or any other nervous organ of sensation, and thus reach the rational mind, when he pleases, without the consent of the will of the subject. Thus constituting a new and perfectly unique personality.

This, I believe, to be the true common sense idea expressed by Jesus Christ, our Saviour, when he prayed to the Father, "Sanctify them through thy truth: thy word is truth." Jno. xvii. 17. And by the Apostle James, when he says of the Father of lights: "Of his own will begat he us with the word of truth, that we should be a kind of first fruits of his creatures." Jas. i. 18. Sanctifying is a personal act. Begetting is a personal act. The Father of lights is the agent, the author, the sole efficient cause. And the word of truth is the sole efficient cause, the immediate and invariable antecedent to the change whenever it takes place. This word of truth, "is the word of salvation." "It is the power of God unto salvation." Rom.

i. 16. "By which also ye are saved." 1 Cor. xvi. 2. "The law of the Lord is perfect, converting the soul." Here, then, vanishes the vexed question, which has been the subject of bitter conflict for ages, viz: Does the direct or immediate power of God, or the motive influence of truth, produce the change of regeneration or conversion? The word of truth and the power of God unto salvation is one and the same thing. In relation to the salvation of sinners of the human family, the almighty God and the word of truth constitute a single personal identity.

Thus we have three persons in the Godhead: the Father, in the relations of Creator and Preserver; the Son, in the relations of Mediator and Redeemer: the Holy Ghost, in the relations of Comforter and Sanctifier. But not the least reference or allusion to the substantive existence or being of the Deity, in relation to time, space, mode, method, or numerical distinction. These three persons are as perfectly distinct and diverse from each other as any three human persons can be. They are neither the same in substance, nor equal in power, glory, or authority. The first in substantive existence is the infinite, eternal, and unchangable Spirit, pervading all space alike, whether occupied by other beings or not. Self-existent and uncaused himself, and the primary cause of all other substantive being. The second is the same infinite being, uniting and acting in the most perfect personal unity, with a finite, created, intellectual moral agent, existing for a time in a material, animal body, and still existing in a finite, created, and spiritual body. The third in substantive being is the same infinite and self-existent Spirit, but acting in a new and different personal relation, on subjects in a different condition, never conceived of by man before his fall. Each of these three personalities is constituted differently from both the others, and sustains to men, the subjects of salvation, a different relation, and performs different works, or different parts of the work of salvation. The first is in authority, power, and glory, and in all his attributes infinitely perfect. The second, in his whole personal work and relations, is subordinate, dependent upon, and expectant of the first. The third is subordinate and perfectly dependent on the other two, both for authority, power, or ability, even to begin the work of moral renovation in the case of sinners.

Till the motive influence of the higher law, that is of eternal truth, is restored and fully established by an adequate atonement, and so embodied as to reach the human conscience through the viciated animal senses of the transgressor, God Almighty is just as destitute of ability or influence to commence the moral renovation of the sinner, as the sinner is of physical power to create a universe. The atonement must come first. Events that are finite, consecutive, and connected in the relation of cause and effect, must succeed in the order of nature. The antecedent must precede the consequent. The cause, instrument, and means must exist, before the consequent changes can begin to take place. The perfect Law of the Lord must be magnified and made honorable, its motive influence must be re-established, before the divine Sanctifier can begin his work of renovation; for he must sanctify them by the motive influence of the truth, as exhibited in that Law. "Sanctify them through thy truth: thy word is truth." The motive influence of that law must be included in the antecedent of all right moral action, and of all moral change for the better.

In affirming three persons of the Godhead I do not pretend, nor intend, to use the word Godhead in the same sense or in the same extent of signification, in which it is sometimes used by men of learning and piety. I do not concur with those theologians who make it synonymous with God, Deity, or Supreme Being. I believe such a use of the word to be solecistic, incongruous, and a breach of the laws of a correct syntax. But I use it in the precise and limited signification which I have endeavored to define.

Nor do I use the word person or personality as meaning all and exactly the same things, when applied to the Godhead, that are intended to be expressed by it in all its various applications to human agents, in human language. Sometimes it is used to designate one individual human agent from others of the same species or class. But in this sense I do not and can not use it, in application to the Godhead. A polytheist might, with propriety, make this use of it, to distinguish the Godheads of his Jupiter, Juno, Mars, and Neptune. But I acknowledge but one God, and know of but one Godhead in relation to human transgressors, and but one class of human transgressors to be saved, and but one Mediator, Jesus Christ, the Almighty Saviour of men. Personality is sometimes used to distinguish the different relations of an individual agent, or the different offices he sustains. "How different is the same man from himself, as he sustains the person of a magistrate and that of a friend." Personality is also used to designate the united concurrent action of any number of human agents. "The whole assembly rose spontaneously at the entering of the king." Here personality, in the singular number and third person, is used to designate the relation and the concurrent action in that relation, of a large number of different individual agents. But in this use of personality there is no reference at all to the nature, or substantive being, or the manner of existence of the different agents concerned. Nor does it convey or imply the least suggestion, in reference to the number or circumstances of these agents, aside from that particular relation, whether they were two, five, or five thousand; whether black or white, rich or poor, wise or simple, civilized or savage. There is no solecism or mysticism in this use of personification; no incongruity of language, no absurdity or contradiction in words or conception. But all is plain common sense language, capable of being understood by every person of common sense and common education. When, therefore, we affirm three persons of the Godhead, we use the terms person and personality in the common sense meaning of the words, according to the usage of the best writers and speakers of the language. And we use this language, and thus personify the Godhead, because we can not conceive of any other language, or any other method by which it is possible for God, angel, or man, to convey to a sinful man any consistent, intelligible, or rational conception of the nature of salvation from sin; or of the manner, means, and influences by which God does or can save a sinner from the penalty of his perfect law; and also because this is the method the Holy Ghost uses in the Bible to communicate the knowledge of this subject to men. It involves no solecism, absurdity, or contradiction. It is easily understood by all persons of common sense, who wish to understand and are willing to bestow the necessary thought and reflection. And there is not the least danger of its being misunderstood, to affirm the contradictory mysticism of three Gods being one God, or of three substantive beings constituting but one divine essence.

But when the orthodox trinitarian affirms that the one true God, the Deity or the Supreme Being, exists in a trinity of persons, he commits a manifest solecism, he utters a real absurdity, he asserts a positive contradiction, both in words and in thought. He thus exposes himself to the just censure and easy refutation of his adversary. Trinity necessarily involves plurality, but plurality is not predicable of an infinite, omnipresent, and unchangeable Being without great absurdity and contradiction. The Bible declares, "The Lord our God is one Lord." Deut. vi. 4. On the other hand, when the professed unitarian affirms that "Three persons in the Godhead" means that there are three Gods, or in any way, shape or manner, implies or involves a plurality of Gods, or a plurality, or the least variety in the divine essence, commits the same solecism, and utters just as great an absurdity. He totally ignores all distinction between substantive being and personality; confounding them as identical, or essentially coëxistent; and then transfers the personality, which we ascribe, and which exclusively pertains to the relationships that God sustains towards sinful men, to the substantive being of God, or to the divine essence. Whereas, the personalities of the Godhead have no more reference to the substantive being of God than the phases of the moon have to the physical substance of the material sun. Every schoolboy of common sense knows that the various phases of the moon are produced by her own motion, constantly varying her relations, in space and position, to the light of the sun. And every theologian, who pretends to think and reason, ought to know that the personalities of the Godhead have their existence only in the varied relations which exist between God and sinning men; and that all the variety in these relations is produced by the voluntary action of sinners in relation to the perfect law of God. But the parties who had conceived these conflicting dogmas fell to loggerheads about their different mysticisms, each contending for the truth and divinity of their own absurdity and contradiction, as an essential doctrine of godliness. And thus the conflict of ages has been kept alive, and time and treasure, thought and labor enough wasted to have evangelized the world and saved its millions ages ago; while the entire subject of all this controversy, and the sole cause of the inconceivable loss and misery, has been a perfect myth, without the shadow of basis or cause, either in the nature or relations of any existent being or thing in the universe.

But every common sense reader of the Bible, who feels interest enough on the subject to consider and reflect on what he reads, knows that three distinct persons are there described, as sustaining distinct personal relations to fallen men; and as each performing distinct personal agencies, or works, which none but an agent of infinite wisdom, power and goodness can perform. And in all this he discovers no inexplicable mystery beyond the sphere of human intellect to understand or comprehend. Still we constantly hear from the pulpit, and read in books of theology and practical religion, of the profound and inexplicable mysteries of godliness involved in this subject. We are often exhorted to believe, without doubting or hesitation, and warned against the damning sin of doubting propositions which contradict every intuition of human intellect, and every fact of human experience, and the whole system of revealed truth. How, says the godly teacher or writer, the infinite, unchangeable, and true God exists in three distinct and different persons, we cannot explain nor understand, even if God should declare it unto us, because it is a subject infinitely above the sphere of human intellect. But it seems that these learned teachers have not been able to understand, though God has often told them very plainly, that he existed and still exists, antecedent to, and independent of, all personality or personal relation to the children of men: and, as far as we know, of all created or finite beings. To be sure, there is no Christianity, and, as far as we can conceive, no salvation without the doctrine of the trinity and the incarnation of the Deity. But Paul told Timothy that this great mystery of godliness was manifested in the flesh. If manifested in the flesh, it must be plain to the understanding of every human intellect in the flesh, who is willing or wishes to understand. Perhaps it would be as well, and as safe, to let the people of only common sense believe, if they will, what Paul teaches on the subject, as to wrap up the whole in ever so profound a fog of mysticism; especially since persons of only common sense are in the habit of believing practically only what they are able and permitted to understand.

But the source of all this error, mysticism and controversy, may be seen in the confounding of personality with substantive being, as identical, or, at least, as something essential to and coëxisting with substantive being, and in using the word Godhead as synonymous with Deity. Whereas, personality pertains exclusively to the relations of moral agents. It is an absolutely necessary and most useful contrivance in every human language, to express, by varying the forms or positions of words, the varying circumstances of these relations, and of the duties and obligations resulting from them. The relations of the infinite and unchangeable God to sinning men must necessarily change and vary, as the character, condition, and circumstances of the sinner change. But in the substantive being, character, purpose, and will of the Supreme Being, there is no numerical distinction, no variableness, neither shadow of turning. When, therefore, the professed trinitarian predicates personality of the Supreme Being, or affirms that the one living and true God exists in three, (or even in one person,) he contradicts himself, and utters a gross absurdity, which can not be reconciled with the truth of God or the nature of personality; for the very nature of personality necessarily involves the idea of change, of variety, of plurality. Personality, even in the singular number, is never used but to distinguish, by his relations, an individual of a particular nature, genus or species, from other individuals of the same kind, and, therefore, necessarily implies that others of the same nature, genus or species, do actually exist at the time.

Also, when the professed unitarian predicates personality of his **God** as something essential to his nature, or as qualifying the manner of his existence; or when he affirms that a plurality of persons in the Godhead implies a plurality of Gods, or any variety or numerical distinction in the divine essence, or the least shadow of variation in the Supreme Being, he falls into the same error, contradiction, and gross absurdity. He confounds personality and substantive existence as an identity, or as essentially coëxistent: and uses the word Godhead as synonymous with God or Supreme Being. Therefore, the single or individual personality which he ascribes to his God, necessarily implies that there are a variety of Gods, from whom it is necessary to distinguish the identical Being, which he worships as his God. But when this one personality is added or predicated, when he has called him the person of the one God, or the one God person, or the God of one person, or the personal substance of the one God, and varied the one person of his God by all the shades of meaning and all the modes and forms of expression and exposition that human language can furnish, the distinction is not yet made. He has not told himself, or any other created intellect, who his God is, or what he is, how he exists, or whether he exists at all, or has any substantive being, or is only a mere fiction of the imagination. He has not yet expressed, even to his own perception, or the perception of any other human intellect, which of the "Gods many and Lords many" he worships, or how his God differs in any respect from the ten thousands of Gods that float in depraved human imaginations. Some other word, which refers to the relations of moral beings, must be added, before personality will express any meaning at all, or qualify any substantive existence. The reason of this is, because personality refers, or has respect to the relations of moral agents, and to nothing else; and exists only in the construction of human language to express the varieties of these relations. We may, therefore, defy the unitarian, the trinitarian, and all the doctors of theology and professors of philology on the earth, to show any meaning, sense, signification, use or influence of personification, in any of its forms or varieties of expression or shades of meaning, when abstracted from, or predicated of any thing else than those relations of moral beings which involve duty and obligation.

I believe in the one infinite, self-existent Spirit as the only true God. And I believe him to be omniscient, omnipresent, and eternal; infinite in wisdom, power, and goodness, and in every other attribute essential to Deity. But with respect to the nature of the divine essence or substance, or the manner in which he exists, and with respect to the essential attributes of his being, I know nothing and can believe nothing, except what he has definitely and distinctly revealed to me, and made plain to my understanding and comprehension. I am a finite being. My intellectual endowments and moral susceptibilities are all finite, limited, and imperfect. And, therefore, all my perceptions, conceptions, ideas, or mental images of God, his essence, substantive being, mode of existence, purposes, acts, and ultimate designs, however enlarged and magnified by my little finite intellect, are still, and necessarily infinitely inadequate, and infinitely short of the true ideal of the infinite and eternal God. If, therefore, I attempt to infer, or deduce any proposition, dogma, or affirmation, as a fact or truth, from my inadequate conceptions of the divine Being, his nature, attributes, purposes, and designs, it is impossible for me to know, whether my inference is true or false. And there is necessarily but one chance or probability, among an infinite number to the contrary, that my inference or affirmation may be true. And I have never seen, known, heard, or read of any human agent in the flesh, since the fall, that ever had or was able to form any adequate, definite, explicable or understandable conception of the nature of the divine Essence, or the manner of his existence, or action; or of the extent, method, or number of his decrees, purposes, or designs, any farther than God may have communicated to him by direct, express and comprehensible revelation in human language. I have, therefore, repudiated all inferences, dogmas, and affirmations, drawn from the finite, inadequate and imperfect conceptions of fallen men, concerning the infinities and eternities of the divine Being, his attributes, purposes, and works.

I believe that this self-existent Spirit, the living and true God, is the Creator of all other substantive beings, and that he therefore existed antecedent to the existence of any other being, and of course antecedent to any relation or personality of beings. For I can not conceive of relationship, as existing antecedent to the existence of the beings, who sustain the relation, and in whom alone the relationship has existence. And I can not conceive of personality but as qualifying some relation involving obligation and duty. God must, therefore, have existed before he sustained any relation to any other being, or any obligation, duty, or personality. But when God created other and finite moral beings, he, by that act, brought into existence various relations, involving obligations and duties. And by the same act, also, he created the necessity of language, or some medium of intercourse or communication among moral beings: and also the necessity of those varied forms of language which are used to designate the varieties of personal relation. To meet these necessities in the case of men, God taught Adam the use of articulate sounds, as signs of things and thoughts, and thus constituted a medium of intercourse between himself, the moral Sovereign, and his human subjects. Hence, the personal Logos, or Word, which, at the beginning of the dispensation, or reign of grace, was with God, and was God, viz: the self-existent Creator, the I Am, holding verbal intercourse with man, his creature and subject. This personality, or personal relation, was very properly and significantly called the Logos, or the Word, from the fact, that the only medium of intercourse between the correlatives of this relation was verbal. The finite correlate existing, only in perfect personal unity with a physical organization of material substance, the infinite spiritual Correlate, could reach his finite intellectual and moral susceptibilities only by locomotion produced in his physical organs of sensation. Thus we see God teaching Adam the use of articulate sounds as a medium of intercommunication. Gen. i. 19, 20. The personal Logos commenced existence immediately after the creation of man. Any supposed antecedent existence is an impossibility, involving a positive contradiction.

When Adam brought sin and its consequent death into the world, he also created new and varied relations between himself and the moral Sovereign of the universe. Infinite goodness towards the guilty transgressors, of course, assumed the relation of Saviour to the sinful race, including all the subordinate relations of Mediator, Redeemer, Advocate, Prophet, Priest, King, Sanctifier, Comforter, etc. Now, I use the term of Godhead, to signify all these varied relations which God, the moral Governor of the world sustains to sinning men. And I find it not only very convenient, but absolutely necessary, to use those forms of human language which are contrived to express the distinctions of personal relations, in order to speak, write, or even to think any thing intelligibly, in reference to these relations, or to the obligations, duties, and interests growing out of them. And God, himself, in condescension to our infirmities, or in consequence of the limited, imperfect and perverted condition of our endowments, is under the same necessity of using these same personal forms of language in order to make known to us his will and purposes concerning these new relations created by transgression.

While, therefore, I believe in a trinity of persons in the Godhead, as confidently as in my existence, I also believe, with the same confidence, in the perfect unity of the Deity, as a single identical and spiritual Substance, or Being, without the least shadow of numerical distinction, or variety in his essence or mode of existence. I claim, therefore, to be in faith and doctrine a true, orthodox, and consistent unitarian. And, with the same unhesitating confidence, I pronounce every person, who affirms that God exists in three persons, to be in faith and doctrine a real polytheist.

It may be possible, that my knowledge, belief, and affirmations on this sublime and awful subject, are mere delusion, error, or falsehood. I am a finite, fallible, fallen and depraved creature, liable to err as well as my fellow sinners. I have, in times past, erred, have been deluded, self-deceived, and deceived by venerable and pious human authorities. I have perverted the truth, and have loved darkness rather than the light of truth. This was the natural consequent of my evil doing, according to the law of sin and death. But in reference to myself, my present knowledge, belief, and affirmations on the subject, are of that peculiar kind, which seem to me to be absolutely infallible. First, because I know intuitively, and can not avoid knowing, and am necessarily conscious, and can not avoid being conscious of my own existence. And I know, intuitively, and can not avoid knowing, that I acquired this knowledge of my existence, through the sensation of a physical contact, of other substantive being. Thus, I intuitively acquired, and could not avoid receiving the knowledge of the existence of other substantive beings besides myself. And I also know, intuitively, that God has so constructed, and combined together my physical and intellectual endowments and moral susceptibilities, that it is impossible for me to know, conceive, or be conscious of my own existence and the existence of other substantive beings, or of any change whatever, without at the same time, or immediately subsequent, conceiving of, and knowing, intuitively, the existence of an efficient antecedent or adequate cause of the existence of such beings and changes. The only adequate and primary cause, possible to my conception, of the existence of all finite beings, is the infinite self-existent Spirit. Thus, I intuitively know the existence of the infinite, eternal, and self-existent God, and his essential attributes of infinite wisdom, power, and goodness. I believe also, and I think that I know, intuitively and necessarily, that this intuitive knowledge of God, and his relations as Creator, Preserver, and moral Governor of the universe, is the first, most immediate, direct, express, infallible, and unmistakable revelation which God ever made, or can make to a created intellect. This knowledge, belief or intuition of this primary revelation from God, is no inference of a fallible, depraved creature, no result of a process of human ratiocination, but is immediately resultant from the relations constituted by endowing the animal man with moral susceptibilities, and thus constituting his human nature, making him an accountable creature, a subject of moral government, and capable of forming moral character, contracting merit or guilt, and receiving reward or punishment. The process of the reception of this intuitive knowledge may be interrupted by the inexperienced and physically depraved human agent, being deceived and induced, as Eve was, to transgress some law or obligation resulting from these relations. The immediate consequence of the first evil doing, according to the law of sin and death, is the closing of his intellectual vision against this light of truth. "For every one that doeth evil hath the light," etc. Jno. iii. 20. And by wholly engrossing and occupying his mind with the objects of animal and sensual pleasure, he may, by continuous, positive, and habitual effort, exclude this kind of knowledge from his thoughts and memory for a time. But being intuitive, natural and necessary it must and will return in due time, either in the present state of probation, or the future state of retribution. If voluntarily received and submitted to in the state of probation it will be saving, otherwise condemning.

But, besides this intuitive knowledge, I know and believe that what I have endeavored to state, is eternal truth, by the infallible testimony of this same self-existent God, of infinite wisdom, power, and goodness. This testimony he has given in the second person of the Godhead, constituted by the perfect personal unity of himself with the man Jesus of Nazareth. This testimony is perfectly adequate to found the most perfect and infallible knowledge and belief; it being the concurrent and united testimony of two competent, infallible witnesses, a sinless human being and the unchangeable God of truth. He has caused it to be recorded in the Bible, but it was first given and taken, illustrated and recorded on the day sin entered the world, in the memory of the human family; by typical symbols, visible, tangible and audible, adapting it most perfectly to the fallen condition of man at that time. The recording on paper or parchment became necessary, as the human race degenerated, and human memory became an incompetent and unsafe medium of transmission. The certainty and infallibility of my knowledge and belief, founded on this second revelation, depend solely on the unchangeable truth and veracity of the self-existent God. And what makes it entirely satisfactory to me, is the fact, that it harmonizes and agrees perfectly with the primary revelation, or the normal intuitions of uncontaminated human nature, and with the infinite wisdom, power and goodness of the divine author. My knowledge of what I have stated and endeavored to illustrate is, in this aspect of the subject, the knowledge of faith, or perfect confidence in the truth of a competent and infallible witness. And with Paul, I think "I know whom I have believed."

I have also an experimental knowledge of the truths I have stated. I have tested these things whereof I affirm by actual and personal experiment. I have believed in the man Christ Jesus as the Redeemer, the Mediator, the propitiation, my Prophet, Priest and King; and have entrusted to his disposal my entire interests, present and future. The result of this experiment has been that I have seen, felt, and experienced the infinite wisdom, power and goodness of the self-existent God, in personal unity with that word of truth contained in the Bible, constituting the higher law of the Lord, which "is perfect, converting the soul," the gospel of Christ, the power of God unto salvation, and the law of the Spirit of life in Christ Jesus, freeing me from the law of sin and death. This experiment I have repeated continuously, from time to time, for more than half a century, in my own case; and witnessed the same in the cases of scores and hundreds of other sinners who professed to hope in a moral renovation. And I have never seen, heard or read of the human subject that had ever experienced, or felt, or known any moral change for the better, but what had been produced by the motive influence of truth, or the will of God embodied in human language, and acting as an essential constituent of a composite divine person, viz., the Holy Ghost. The divine Mediator and Saviour of men has never, to my knowledge, desired or asked God to produce any moral or saving change in any sinner of the human race, but by the motive influence of truth thus applied. "Sanctify them through thy truth: thy word is truth." Jno.

xvii. 17. And I have never been able to learn, though I tried for years, that it was possible, even for omnipotent God, to produce any saving or moral change for the better, by any other influence in the universe besides the motive influence of truth, persuading the subject to cease doing evil and begin to do right. Therefore, I do not and can not know how to begin to doubt the truths which I have endeavored to state concerning the divine persons, and the manner in which they are constituted. But I do know that what I believe and affirm concerning the persons of the Godhead, the incarnation of the Deity, and the perfect unity of the self-existent Being, is actual knowledge of the truth of God.

Yet I know nothing at all, have no definite, or adequate, or expressible, or communicable conception, idea or notion of the real nature of the divine essence, or of the manner of his existence, or of any numerical or other distinction in his being, or of his essential attributes, (farther than included in his infinite wisdom, power and goodness,) nor of the extent of his purposes, volitions and designs. Being a finite, frail, and feeble creature, I feel totally incompetent adequately to conceive of infinities, or to wield them successfully in ratiocination. I must, therefore, be excused for omitting them while treating of created subjects and events. If, however, I have succeeded in giving an intelligible analysis of my own thoughts on this subject, the practical results of the discussion may be easily apprehended.

1st. These two essential and fundamental doctrines of Christianity, the incarnation of the Deity and the trinity of persons in the Godhead, thus divested of mysticism, are left plain, simple, Bible truths, fully manifested and plainly revealed to the understanding and entire comprehension of all fallen men who desire to understand them, and are willing to bestow the necessary thought and attention. But this by no means implies that all men will understand or believe these doctrines while in the flesh. Many men are evil doers, and every one that doeth evil hateth the light of truth, neither cometh to the light. Nor does it imply that all Christians will correctly or fully understand and believe; though no man can be a real Christian without apprehending and practically believing them. Nor does it imply that even the majority of Christian ministers and teachers, at any particular period, have or will understand these sublime doctrines in all their relations and influences. It must appear vanity and presumption for any uninspired teacher to pretend perfectly to understand them in all their relations, importance, and bearings; because all men, even the most wise and holy, are liable to be influenced more or less by the law of sin and death, that is, by falsehood. But it does imply that the whole truth concerning these sublime doctrines, so far as they are connected with or may in any manner modify the Christian system of doctrine, or the work of man's salvation, is clearly revealed: so that every human agent who is interested or needs salvation may, by a proper use of his natural endowments, understand and fully avail himself of their influence and benefits, in performing his whole duty and securing his own everlasting salvation. So much, at least, the Apostle Paul has told us, 1 Tim. iii. 16: "God was manifested in the flesh, justified in the Spirit, seen of angels, preached unto the gentiles, believed on in the world, received up into glory."

2d. In the light of the few facts stated, respecting the meaning of the term Godhead, and the nature of personality and its uses, a plain common sense meaning is reflected from every word and sentence in the Bible which mentions or alludes to the subject of the trinity, divine personality or incarnation; a meaning definite, clear, precise, and easy to be understood and comprehended by any human intellect sufficiently developed to distinguish between right and wrong, and transgress the higher law: provided such intelligent is desirous and willing to know and understand, and willing to bestow the necessary thought and attention on the subject.

For example, the declaration of the Psalmist, (Ps. ii. 7,) in the person of the infinite, self-existent God, he affirms, "Thou art my Son; this day have I begotten thee." Here the relation of sonship is affirmed. The exact date of the commencement of this relation is stated. "This day." Meaning the very day, because it can mean no other, than the day when the Holy Ghost came on the virgin, and the power of the Highest overshadowed her. Therefore, (said the angel,) that holy thing, which shall be born of thee, shall be called the Son of God. Luke i. 35. The method in which this relationship was created, and the agents concerned in producing it, are unmistakably designated. "The Holy Ghost, the Highest, a virgin espoused, and the virgin's name was called Mary." But though the Sonship was then and thus constituted, no personality could attach to the relations, or to the human correlate, till the moral susceptibilities of the child Jesus were sufficiently developed to understand the nature of law, to feel obligation and obey his heavenly Father. Therefore, the personal form of language was omitted in the description, and this Son of God, after his birth and begetting by the power of the Highest, must be called a mere thing; a holy thing, to be sure, in the tropical sense, as other things consecrated to the service of God; but in itself a mere thing, as destitute of personality and moral character as any other human animal at its birth.

Again, Jno. i. 1, 2, "In the beginning was the Word, and the Word was with God, and the Word was God. The same was in the beginning with God." Here the personality of the Logos is definitely fixed in the finite, in relation to time. The commencement of the relation is located precisely at the beginning of the mediatorial kingdom, or administration of grace to apostate men, over which this person was constituted King, Mediator, Redeemer and Saviour. As the relation of Sonship did not then exist between God and men, in the literal sense, and as the administration of the kingdom of grace commenced by a revelation of the purposes of God concerning the fallen race in pronouncing sentence on their tempter, the Logos, or Word, was the proper, and the only proper term to designate the new personality then, there, and thus constituted. And Moses has dotted down the date of this new personal relationship between God and man in the cool of the very day, when the subjects of grace came into existence by eating the forbidden fruit. Gen. iii. 8. Just when the will and gracious purpose of God, embodied in human language, first fell on the physically depraved animal organs of human sensation; in the very act which commenced the administration of grace to the guilty culprits; the first act of Mediatorship ever performed; at the very point of time and place in the garden of Eden where God, in the person of the divine Logos, convicted the first sinner of the human family; and in the person of the divine Comforter, the Holy Ghost, or word of truth, converted, regenerated, gave peace and comfort to the first penitent believer in the Mediator. "In the beginning was the Word." Jno. i. 1. After the incarnation these personifications of the Deity are very properly and significantly designated by the names Son and Holy Ghost. "And the Word, or Logos, was made flesh, and dwelt among us, (and we beheld his glory, the glory as of the only begotten of the Father,) full of grace and truth." Jno. i. 14. Here is no mystery; nothing inexplicable; nothing above the comprehension of any common sense reader who is willing to think and understand.

The passage, Isa. ix. 6, and its parallel, Tim. iii. 16, have been often represented as full of profound and awful mysteries, utterly inexplicable and incomprehensible to all human intelligence. But there is nothing mysterious or incomprehensible in the truth that an omnipresent God, of infinite wisdom, power and goodness, should be able to assume any relation to any of his works, at any time or place, provided the relation does not involve a contradiction; or to put himself in the most perfect personal unity with any being who occupies any portion of that infinite space which he pervades but does not occupy. Now, in the light of this plain common sense truth, these passages are just as easily understood and comprehended as the history of the child Jesus, or any other child that was ever born. The manifestation in the flesh, the childhood, sight by angels, government shouldered, the Wonderful, the Counsellor, the Mighty God, the everlasting Father, the Prince of Peace, all follow each other in perfect harmony with universal common sense. To be sure, the subjects treated of in these passages are the most mysterious, profound, sublime and glorious, ever conceived by created intellect. But the facts stated concerning them in this language are just as easily understood, by those willing to understand, as the simplest facts that pass before their senses daily. And they are facts that perfectly concur, in all their relations and connections, with the normal intuitions of unperverted human intellect or common sense.

3d. We learn, from this discussion, that the common sense and perfectly intelligible testimony of God, in the Bible, puts every thing pertaining to the trinity, the incarnation, the Mediator, the Redeemer, the Son of God, the Holy Ghost, the Comforter, their works of grace and the saving consequences to fallen men, as far as they pertain to Christianity, entirely within the sphere of the finite, in relation both to time and space; and thus brings them within the proper and legitimate sphere of human intellectual comprehension; and thus divests the Christian system of doctrines of one numerous category of incomprehensible dogmas and inexplicable mysticisms, which are constituted by predicating infinities and eternities of created finite beings, relations, endowments, qualities, etc. Such, for example, as the eternal Sonship of Jesus Christ, eternal generation of the Son, eternal procession of the Spirit, eternal punishment, eternal misery, infinite evil of sin, infinite guilt, infinite justice, grace, mercy or goodness, conferred on finite objects. In all the relations existing, or that may exist, between God and his creatures, one of the parties of the corelation necessarily exists in the infinite, and the other in the finite. When, therefore, the infinites and eternals of the self-existent Deity are predicated of the finite creature, a solecism is perpetrated, a gross absurdity is uttered, a positive contradiction is affirmed, and the result is infinite nonsense or mysticism. But the pure light of revealed truth, with all the normal intuitions of human intellect and the dictates of common sense, place these inexplicable dogmas of eternal beginnings and infinite finitudes in the category of theological romance or metaphysical fiction. We are not quite able yet to force infinities into finite dimensions of either time or space. Nor can we add supernatural power to omnipotence, till we first find a beginning or end to infinity.

Hence those religious teachers, who can find no influence in the universe adequate to any saving change but the supernatural power of God, are in the habit, whenever they introduce the subject of moral renovation, of undeifying the Deity himself, to make room for the introduction of their own supernatural mysticism.

4th. If our positions respecting the meaning of the terms Godhead, personality and incarnation, be correct, it is very easy to see, in the light of this discussion, that the principal topics of controversy between Arians and Trinitarians, or Unitarians and orthodox Calvinists, which have disturbed the Church and the world for ages, and depopulated and deluged with innocent blood vast provinces of Christendom, are mere theological romances, the visionary productions of depraved human imagination; and that these inexplicable romances (called mysteries of godliness) have no more relation to Christian theology, and can have no more influence on the relations, duties, interest or conditions of moral agents, than the dreams of lunacy. But when Christianity shall be divested of these infinite predicates of finite beings, relations and qualities, and similar mysteries, the conflict of ages will pass from the Church, as harmlessly and as quick as the astronomer's awful monster, with a proboscis forty miles long, left the moon when the midge left the lens of his telescope. And then the splendid intellectual talents, the vast amounts of labor, time, treasure and effort, which for ages have been wasted in the conflict, may be appropriated to propagating the gospel of Christ, "the power of God unto salvation." And the possibility of evangelizing the world may again become visible, as in the first century, after the day of Pentecost.

III.

THE LAW OF SIN AND DEATH.

INTRODUCTION.

In the seventh and eighth chapters of the Epistle to the Romans the Apostle describes a law, which he found still abiding in his members, after his regeneration, and bringing him into captivity, to the law of sin. This law he contrasts repeatedly with the law of God, and with the law of his mind, and shows their perfect contrariety and opposition to each other. In chapter vii. 24, he represents the influence of this law of sin and death as a most grievous burden and profound affliction to his soul. But at the same time, he rejoices with thanksgiving in the sure prospect of perfect deliverance from this affliction, through Jesus Christ our Lord. In chapter viii. 2, he ascribes his deliverance from the law of sin and death, to "the law of the Spirit of life in Christ Jesus." We learn also from the whole context, that this law of the Spirit of life in Christ Jesus, can mean nothing else, less or more, than the law of God and the law of his mind, or that law, obedience to which, had since his conversion, become the generic volition of his mind, or the ruling purpose of his soul. This law of the Spirit of life in Christ Jesus consists of that entire revelation of the will of God to men for their salvation, contained in the Bible, including the moral law and the gospel of Christ, with all the illustrations of the same, contained in the history and ordinances of the church. The Apostle tells us, chapter viii. 3; that this higher law was weak through the flesh, antecedent to the revelation of the great mystery of godliness, the incarnation of the Deity. Previous to such revelation, or exclusive of that important fact, the moral law was not competent to deliver the sinner from the law of sin and death. But when this mystery was revealed to the sinner, who had fallen under the influence of the law of sin and death, it became able to save the soul of the believing sinner. Or, it became what Paul affirms of it, "the power of God unto salvation to every one that believeth." Or, as David describes it, it was "perfect, converting the soul." Or, as expressed in this connection, it became "the law of the Spirit of life in Christ Jesus," freeing the believing sinner from the influence and consequences of his past transgressions. That this is the true meaning of the passage appears obvious from the effect and final result ascribed in the subsequent context. The effect was "That the righteousness of the law might be fullfilled in us, who walk not after the flesh, but after the Spirit." The final result ascribed was the deliverance of the creature itself, that is the regenerated believer, "From the bondage of corruption into the glorious liberty of the children of God;" or, into the adoption, to wit, the redemption of the body.

Now if this law of the Spirit of life in Christ Jesus, free the sinner from the law of sin and death—If it convert the soul—If it be able through faith to save the soul, and be the real power of God unto salvation to every one that believeth—If the law of sin and death be a perfect contrariety to the law of the Spirit of life in Christ Jesus—If the contrast which the Apostle exhibits in the passages quoted, be a true and just contrast—If so, we may infer with entire confidence, that a correct analysis of the law of sin and death, must exhibit the true theory of human depravity; or, of that state of sin, guilt, and misery, from which God the infinite Spirit saves sinners, through the redemption wrought by Christ. If the law of the Spirit of life in Christ Jesus, furnish a complete remedy for the plague of sin and its fatal consequences, then the law of sin must, when analyzed, develop the entire cause of the disease, and its consequents, from which the sinner is saved.

In order to obtain a correct analysis of the law of sin and death, it will be necessary: 1st. To ascertain what sin is, how it is created, and what is its specific nature. 2nd. To define the true signification of the term law, in this peculiar relation to sin. 3d. To trace the process by which sin operates on the subject from its first inception, till it issues in death.

CHAPTER I.

SIN.—HOW ORIGINATED.—ITS NATURE.

1st. WHAT is sin? The thing called sin is by Paul very often personified, and a variety of agency, action and consequents ascribed to it. But the meaning of the word sin, is perhaps as definitely fixed, and as precisely limited to a single thing, as the meaning of any other word.

It is a very few times used metaphorically in the Bible to signify a propitiatory sacrifice for sin. Perhaps once or twice, to signify the punishment incurred by sin. "And the calves of Jeroboam are once called the sin of Samaria." But the literal meaning of the word, is uniformly limited to one identical thing; and our inquiry relates to that very thing: the thing that incurs guilt, and that exposes the author to penal suffering. In the First Epistle of John, iii. 4, we have a clear, full, and precise definition of sin, by the inspired Apostle. "Whosoever committeth sin, transgresseth also the law, for sin is the transgression of the law." This definition fixes the meaning of the term sin to a particular relation, and limits it exclusively to that specific relation alone. The particular relation to which sin is limited by this definition, is the relation which the voluntary action of a moral agent sustains to the law of God, when such agent transgresses that law.

The use of the relative "whosoever," extends the meaning of this definition to every sinning agent of the human family, and to every act of transgression, of each sinning agent. The use of the adverb "also," identifies exclusively every act of transgression, with the odious thing called sin. And the use of the conjunction "for," unites inseparably every thing that may be called sin, or sinful, to the specific relation, designated as transgression of the law. "For sin is the transgression of the law." So that to predicate sin of any thing that does not amount to actual transgression, or does not sustain that specific relation to the law of God, is solecistic and false. Or to impute sin to any agent, whose character does not include that relation to the law, is a false and slanderous accusation. "For sin is not imputed, when there is no law," Rom. v. 13; "And where no law is, there is no transgression." Rom. iv. 15. It is therefore perfectly obvious that certain antecedents must in every case exist, before it is possible that sin should exist.

1st. A supreme moral governor, whose rightful prerogative it is to enact laws, or prescribe a rule of moral action, must preexist. 2nd. A moral agent capable of understanding law and feeling obligation. 3d. A law actually pronounced, or enacted by the rightful Sovereign. 4th. The agent must have known, perceived, or understood, what the law required, and must have felt the obligation which the law imposed. 5th. He must have been free to act, and must have possessed the ability to act, either in obedience or transgression of the law, according to his own volition or choice. 6th. Some motive influence to act must have been perceived, felt, or supposed by the agent. 7th. The agent must have really acted, and must have put forth that particular kind of action, or acted in that manner or direction, which constitutes transgression of the law before sin could exist.

The common sense of all mankind, the intuition of all human intellect, teaches the absolute necessity of the existence of all, and of each of these antecedents, before sin can possibly exist in the case of any human agent. The Bible uniformly, distinctly, and without any exception, teaches the same absolute necessity. "For by the law is the knowledge of sin," Rom. iii. 20; "For where no law is there is no transgression," Rom. iv. 15; "Nay I had not known sin, but by the law: for I had not known lust except the law had said thou shalt not covet," Rom. vii. 7. The only law recognized in the Bible as binding on human agents, or, as giving moral character to their voluntary actions, is that higher law of the Lord, which is perfect, converting the soul, which Paul calls the gospel of Christ, the power of God unto salvation, and by which he affirms, all men shall be judged, and the retributions of his moral kingdom be distributed, "in the day when God shall judge the secrets of men by Jesus Christ according to my gospel," Rom. ii.

6-10; "But sin is not imputed, when there is no law," Rom. v. 13.

No person of common sense, when as a magistrate, judge, or juror, he is called to judge of the conduct of his fellow creature, ever imputes crime to him, till he is convinced of the existence of all these antecedents. If any one of them is lacking, or is not fully proved to have existed, by the testimony exhibited, his verdict is, not guilty. And the Bible contains not a word or syllable imputing sin or guilt to a human agent, where all or any of these antecedents is not affirmed, or necessarily presupposed.

Hence, those persons who predicate sin, or guilt, or innate moral depravity, of human nature, or of any human agent, or of any endowment, emotion or susceptibility of a human agent, antecedent to the voluntary action of such agent, under the motive influence of law, or before he has actually transgressed, are in a great error. They err in affirming what they do not know; and what their own common sense, or the normal intuitions of their own intellect tell them is false. They err in affirming what contradicts the word of God, and the eternal and unchangeable principles of moral rectitude as conceived by themselves. When they quote the word of God to prove their affirmations, they misunderstand, misinterpret, and grossly pervert and falsify the scriptures. For example, they quote Eph. ii. 3. "And were by nature the children of wrath even as others," to prove that human agents are born sinners, are morally depraved when they come into the world, and are guilty before they have done any thing, or known any thing, or commenced voluntary action. But the Apostle says nothing of the kind in that passage, nor makes the least allusion to the character or condition of human agents at their birth, or antecedent to their voluntary action, under motive influence of law. The Apostle tells us, that the saints at Ephesus, and himself also, at the time of their conversion, had become liable to suffer wrath, as the natural consequence of a continuous course of actual voluntary transgression of the law of God; or, as the natural result of walking in time past, according to the course of this world, according to the prince of the power of the air, the spirit that now worketh in the children of disobedience, and having their conversation in the lusts of the flesh, fulfilling the desires of the flesh and of the mind. The condition expressed by the metaphor " children of wrath," is a condition acquirable only by actual transgression of the law of God, by deeds done in the body. And whenever scripture is quoted to prove innate moral depravity or sin, or guilt, or liability to penal suffering, antecedent to positive transgression of law, it is perverted, and the testimony of God is falsified.

The inquiry may here be suggested, how does it happen, that so many learned, great, and pious theologians, have for ages thus erred and perverted the language of inspiration ? I answer, it has so happened, because their own minds have been first perverted by adopting the false pagan dogma of Platonic philosophy, that every antecedent is of the same nature and moral quality as its consequent, and that the consequent always derives its moral character from the antecedent. That is, the sinner commits sin solely because he was a sinner, before he committed sin.

It is true that human agents, in consequence of the sin of their antecedents, are born with a depraved physical organization. They come into the world, and commence their existence in a vitiated, frail, sickly and dying animal body. In consequence of this, their animal instincts, appetites and passions, are vitiated, disordered and precociously developed, and often become uncontrollable, before the moral sense begins to be developed. While on the other hand, the intellectual and moral susceptibilities, for want of a healthy and elastic physical machine, or animal body, are for a length of time, more or less, retarded in their development, and in a large proportion of the race, are never developed at all into a moral agent, or, an accountable subject of moral government, while they continue in the flesh. In the case of those human agents who live to develop their moral sense, and begin to form a moral character, these vitiated animal instincts, appetites and passions, increased and aggravated by social circumstances, by defective and vicious training, and foolish indulgence, have generally surrounded them with numerous motive influences tending to induce them to commit sin, when they commence moral agency. After their intellectual and moral susceptibilities are sufficiently developed to act under the motive influence of law, and give moral character to their actions; these motive influences to sin, prevail in their partially developed minds, over the motive influences of the law, and they choose to transgress, rather than obey. And each one for himself originates sin, incurs guilt, contracts moral depravity, and commences the formation of a sinful character. Each one by the free voluntary action of his own will, in view of such motives as are present in the case and at the time, gives that moral hue to his action which constitutes it a sin. And this vicious and odious hue, which constitutes the sin, exists and is seen only in the relation which the voluntary action sustains to the law of God. It is this relation to the law called transgression, which alone is ever called sin in the Bible. And the sin is exclusively the sin of the agent, who puts forth the act of transgression: it constitutes a portion of his moral character, because he is the sole author and cause of its existence. He created it; he brought it into being by his own voluntary action. His volition was the immediate and invariable antecedent. Thus, every individual human agent to whom sin is imputed in the word of God, or, can be justly imputed, or whose character sustains the least taint of moral evil, has himself originated the same, by the free voluntary action of his own will under motive influence of the law of God.

So much for the present may suffice concerning the origin of sin, in the case of every individual in whose character, condition, or relations, the thing exists. And so much the common sense of all men, and the uniform testimony of the word of God, teach us without exception or contradiction.

With respect to the nature of sin, we have already discovered that it is the distinguishing quality of a certain specific relation. Its opposite or contrast is called holiness, or righteousness, which qualifies another and perfectly opposite relation to the law of God. These two qualities distinguish all the relations of all the voluntary actions of moral agents, to the law of God, into two classes, good and bad, right and wrong, holiness and sin. And the characters of the agents or authors of such actions, are distinguished into good and bad, holy and sinful, only by the qualities of these relations to the law of God. The moral characters of the subjects of the divine government are made up exclusively of actions bearing such relations to the higher law.

As the relations of things have no actual existence separate from the things thus related, so also the qualities of such relations, can have no substantive or real existence separate from the relations thus qualified. It is obvious, therefore, that sin can have no real existence in the abstract, but can only co-exist with the relation it qualifies. And that relation can only co-exist with the action thus related. But action considered abstractly, that is, separate from the agent, or cause of it, and his relations to the law, and the lawgiver, is a mere event without any moral quality or desert. Suppose the action to be a stroke, which causes the death of a man. If the author of it be an idiot, or a brute animal, or if it be caused by a piece of wood, moved by physical influence only, there is no sin committed, because there is no relation in the case, to which that quality can attach. And there is no such relation, because there is no agent, whose action can sustain such relation. Volition under the influence of conscience, or the moral sense, being an essential attribute of the agent, who can sustain such relation. Therefore, sin, in its very nature, and guilt its immediate consequent, are inseparable from the agent, who originates, or brings into being the sinful action. It pertains exclusively to his personal identity, and can no more be separated from him, and become the sin and guilt of another, than his identity can be separated and become the identity of another agent.

Again, such is the nature of sin, that it can not be truly predicated of any person or thing, but a free moral agent, acting under the motive influence of the higher law, or of the character or voluntary action of such agent. The relation, which sin qualifies, is relation to the law. But the act can have no relation to law, unless it be performed under the motive influence of the law, either in concurrence with, or against it. And the agent can sustain no relation to law, nor act with any reference to law, till he understands what the law requires. The law may exist, and exhibit paramount obligations to act in a certain method, but it can exercise no motive influence on any agent, till such agent understands the requirements of the law, and feels obligation imposed by the law. Therefore, because my sin is created, brought into existence, or caused to be, solely by my voluntary action in transgressing the law, it necessarily follows, that the agency of no other being can ever make me a sinner, not even omnipotence. The sin of other agents may bear the relation of remote antecedence, to my sin, and may thus present motive influences to induce me to sin. But they cannot cause the existence of my sin, because every intelligent being is a cause, an adequate cause, an efficient cause, an original cause, and the sole or only cause of his own actions. Motive influences may be necessary antecedents to voluntary action. But they cannot be immediate antecedents or cause to the moral quality of voluntary action. For the moral quality of the action is always created by the volition or choice of the agent, in view of these antecedent motive influences; and because no antecedent can be the cause of an event, but an immediate and invariable antecedent. If it be not an immediate antecedent, some other antecedent must intervene as the true cause. If it be not an invariable antecedent the event, or change, may take place without it, and therefore cannot depend upon it in the relation of cause. Thus the volition of the agent always intervenes between the moral quality of his action, and all motive influence to act, either right or wrong; and every agent, in order to act responsibly and give his actions moral character, must necessarily act with entire freedom and perfect ability to concur with or reject and resist, either the less or the greater, the most powerful or the weakest motive influence, according to his own choice. And because the higher law, with its paramount motive influences, must necessarily be present when it is transgressed, sin cannot be committed but in opposition to the strongest motive influence present, and no motive influence can cause or necessitate the moral character of voluntary action, either good or bad. Therefore the existence of sin, antecedent to the voluntary action of the subject, under the motive influence of the law of the Lord, is an absolute moral impossibility.

CHAPTER II.

THE LAW OF SIN AND DEATH DEFINED.

In what sense is the word law used, when predicated of sin, as in the phrase "the law of sin," used by Paul to the Romans? There are two significations of the term law, as used in the Bible, the one literal and the other metaphorical. When used in the literal sense, it always signifies or implies some rule of action, prescribed by rightful authority, imposing obligation on an intelligent moral agent. In this primary and literal sense the word is used in a great variety of relations, both in the Bible, in other books and in common parlance. Thus we read of the law of the Lord, the moral law, the law of the state, the municipal law, the law of nations and the law of nature. In all such cases a rule of action by rightful authority and obligation imposed are expressed or implied. But in this literal sense it can never be truly or properly applied to sin. For sin in all its aspects, in every possible relation, is transgression of the law. But in the metaphorical sense law is often used to signify any uniform or invariable method, in which relative changes succeed each other. Thus in reference to animal development, we speak of the laws of animal life and health. In this sense we have the laws of vegetation, the law of gravitation, and a great variety of physical laws. In all these cases there is implied certain invariable conditions, and a uniform method, in which the successive changes take place, to reach the ultimate result. And if these conditions fail, or this method be interrupted, the result must fail. Such is the law of sin and death.

The process by which, in the case of any human subject of moral government, sin issues in death, is supposed to depend on certain conditions, and to proceed in a certain method, and when these fail or are interrupted, the result will not come to pass. If in the present state of probation under the dispensation of grace, any human agent transgresses the law of God, he thereby becomes a sinner, and puts himself voluntarily under the motive influence of the law of sin and death. Though the sin of his predecessors has had a most malignant and lamentable influence on his condition and circumstances as an intelligent agent and sensitive being, even before his actual transgression; yet he himself remains innocent. The malignant influence has not yet reached his voluntary action, nor attainted his moral character with pravity or guilt. His nature, as an intellectual being, as a moral agent, and a subject of moral government, is as free from sin, and as incapable of penal infliction and suffering, as it was the moment it came from the hand of the infinite Creator, in the case of Adam. Because he hath not yet transgressed; and because under God's free and perfect government, innocent subjects are not made slaves, because some of their ancestors were vile enough to sell themselves into bondage.

The great leading principle, or first section of the law of sin and death, is well defined by the Saviour, in his discourse with Nicodemus, John, iii. 20; "For every one that doeth evil hateth the light, neither cometh to the light, lest his deeds should be reproved." This definition is very plain, simple, and and easily understood. It was perfectly illustrated and its truth confirmed, in the case of the first transgression ever committed by a human agent. It is also experimentally proved and perfectly understood, by every agent who commits an evil deed. He declares by his actions, as Adam and Eve did, that he understands it, that he sees it, that he feels and knows it, in every nerve of his body, and every emotion of his soul. Or, as Job describes the murderer, the thief, the adulterer and burglar; see Job, xxiv. 13–17; "They are of those that rebel against the light; they know not the ways thereof, nor abide in the paths thereof. For the morning is to them even as the shadow of death; if one know them, they are in the terrors of the shadow of death." The process by which this definition is confirmed, may be thus explained. The first sin, that a human agent ever commits, is committed in the light, and under the motive influence of the higher law; for it is impossible to commit sin, or that sin should come into existence at all, in any other circumstances. For the very nature and being of sin depends exclusively on its relationship to that law, as the apostle affirms. "Nay, I had not known sin, but by the law: for I had not known lust except the law had said, Thou shalt not covet," Rom. vii. 7. As soon as the first evil deed is perpetrated, the light of truth shining in his own intellectual nature, reflects from that perfect mirror, his true character, depicted in all the odious deformity and blackness of guilt; with death standing right behind him, with his scythe already swung to cut him down, and the flames of hell rolling to receive and torment his guilty soul. For we must here remember the perfection of the law of the Lord, which executes its penal sanction, by its own moral influence, independent of all other agencies or influences. As in the case of Adam, "In the day thou eatest thereof, thou shalt surely die." And but for the interposition of grace, they had sunk to perdition, and the whole race been extinguished that very day. But every sensitive being is by the Creator endowed with a strong and adequate array of instincts, appetites and passions, for his own protection, preservation and defence. These endowments are an essential part of his nature. Without these no species of sensitive beings could be kept long in existence. These instincts, appetites and passions are all in themselves perfectly innocent or without moral character, and in the normal state of human agents, were always under the perfect control of the reason, will and conscience. But they may by mismanagement, provocation and undue excitement, become vitiated and uncontrollable. Yet they are always ready, on the first emotion of fear, or pain, or apprehension of danger, to act for self-defence, and immediately call into action every other endowment, mental and physical, for the same purpose. But the very first reflection of the guilty conscience, after transgression, presents a specter, which awakens the most horrific emotion of terror, shame, self-abhorrence and painful anticipation. The light of truth in the higher law, because it reflects or discovers this horrid specter to the conscience, seems to the deluded sinner, to be the cause of all his bitter emotions, his shame, fear, and painful apprehensions. Therefore he hates and shuns it, and all his self-preservative endowments are arrayed against the light, and every means of excluding it is put in requisition. And the only successful means is to employ and engross the entire intellectual endowment of the agent, in physical attainments and sensual enjoyment. In this manner the law of sin and death operated in the case of Adam and Eve. And in the same manner it operates in the case of every transgressor; as Job describes in the passage quoted, "The morning is to them, even as the shadow of death." But this is all voluntary self-deception, or lying to his own understanding and conscience, or as Isaiah expresses it, having a lie in his right hand. Not the light of truth, but his own transgression is the sole cause of all his sufferings and slavish fears. The light of truth in the higher law, is the only medium, through which he can see his true character. But in transgressing he voluntarily yielded himself to the guidance of falsehood, and still chooses to be deceived, rather than return to the direction of truth, the only rule of duty. Eve knew that the serpent lied, and that to transgress was wrong, but she chose to try the experiment of yielding to a lie, for the sake of the promised pleasure. And every transgressor, who commits an evil deed, does the same. He knows what is right and does what is wrong, he chooses deception, prefers falsehood to truth, and loves darkness rather than light; because the light reproves his evil deeds, or reflects his deformed, polluted character, the sight of which is tormenting to his soul. This hating the light of truth, and turning from it, rejecting it as a rule of action, and closing the mental vision against it, is a second transgression of the higher law. For the very first intuition of conscience, after the conception of a supreme moral governor, is, "Thou shalt keep my commandments, and do all my will." And the written law is full of similar injunctions. And it is an evil deed of a higher order, and of a more aggravated and malignant criminality, because committed more directly against the person, and sovereignty of the lawgiver. For the light of truth, thus hated and rejected is nothing else, but the perfect law of the Lord. And this higher law is nothing else, but the holy will of God, his eternal purpose, his unchangeable decree, the pure desire of his soul. That is, it is God himself, who is light and in whom is no darkness at all, emitting the light and glory of his infinite perfection, for the life and felicity of his intelligent creatures.

This second step of moral depravation, under the law of sin and death, sweeps away the whole first table of the higher law, from the conscience of the sinner. It is a positive act of high treason against the government of heaven, and against the person of its holy sovereign. His first transgression might have been a mere trespass against some temporal right of his neighbor, or only a violation of some law of animal life or health, against his own interest or comfort. But hatred of the light, and aversion to it, is actual rebellion against the law of the universe, against the law of love, the source of all happiness, even against the law of the Spirit of life in Christ Jesus, the only saving influence in the universe. God himself is the real object of all this hostility to the light of truth, for "God is light, and in him is no darkness at all." And this same advancing step of moral depravation is repeated at every successive voluntary act of transgression, till the sinner repents, turns and submits cheerfully to the influence of the higher law. It is easy, therefore, to see, that the very first section of the law of sin and death, is sufficient to account for any aggravated depth, or degree, or extent of moral depravity ever exhibited, or seen, or felt, or conceived of, by any human agent in the present state. It is equally plain that the process of moral depravation, where no hindering influences are interposed, may be very rapid, and reach an extreme depth of degradation and guilt, in a short time.

CHAPTER III.

THE INFLUENCE OF HABIT.—HOW CONTRACTED.

The next thing to be observed respecting the law of sin and death is the influence of habit. Human agents are creatures of habit. The sinner by his first act of transgression commences a habit of sinning. The next and every subsequent repetition of transgression, strengthens the habit and increases the facility of sinning. According to the Saviour's definition of the law of sin, the habit must strengthen with every successive emotion of hatred of the light of truth, and with every effort mental or physical to evade the light. The process of moral depravation, must therefore be extremely rapid; and the habit of evil doing, hating the light, and evading reproof, must very soon become inveterate, or what is called second nature, because it seems perfectly natural. And it is perfectly natural, though commenced years after the agent was born, because it is the natural consequence of continuous repetition.

The rapidity of this process was clearly illustrated in the case of Adam and Eve. In a single day they acquired such a habit of evading the light of truth, that they could not answer their Maker the plainest question, without prevaricating and trying to hide their true character. Similar illustrations we have constantly before us in the history and experience of human society. The influence of habit in directing the actions of rational agents, even against the most settled purpose of their wills, is constantly exhibited in the conduct of mankind. And every person who has lived but a short time, and had but a limited experience in the world, knows how soon habits are acquired and how inveterate their influence becomes.

David, the man after God's own heart, whose most settled and general purpose for many years, had been to obey the law of God, gives us a striking example of the influence of habit, in the matter of the wife of Uriah. But the experience of Paul recorded in the seventh chapter of Romans is perhaps the most perfect illustration of this subject. He had antecedent to his conversion, contracted vicious habits. But they were not merely sensual indulgences and vulgar transgression, such as constitute what is commonly called a vicious character. He was an eminent professor of religion from his childhood; brought up in the straitest sect of the only true church; liberally educated, and faithfully instructed in law and theology, by the most renowned professor then living. He personifies his sinful habits under the title of sin, and declares that sin had wrought in him all manner of concupiscence, that he was sold under sin, that he was a child of wrath, even as others. And even since his conversion, he was such an abject slave to sinful habits, that when he would do good evil was present with him, and the good that he would do, he did not, but the evil which he would not, that he did. He represents his character antecedent to his regeneration, by the appropriate and significant metaphors, of a death in trespasses and sins, and of children of wrath, and describes the method and whole process, by which he had brought himself into this wretched condition.

"And you hath he quickened, who were dead in trespasses and sin; wherein in time past ye walked according to the course of this world, according to the prince of the power of the air, the spirit that now worketh in the children of disobedience: among whom also we all had our conversation in times past, in the lusts of our flesh, fullfilling the desires of the flesh and of the mind; and were by nature the children of wrath, even as others," Eph. ii. 1, 2, 3. Now this description tells us, as plainly as language can express it, that Paul and the saints at Ephesus had brought themselves into this condition of moral imbecility, or death in trespasses and sin, and made themselves children of wrath by their own voluntary action in transgressing the higher law. For trespasses can not be committed, or brought into existence at all, but by voluntary overt action of the subject. Paul, by a continuous series of actual transgression, which he describes, by having his conversation in times past, in the lusts of the flesh, fullfilling the desires of the flesh and of the mind, had contracted such habits of sinful indulgence, that after his conversion and comparative freedom from the law of sin and death, and after many years of experience in a life of faith and holy obedience, to the law of the Spirit of life in Christ Jesus; he still found these habits cleaving to his flesh and controlling the actions of his physical members, and often prevailing against the desires of his better mind, and the firm purposes of his renewed and sanctified freewill; and also against the paramount motive influence of the higher law, which he had resolved fully to obey.

And every true believer knows by experience, that habits contracted in the flesh, by sinful indulgence of vitiated appetites and passions, adhere to the flesh, with invincible tenacity. And every person of common sense is intuitively conscious that he has no sin, or guilt, or moral depravity, but what he himself has contracted by transgressing some law. It is therefore perfectly evident, that neither Paul nor the saints at Ephesus, nor any of the faithful in Christ Jesus, ever had any sin or guilt, or moral depravity, or liability to wrath, but what they had contracted each for himself, by his own voluntary action in transgressing the law of God.

CHAPTER IV.

ORIGINAL SIN, ETC., THE TRUE SOURCE OF ERROR.

This law, which Paul saw in his members, consisting in habits of transgression and aversion to the light of truth, warring against the law of his mind, is the very thing, which has, for ages, by many pious and learned divines, been called original sin, innate moral depravity, the corruption of the whole human nature, a sinful nature, a guilty nature and a native propensity, disposition, or inclination to sin. It has also been extensively represented as the total depravity of human nature, and total inability to do right or perform any right moral action. It has also been represented as existing in every individual of the human race since the fall, in the very first moment of his being, antecedent to knowledge, volition and action of every kind and degree. It has been asserted also that this corruption of nature is the cause of all the actual transgression in the world. But sin in its very nature and in all its forms, aspects and relations, is necessarily subsequent to voluntary action, under the motive influence of law, and is invariably, wherever it exists, the consequence of such action in transgression of law. And when we analyze the process of moral depravation, we find that this proclivity to sin, aversion to the light of truth, hatred of God and his law, and everything else included in the definition of original sin, by its orthodox defenders, is subsequent to actual transgression of law, and is the natural consequent of transgression. All sin has relation to law on one hand, and relation to a sinning agent or subject on the other. All sin and sinfulness must be found somewhere in the relations of these two subjects to each other. And we actually find all sin and sinfulness to be the distinctive quality of that variety of relation, which voluntary action sustains to the law, called transgression. As no relation exists before the subjects of it exist, therefore sin cannot exist antecedent to knowledge, volition and action. But original sin, according to the definition of its advocates, is something existing before its immediate and invariable antecedent, that is, existing before the cause of its existence, a consequent existing before its antecedent, a creature existing before its creator. To avoid this solicism a variety of hypotheses, equally solecistic have been invented. Such for example as a covenant formed before the parties to it existed; a seminal presence of all men in the first man, before the second man was created, or began to exist; a sinning by proxy; and last of all, a judicial punishment inflicted on myriads of innocent subjects, for a single offence of a remote progenitor. See *Hodge on Romans*, v. 12-19.

But the great error, in the dogmas of original sin, does not consist in affirming the innate depravity of the whole human race. For all the race, since the fall, are born physically depraved. This is the natural consequence of the sin of their depraved antecedents. But this physical depravity is a perfectly innocent infirmity. No moral evil, no guilt, no liability to penal suffering, can attach to the subject, for this kind of depravity. Because the subject has had no agency, no volition, no participation, in any way or manner, in causing this depravity, or in bringing it upon himself. Nor does the error consist in affirming that men are naturally depraved, even in the moral sense. For the natural consequence of transgression is moral depravity, and a continuous course of transgression always accumulates moral depravity, or strengthens the habit, and increases the facility, of sinning. Nor does it consist in affirming that all men are sinners. For all human agents, who live to develop manhood and form a moral character, do commit sin, and are morally depraved and guilty. But their moral depravity and guilt, being the consequents of their sin, are necessarily subsequent to, and caused by, their own actual transgression of the law. Nor does the great error consist in affirming that all men have a strong inclination, propensity or bias to sin, or that these traits of character are natural to all men. For these habits, as already shewn, are the natural consequents of transgression, and solely acquired by repeated transgression; according to the law of sin and death.

But the error, the absurdity and falsehood of the dogmas of original sin consist: 1st. In imputing sin, moral pravity and guilt to human nature. Human nature is the work of God. If it be sinful, God is the sinner, who made it so. For no other agency in the universe, but God's, ever had any hand in constituting human nature what it is. And human nature is identically the same thing now, that it was when God created it, at the beginning. The same in sinful men as in holy men. The same in Jesus Christ, as in the whole fallen race of Adam. He was of the same genus, man, intellectually, morally and physically, as all the race he came to save. He partook of the physical infirmities of man, even of those contracted by actual transgression. "God sending his own Son in the likeness of sinful flesh, and for sin, condemned sin in the flesh," Rom. viii. 3. "He took on him the seed of Abraham. Wherefore in all things it behooved him to be made like unto his brethren, that he might be a merciful and faithful High Priest in things pertaining to God, to make reconciliation for the sins of the people. For in that he himself hath suffered being tempted, he is able to succor them that are tempted," Heb. ii. 16-18. Yet he was without sin, holy, harmless, undefiled and separate from sinners. And human nature must continue to be the same in the future as in the present state. For the moment any change takes place in the nature of any agent of the human race, he ceases to be a human agent: he ceases to be answerable under the laws that govern human agents; and he ceases to be accountable for any past human actions he may have committed. Because change of nature destroys personal identity. Besides, sin does not belong to nature in any sense whatever, but pertains exclusively to moral character, and therefore cannot, but falsely, be predicated of human nature in any case. To affirm sin of human nature, understandingly, is indeed slandering the Maker and Redeemer of human agents. It is pronouncing innocent babes guilty before they commit sin. It is pronouncing innocence guilty of crime. It is, therefore, unjust, absurd and false.

2d. The next gross error is committed, in affirming moral pravity, guilt and penal suffering of the whole race, antecedent to knowledge and voluntary action under the motive influence of law. But we have already shewn the impossibility of the existence of sin or guilt or penal suffering, in the case of any human agent, antecedent to his voluntary action under the motive influence of law. And everybody knows that motive influence antecedent to knowledge is impossible; and that the whole race are born destitute of knowledge, and continue without knowledge of law or moral obligation for years; and that a large proportion of the race die without knowledge of the law, and, of course, die in perfect innocence, as they were born.

3d. Another very great error and absurdity in this category, is the total inability of unregenerate human agents, to perform right moral action, or to do good. We often hear from the pulpit of the total inability of all men to obey the law of God, or perform any act that is truly good according to that law, or to comply with any of the requisitions of the gospel of

Christ. And at the same time, and by the same teachers, we hear these imbeciles denounced as the most guilty and depraved sinners for not doing what they are totally unable to do. Yet every human agent, who ever acted under motive influence of law, or who ever began to form a moral character, knows intuitively, that where ability to perform duty is wanting, no obligation can be imposed by any law or authority; that where ability is wanting, sin or crime cannot be committed by any agent, and guilt cannot attach in any case. And the word of God, from beginning to end, in every precept, command or reproof, implicitly teaches the same; and never in a single instance imputes sin, where ability is wanting. Inability to avoid any particular action, always divests that act of criminality, and the actor of guilt, however injurious it may be. If inability to do right and to avoid doing wrong, is true of any human being, his action is no longer agency in the moral sense, but only instrumentality. Because it can have no relation to law, and therefore no moral quality or character, either good or bad. Such a being is not a subject of moral government, because there is in him, no basis for obligation to rest upon. He cannot be conscious of guilt or penal suffering, or of merit or reward. He cannot be justly punished.

The strength of vicious habits, though it may have become a law in the metaphorical sense, and exercised a controlling influence over the actions of the agent for the time being, yet necessarily implies the possession and actual employment of all the endowments, susceptibilities and faculties, and therefore all the ability, for both good and bad action, which constitutes a moral agent, or an accountable subject of moral government. This must be his condition, as long as the subject is on probation under grace. For the habit, propensity, or whatever else you may call it, was first contracted by actual transgression of the law, and its whole strength and influence have been accumulated by repeated transgression. And though the habit may have been so inveterate, as to repeat the act, without awakening any recognition by conscience at the time, or leaving any record in the memory, still the endowments, the susceptibilities and faculties of the agent continuing the same, his ability both physical and moral must continue to be the same as before he began to contract the habit. Even in case of those habits of vicious action which had become generic, controlling and inveterate, before the agent was capable of giving to his actions any moral character at all, before he knew anything about law, or was conscious of obligation, still this inveterate habit constituted no inability, at the time he first committed sin by indulging it. For if it had constituted real inability, it would have been impossible for him to have committed sin at all. He must have remained innocent still. For ability to obey the law is always a necessary antecedent circumstance in order to transgress it; ability to obey and transgress being identical.

Wherefore the apostle, in describing his experience under the law of sin and death, never intimates the least inability, either moral or physical. Previous to his conversion, he was alive without the law, not without ability to obey the law. But he had contracted such a habit of evading the light of truth in the law, that he felt no compunctions of conscience, in a continuous course of sinful indulgence. He seemed to himself to be alive in the moral sense, though actually dead in trespasses and sins. After his conversion he still continued partially subject to the law of sin and death. But it now seemed like bondage to him. He felt as if he was sold under sin. But this bondage to sin, this proclivity to sinful indulgence, constituted no inability in his case. Because he was fully conscious of willing and doing right at the same time; that is, of exercising all the ability of a moral agent, an accountable subject of moral government. "So then with the mind, I myself serve the law of God, but with the flesh the law of sin." And while he groaned under the body of this death, he also exulted in thanksgiving to God, through Jesus Christ our Lord, that he himself was freed from this law of sin and death. "For the law of the Spirit of life in Christ Jesus, hath made me free from the law of sin and death." It is therefore perfectly obvious that the law of sin and death inflicts no inability on the subjects of it; and equally obvious that the law of the Spirit of life in Christ Jesus imparts no ability, in freeing his subjects from its bondage. The change from the influence of the one, to that of the other, or from an unregenerate state to that of a regenerate believer in Christ, involves no change of ability in the subject. The entire influences of both the law of God and the law of sin, are motive influences. The influence of truth constitutes the whole influence of the law of God, or the law of the Spirit of life in Christ Jesus, even the whole power of God, to produce any moral change for the better. And the motive influences of the law of sin, are those motive influences produced and presented to the intellect of the agent, through the false conceptions of things, created by the morbid instincts, appetites and passions of his animal constitution, and the surrounding circumstances of a sinful world. Falsehood includes all the motive influence in the universe, to moral evil.

This is farther illustrated, by what is said in the subsequent verses. "For what the law could not do, in that it was weak through the flesh, God sending his own Son, in the likeness of sinful flesh, and for sin, condemned sin, in the flesh: that the righteousness of the law might be fullfilled in us, who walk not after the flesh, but after the Spirit." This weakness did not lie in any imperfection of the law. "For the law of the Lord is perfect, converting the soul." Nor did it consist of inability in the subject: but in the strength of that sinful voluntary, habit, of hating and evading the light of truth, which shines in the law. The glorious provision of grace for the salvation of transgressors, by an atoning Mediator, contained in the higher law, could not be apprehended by the guilty sinner; because by the first section of the law of sin and death, his intellectual vision was closed against the light of truth. It was necessary therefore that a special revelation of this provision of grace, and an illustration of its nature, adapted to the condition and mode of conception of the fallen creature, should be made. This special revelation was made on the very day that Eve eat the forbidden fruit, and the subject fully illustrated by a typical representation of the sacrifice of the incarnate Mediator. God sending his own Son, in the likeness of sinful flesh, by a sacrifice for sin, condemning sin in the flesh; brought out the full glory and perfection of the higher law in all its motive and saving influence, to the apprehension of the depraved transgressors. This was the light that freed Adam and Eve from the law of sin and death, and saved them from the penal consequences of their transgression, introducing them to a life of faith in the promised seed of the woman. This was also the commandment that came to Paul when he was alive without the law. The command to look to this illustration of the infinite perfection of the law of God. It was the motive influence of the light of this law of God, reflected from the cross of Christ, which slew Paul and thus freed him from the law of sin and death; and at the same time quickened him, from the death in trespasses and sins, to a new life of faith. And the design of this was, "That the righteousness of the law might be fullfilled in us, who walk not after the flesh but after the Spirit." Not that we might be made righteous or justified by having the righteousness of another transferred or imputed to us; but that we might in due time, by a perfect renovation of moral character, exhibit in our own persons the righteousness which the law requires.

There is not indeed the least allusion, in this whole description of the Apostle's experience, to any want of ability in the subject, or to any increase of ability in effecting the moral change, which he experienced. But it all necessarily implies the perfect ability of the subject, to obey either the law of God or the law of sin, in view of the motives which they presented, according to his own free choice. The habit of obeying the latter, had been previous to his conversion the generic, predominating choice of his will, and was no burden to him. But since conversion, it was like a body of death to him, even though by the motive influence of the former, he had been, in a good measure, freed from that bondage, and exulted in prospect of a perfect emancipation.

CHAPTER V.

THE LAW OF SIN.—LOCATED IN THE FLESH.—RELATION OF ADAM'S SIN TO THE CHARACTER OF HIS POSTERITY.

This brings us to another important fact in the analysis of the law of sin and death. The Apostle found this law located in his flesh. His physical members, or animal endowments, were the seat of the motive influences, which prevailed against the law of his mind. His animal instincts, appetites and passions, were the mediums through which the motive influences of the law of sin operated, to control his voluntary actions against the generic desire of his regenerated will. "For I know that in me (that is in my flesh), dwelleth no good thing." —"I find then a law, that when I would do good, evil is present with me." Again the perfect deliverance from this law of sin and death, for which he waited in confident hope, even while he groaned under the body of this death, was "the redemption of the body." When the body should be redeemed from the physical consequences of transgression, then the salvation of the believer would be perfected in the glorious manifestation of the sons of God. It is worthy of special observation, that in this whole description, the Apostle keeps up a perfect and exclusive contrast, between the flesh and the mind, the physical and intellectual endowments of the creature. This contrast runs exactly parallel with the contrast between sin and righteousness, and between the law of God and the law of sin and death. Thus showing, that all the motive influences which excite to sin, have their origin in, and act only through the flesh and the animal endowments.

This parallel contrast suggests to us the true scriptural and evangelical theory, of the relation between Adam's sin and the moral character and condition of his posterity. Adam transgressed by eating the forbidden fruit. By that sin he incurred guilt, and became morally depraved, and liable to the penalty of the higher law. By the same act of transgression, he became physically depraved. His animal or physical constitution was disordered, diseased, vitiated, and became subject to pain, sickness, and death. But this physical depravity, or vitiosity of his animal constitution, was no part of the sin or guilt of that transgression. Eve was not to blame, or guilty, for the physical pain and shame she suffered. This was a mere physical consequence of the transgression committed. It lay entirely without the moral sphere, and belonged exclusively to the physical system of things. It was a mere animal affection; a disorganization of animal substance. It consisted wholly in locomotion. The very nature of the thing necessarily excludes all moral quality or character from this kind of depravity. But this is the only depravity which Adam, by natural generation, transmitted to his posterity; and which has been transmitted from one generation to another ever since. And this is the only consequence of his eating the forbidden fruit, which is in its nature transmissible by any power, influence, or agency in the universe. All moral character adheres in personal identity, and is therefore incapable of transmission in any way, shape or manner. The posterity of Adam can therefore derive no moral pravity, guilt, or penal infliction, from his sin, or the sin of any antecedent, but must remain perfectly innocent, till by personal transgression of the law of God, they contract guilt.

Physical pains and the dissolution of the body were involved in the consequences of eating the forbidden fruit, not because they constituted an essential part of the penal sanction of the law of God, but because the accountable subjects were then existing and acting in a physical organization; and the execution of the penalty of everlasting destruction from the presence of the Lord and from the glory of his power, must necessarily destroy such a delicate organization. But there was no penalty executed at that time, either on Adam or any of his posterity. Nor has there been since, nor ever will be, or can be, for that particular transgression. For the Divine Mediator interposed and stopped the execution as soon as it began, before the limited time expired. He exhibited to the guilty culprits, the gracious provision of the law of the Lord, for the redemption of fallen men, through a propitiatory sacrifice of a mediator. This melted the hearts of the human offenders. They repented, believed and hoped. They were pardoned. They were graciously received, taken into the favor and protection of the Mediator. They were justified, not in the legal or judicial sense, but in the evangelical or metaphorical sense. All the guilt and liability to punishment incurred in that transaction, up to the moment of their repentance, was absolved, wiped away and forever annihilated. The law of the Spirit of life in Christ Jesus also, beaming in their souls through the promise that the seed of the woman should bruise the serpent's head, freed them from the law of sin and death, as it did Paul, though it still adhered in their flesh, as it did in his. And that very night, before the meeting was adjourned, they were constituted a church of redeemed sinners, and received a sacrament exhibited in typical symbols, which has distinguished the true church from that day to the present; but which since the incarnation is exhibited in representative symbols, instead of typical. The sacraments of the church have always been the same in design, meaning, and moral instruction, viz., plain, simple and significant symbols of the great mystery of Godliness, God manifested in the flesh, giving himself a ransom for all. (Not a hidden mystery that cannot be understood even by those to whom it is revealed, but a revealed mystery, explained and illustrated for the purpose of being understood and believed.)

Thus the guilty and depraved transgressors were saved morally from the guilt and penal desert of that sin. But their bodies, their animal organization was still vitiated and diseased, and subject to the law of sin and death. This moral renovation of character, or freedom from guilt and spiritual bondage of their will, was effected, as in the case of Paul, by the motive influence of truth, exhibited in the law of the Spirit of life in Christ Jesus. When the commandment came he died unto sin, and in the same spiritual, or moral process, he was quickened unto righteousness, so that henceforth he, with his mind, served the law of God. But the law of sin still remained in his flesh. Physical depravity is not removed by motive influence of the light of truth. No act of grace or absolution could heal the diseases of the flesh, or destroy the influence of animal instincts, passions and appetites, nor of vicious habits long indulged. The flesh is a physical substance; therefore none but physical influence could produce the change necessary to free the flesh from the physical consequences of transgression. This freedom, we are assured, shall be effected in the resurrection, "When the dead shall be raised incorruptible and we shall be changed. For this corruption must put on incorruption, and this mortal must put on immortality," 1 Cor. xv. 52, 53.

CHAPTER VI.

THE NECESSITY OF DISTINGUISHING BETWEEN THE MORAL AND PHYSICAL SPHERES.

WE here come to the necessity of the distinction between the moral and physical spheres; between the material and spiritual organizations which combine to constitute the living man, the accountable subject of moral government, in this present state of probation under grace. Man is constituted of a soul and a body; a spiritual, immaterial, invisible and intangible substance, or organization, endowed with intellectual and moral susceptibilities, or faculties. This rational soul is at present intimately united with a material organization, or physical substance, endowed with animal life and organs of nervous sensation. The method of action and the influences by which changes are effected in each of these substances, are entirely diverse from those of the other. And all persons, who have anything to do with human society, (except perhaps a few very learned and superlatively orthodox theologians,) constantly acknowledge and practically apply this distinction. Even the most illiterate and children understand and use this distinction, before they understand the commonest words, by which it is expressed. In attempting to effect or describe any change in either sphere, they seldom mistake the proper influences to be used, or ascribe results to antecedents belonging to a totally different sphere. If a person of common sense wishes his neighbor to change his moral conduct, he does not use a physical machine of twenty horse-power; but he presents to his understanding some of the important truths of the higher law, which are calculated to move his moral susceptibilities. Or if his neighbor is suffering and ready to perish under some ponderous body, that has fallen upon him, he would not stand still and begin to describe, for his relief, the unspeakable love of God in giving his only begotten Son, or the glories of the cross of Calvary, and its power to ease a guilty conscience. If we should see such an exhibition of folly and stupidity, we should be very likely to knock the fool out of the way, and seize hold of the weight that was crushing the man, with all the physical force we could muster.

Indeed, the reality and practical necessity of the distinction between spiritual and material substances, and between moral and physical influences, are among those intuitive truths, which we cannot avoid knowing and believing, just as soon as we have any distinct perception of the subjects of this distinction. If, therefore, when speaking of the character, condition, and changes of human agents, in the present state, this distinction is confounded, forgotten or disregarded, we shall, of course, be involved in solecism, absurdity and contradiction. And this is undoubtedly the source and true cause of the profound and awful mysticisms, which involve the whole subject of the fall and recovery of man, in incomprehensible absurdity. Physical consequents have been ascribed to moral antecedents, and moral changes to physical forces. Mere animal phenomena have been described as moral qualities, and simple moral changes are declared to be the substantial productions of physical influence. Man is represented as annihilating, by a single act of disobedience, all his own power, or ability to do right, and at the same time retaining all his responsibility for doing wrong. And God is described as employing a tremendous physical force, far above and beyond his natural omnipotence, to effect a mere moral change, in a finite, feeble, dependent subject. But when the natural and essential differences of things are ignored or confounded, we may expect no end to absurdities and mysticisms.

Adam, the progenitor of our race, introduced sin into the world. "Wherefore as by one man sin entered into the world." We have a very concise, but very complete and perfect account of this event in the third chapter of Genesis.

Every circumstance which might be necessary for the perfect understanding of the nature, causes, and consequences of that event are plainly stated, in the fewest, but most perspicuous terms. It was a transgression of the law of God. It was an act of voluntary disobedience to a positive command. "Thou shalt not eat of it." The sin of this act consisted exclusively, in the relation which it sustained to that positive prohibition. "Hast thou eaten of the tree whereof I commanded thee that thou shouldest not eat?" If that prohibition had not existed at that time, or if the agents had not heard of it, or known of it, no sin would have been committed by them in that act. Or, if their action had borne any other relation to the command, than that of transgression, the agents must have remained perfectly innocent, and sin could not have entered into the world by that event. It was a free, voluntary act, without constraint, compulsion, or necessity. If it had been otherwise, the authors would have justified themselves from all sin or guilt in the case. Adam and Eve were the sole authors of all the sin of eating the forbidden fruit. Their voluntary choice, that is, they themselves, were the sole cause, the efficient cause, and the only cause of the existence of that particular sin. This circumstance of the event is very clearly stated in the history, and fully illustrated by the conduct of the agents, and confirmed by the sentence of the judge. The offenders both tried to assign some other cause, to impute the sin to some other antecedent, or to throw back the causality of the evil from themselves to something that preceded their own voluntary action. Eve said, "The serpent beguiled me and I did eat." And Adam said, "The woman, whom thou gavest to be with me, she gave of the tree, and I did eat." These were facts in the case; the Judge did not controvert them: the serpent had beguiled the woman by false pretenses; the woman had enticed the man by her example, and blandishments. But the Judge still regarded each party as the author, the cause, and responsible agent of his own sin in the transaction, and pronounced judgment accordingly. And we may safely concur, with the unerring judgment of God, that the sin of voluntary action does not lie in any antecedent motive influence. It is not derived from antecedent influences tending to excite, or to persuade, or entice to a particular course, or kind of action; but is always created or caused to exist, by the volition or choice of the agent, who transgresses any obligation of the higher law.

Another circumstance attending the introduction of sin into the world was, that without antecedent motive influence, the event could never have taken place: sin could have never existed in the human family. Because antecedent motive influence is an essential condition of all moral action, both good and bad. Action without antecedent motive influence is nothing else, and nothing different from physical change, or animal phenomena. To give it moral character it must transpire in the sphere of intelligence and moral judgment. The agent must have some reason, grounds or inducements, either true or false, for acting thus, in order to make him responsable and give moral complexion to his conduct. Sin is transgression of law. It must therefore be committed under motive influence of law. Otherwise it can not come into existence at all. But the moral character or relations of any motive that may precede the voluntary action in any particular case, does not determine or necessitate the moral character of that action. The moral character of every action is determined by the volition, of the agent; and it may be in direct opposition to the most powerful motive influences ever presented to a human intelligence. In order to invest voluntary action with moral character at all, the author of it must see and understand, and feel in his conscience, the motive influences that preceded it: and must freely choose which motive influence he will yield to, concur with, or obey.

And he may, and is always perfectly able and at liberty to

obey the most trifling, insignificant, and feeble motive influences, that can be suggested in the case.

This fact every intelligent agent, who has acted under the motive influence of the Law of God, knows intuitively by his own experience. And the entire history of human agents, by which the higher law is illustrated in the Bible, confirms the fact as an essential and unchangeable principle of all morality, obligation, freedom and accountability. The first sin of our progenitors exhibits a perfect illustration and confirmation of this truth. Previous to their first sin, the accumulation of motive influence to right moral action, was as great as it was possible for them to conceive, or for infinite wisdom, power and goodness to impose upon their moral susceptibilities. The motive influence of the law of God, addressed to them by the supreme Sovereign in person, confirmed by their entire past experience of its eternal truth, its infinite perfection and goodness, and of the perfect utility of obedience; their entire nature, their whole existence, all their intellectual intuitions, and moral consciousness, all their acquired knowledge and experience, all their sensations and emotions, were an accumulation of motive influence to right action. The authority of God expressed in the higher law, is always paramount motive influence to right action. No conceivable influence to the contrary can bear any other comparison with it, than that of finite to infinite. In the case of Adam this paramount influence of the higher law was present with him, before his eyes, in his mind, pervading his whole being and his entire history. In opposition to this, the only influence to transgress was the falsehood of the serpent. And yet in view of this inferior motive influences Adam chose to transgress. He chose freely, understandingly, with knowledge, and free of all constraint. The serpent did indeed beguile the woman, and the woman enticed the man. There were present motive influences both to good and evil, to obey and transgress. But the motive influences to right action, were at the time infinitely more numerous, more important, more powerful and constraining than the motives to wrong action. And Adam knew this, and yet chose to follow the lesser motives to transgression.

It is therefore perfectly obvious, that neither the moral quality nor the strength of antecedent motives, ever determines, or necessitates the moral quality of the subsequent voluntary action of any free or accountable agent. But every agent by his own volition creates the moral quality of every action that he puts forth, and thus creates and determines his own moral character and destiny.

CHAPTER VII.

THE DIFFERENCE BETWEEN THE MORAL AND PHYSICAL.— THE CONSEQUENCES OF CONFOUNDING THEM.

WE are now prepared to describe the difference in the manner of change in the moral and physical spheres, and the different influences, by which change is produced in each. The primary distinction between the moral and physical is, an intuitive truth; it therefore neither needs, nor is capable of illustration. Every intelligent being perceives the distinction, as soon as he is conscious of his own intellectual existence, and no words can illustrate or add to the perception. The moral sphere includes all spiritual being, and its accidents. The physical includes all matter and its accidents. But the method and influences by which change is produced in each of these systems, are totally dissimilar and diverse from those of the other. In the moral sphere, every change of moral character or condition, involves the idea of agency, of choice, of personality, of accountability, and of desert or destiny. We can not form a rational conception of a moral change of character or condition, without personality and the corelation of personal agencies, both of a moral governor and the subject of government. There must also be an actual issue resultant; and that issue must lie just where character is formed, and where destiny is incurred and endured.

Every change in the moral sphere presupposes motive influences in antecedence; that is, it presupposes influences that are perceived or felt only by intellectual and moral susceptibilities; influences that may be contemplated or judged of only by a rational mind, and which can only be weighed and assorted by the moral sense. But after contemplating these motive influences ever so long, and feeling ever so deeply in view of them, we can have no distinct perception of moral change, till we include the idea of an intelligent moral agent personally choosing and acting. And when we have thus attained a full perception of a moral change of character, we necessarily and invariably feel that there is a destiny or desert, or some future consequence, which we can not separate from it. We can not separate it, because it is a constituent of the nature of moral change to be followed by destiny, according to the nature of the change whether good or bad.

Such are some of the antecedents and conditions of moral change. But when we look into the physical sphere, we perceive nothing of the kind, nothing in any degree resembling these conditions of moral changes. All physical change on the very first analysis, resolves itself into locomotion. If you attempt to seek the true cause of any particular change, or any class or description of changes in the physical universe, you can find nothing but locomotion. If you look into the sublime science of Astronomy, and contemplate the vast masses of matter that compose the physical universe; not a single change of phenomenon, but is resolvable into locomotion, or change of relative position in space. Examine all the phyiscal forces ever discovered or conceived of by man, and all the stupendous effects produced by them, both in nature and by art, and still you find nothing but locomotion. Or, investigate the innumerable and wonderful chemical changes that are constanly going on in earth, air, and water, in the animal, vegetable, and mineral kingdoms, yet nothing is discovered but locomotion, or change of relative position in space of the minute constituent particles composing the matter thus changed. Thus you may go through the material universe and not find a single antecedent, circumstance or condition of moral change of character. You may indeed talk about the agency of physical causes, but that agency is still nothing but locomotion. If you trace back a succession of physical sequences in quest of intelligent agency, you find nothing but locomotion, till you arrive at the infinite first cause. But when arrived at that intelligent first cause, you are entirely out of the physical sphere, out of the material universe. God is a Spirit: His agency in bringing material substance into being, lies entirely without the physical sphere, and within the moral, the spiritual. The change produced by His creative agency was not a mere physical change, but a divine production. The antecedent in that sequence was in the moral or spiritual sphere, the consequence was the existence of physical substance. And the very first change after the creative fiat, had for its immediate antecedent locomotion. "In the beginning God created the heavens and the earth. And the earth was without form and void; and darkness was upon the face of the deep. And the Spirit of God moved upon the face of the waters." And the immediate effect was locomotion in the constituent atoms of matter, taking new relative positions in space thus coming into form and taking the distinctive natures of the different substances, as light, air, water, earth, etc. Though the divine agency is not of the physical sphere in any sense whatever, it originated matter, and the laws, by which changes in the material system take place; and can doubtless, by a wise discretionary providence, accelerate, retard, and govern, their action at his own pleasure. But we find no such thing as intelligent agency in all the physical universe, and nothing that resembles or bears the least affinity to voluntary action, or accountability, or to moral character either good or bad. And among all the causes and conditions of physical change there is nothing resembling motive influence in the moral sense. On the other hand, in all the changes of moral character in the universe, there is nothing resembling locomotion. All intelligent voluntary agents, including all sensitive animal organization, can, each in his own proper sphere, originate or produce locomotion. But none but moral agents, who can weigh motive influences, in that perfect scale of moral rectitude, called the law of the Lord, can originate or change moral character, and no power or influence in the universe, can originate or change moral character, but the subject of the change himself. Because his moral character exists only in his personal identity, and consists of the relations which his personal voluntary action bears to the law of God.

When therefore theologians forget this distinction, and apply the same principles, in describing and explaining moral changes which govern physical changes, they necessarily fall into gross errors, profound mysticisms and positive contradictions. It is a universal truth in physical science, that the antecedent and consequent are always of the same nature, and that the consequent derives its nature and character from that of the antecedent. Because all physical changes consist of locomotion, and their immediate and invariable antecedents or causes consist also of locomotion. But this universal axiom in the physical system when carried into the moral or spiritual becomes a universal falsehood; because there is no such thing as locomotion in the moral sphere; and because moral quality has for its immediate antecedent or cause, the voluntary action of an intelligent agent, but takes its moral nature from the relation it sustains to the higher law. It is also true in the physical system, that to find efficient or responsible agency, you must trace back a series of changes to the infinite first cause. But turn to the moral system and this aphorism instantly becomes a positive falsehood; for we find at the first step, as the immediate antecedent of every moral change, an efficient, an intelligent, and accountable agent. Now apply these principles to the inquiry after the cause of the universal sinfulness of all men, who develop a moral character in this life; according to these Platonic axioms, this cause must be as sinful as sin itself, that is, of the same moral nature as its consequent. The theologians in prosecuting this inquiry, find antecedent to the commission of any actual sin, a vitiated physical constitution, and vitiated, disordered and ungovernable animal instincts, appetites, and passions. When the moral sense of the human agent is sufficiently developed, and the higher law is brought to bear on his conscience, they see the motive influences of these innocent infirmities of the animal organization prevailing over the influences of law, and enticing the agent to commit sin, and thus put himself under bondage to the law of sin and death. Here they suppose they have found the doctrine of original sin, the corruption of his whole nature, which is commonly called original sin; and from which, all actual trangressions proceed. This they say, is inflicted on all his posterity, the first moment of their existence, as the punishment of Adam's sin in his first transgression. And the metaphysical acumen of theologians for ages, has been employed and exhausted, inventing, improving, demolishing and defending theories of human depravity and mystical dogmas based on these premises. But the axioms on which all these inventions and improvements rest, when carried into the moral sphere, are not merely not true, but absolutely false. And therefore all the theories and dogmas built upon them are necessarily false and deluding. They all involve contradictions, absurdities and mysticism. They put the consequent before the antecedent. They make men sinners before they commit sin. And thus the whole subject of the moral character, condition and relations of man, his fall and recovery is involved in obscurity and contradiction. This is not my assertion merely, but the most learned and orthodox teachers of theology and biblical criticism, and the most strenuous advocates of original sin, declare that the dogmas which they themselves teach on this subject, are profound and awful mysteries; that they can not be explained by any common sense principles of moral government; that they are totally inexplicable and beyond the sphere of human reason to understand or explain.

And yet they teach that these dogmas must be believed, as fundamental doctrines of christianity, on pain of excommunication from the kingdom of God.

But in my humble opinion, the whole subject of man's fall and recovery is plainly revealed in the Bible, and every change of moral character involved in either, is described in plain common sense language, easily understood by every person of common sense and common education. And the methods, the antecedents, and the consequents of every change involved are described as plainly as it is possible to describe in human language any physical change. And all the inexplicable mys-tories connected with the subject are mere fictions, invented by the corrupt imaginations of sinful men. The only difficulty in understanding the whole process, beyond what is encountered in the plainest domestic concern, consists in the habit of hating and evading the light of truth, which is always the natural consequence of actual transgression. And I believe that there is no inability or difficulty in relation to the subject, in any human agent of common sense, but the influence of habit, or the law of sin and death.

Let us then return to the consideration of that law, and observe how it operated in the case of Adam and Eve. They were subjects of moral government, intellectual and moral beings, and at the same time physical animals. They subsisted and acted in two distinct natures, or in a complex nature, including both the spiritual and the physical. The event of their sinning or their fall, therefore, necessarily involved both moral and physical change. Both moral and physical consequences resulted; and the appropriate antecedents of each were present. And the peculiar method of sequence in both the moral and physical is described and illustrated in the history of that event. There were motive influences both to good and evil moral action presented to the agents. On the one hand the paramount motive influences of the higher law, in as great extent as it was possible for the agents to conceive, for they constituted their entire being, their knowledge, experience and history. On the other hand the lies of their tempter were the motive influences to evil action. We may here observe, that these two kinds of motive influences, include all the influence for the production of moral change in the universe, external to the voluntary acting agent. The law of the Lord which is perfect, converting the soul, and which is identical with the Gospel of Christ, contains the whole truth respecting every existing relation and every relation that may exist in God's moral kingdom, marking distinctly the line between right and wrong, and imposing all obligation to do right and avoid the wrong. Hence this system of truth contains all the influence, which the infinite God can put forth to induce a finite agent to do right, or to produce any change for the better in his moral character. As God is infinitely good, it is impossible for him to have any motive to evil, or to put forth any motive influence to moral evil. Falsehood, the opposite to truth, is the only motive influence left in the universe, that can have any tendency to produce transgression or sin.

In the case of our progenitors both kinds of motive influence were present. But neither the one nor the other, nor both together, determined, necessitated or caused the moral character of their action in the case. These various motive influences must have been considered, weighed and compared by an intelligent moral agent, and an act of choice or volition must have been put forth by such agent, deciding which kind of motive influence the agent would obey, before either right or wrong, holiness or sin, or any moral quality or character could result in the case. But the immediate consequent of such voluntary action under motive influence of the law, was in the case of Adam and Eve a moral change. They concurred with the motive influences to transgression and became sinners. Their own voluntary action in such circumstances, was the sole cause, the efficient cause, and only responsible cause of their sin. The immediate consequence of their transgression was consciousness of guilt. This was followed by a host of the most painful, terrific and horrid emotions they were capable of conceiving. Fear, shame, self-condemnation, self-abhorrence, hatred of the light, and anticipation of future penal consequences. All this process and change of character and condition was in the spiritual or moral sphere. All the antecedents and consequents thus far were moral sequences. No physical or material influence, force or causality, is to be found in the whole process.

But Adam and Eve were material animals, as well as moral agents. They had a physical, as well as a moral constitution. Their physical constitution was brought into action in effecting this moral change; and physical consequences resulted. While the moral and physical are combined in the same personal agent, their antecedents and conditions must mutually effect each other; and may either retard or accelerate, or wholly prevent the development and action of the other.

Hence this first change of our progenitors to moral evil, produced a corresponding change in their animal organization to physical evil. This change, like all physical change, consisted in locomotion and in nothing else. The healthful locomotion of the animal functions was interrupted, disordered and became painful and sickly, tending rapidly to dissolution. But it included nothing that bore the least resemblance to moral change or to moral character, good or bad. It exhibited not a single trait or circumstance that characterizes moral change, or that is necessary to constitute moral character. Who ever thought that Eve committed sin, in blushing at her own nakedness when discovered, or in shivering and feeling uncomfortable in the cold raw atmosphere, or instinctivly seeking the fig-leaves to cover herself? Whatever you may think, God did not think there was any sin in these physical consequences, for He kindly encouraged her by furnishing skins and making garments to clothe them. Or who ever supposed that there was any sin in suffering by the tooth-ache, a broken limb, or a fever? The thought is preposterous.

But this physical change reacted very powerfully on the intelligents, who were the accountable authors of the moral change. The pain, the physical suffering, the anticipation of speedy dissolution of the body, presented a very numerous and powerful array of motive influences exciting to renewed action to escape these pains and fears. The natural tendency of these motive influences, if viewed in the light of truth, would have been to lead to repentance and immediate return to obedience. But by the very first section of the law of sin and death, this array of motive influence to recuperative action was converted into falsehood; that is, into motive influences, leading the sufferers into other and still more aggravated acts of transgression. Viewed in the light of truth, the physical consequences of sin, would in all cases only excite to repentance and perfect reformation. But the evil doers had put themselves under the law of sin and death, by the first transgression. "For every one that doeth evil hateth the light, neither cometh to the light, lest his deeds should be reproved." They therefore looked at the physical consequences of their sin, not through the perfect mirror of truth, but through the vitiated medium of their animal instincts, appetites and passions. And through this false medium their sufferings seemed to them to be the consequence of the perfect law of God, instead of the consequence of their own voluntary transgression. They therefore hated the light and refused to contemplate their own character, condition and interests by this perfect standard of rectitude and beneficence. Thus the habit was contracted, the law of sin confirmed, the habit of hating the light of truth, of hating God and his law, the habit of contemning all divine authority, and hating all righteousness. And the moral depravity of every descendant of Adam, who becomes a sinner in this world, begins, and is contracted in the same manner, proceeds by the same process, under the same law of sin and death, or in the same invariable method. And every successive volition, action or emotion in that direction adds strength and momentum to the habit, and multiplies motive influences to sinful action. And every new relation, into which any agent introduces this course of conduct, originates a new series of moral sequences for evil action, and thus doubles the rapidity by which moral depravity is accumulated, and the motive influences to evil action multiplied.

In the history of the fall, we are distinctly informed that such was the morbific character of the physical change produced by eating the forbidden fruit, and such the rapidity of the process of both the moral and physical depravation, that death, but for the interposition of grace, would have been the necessary and inevitable consequence in the short space of a single day. "For in the day thou eatest thereof, thou shalt surely die." The beautiful animal organization, so fearfully and wonderfully made, and so perfectly adapted for all physical utility and enjoyment, reduced to common dust again in a single day, presents a most terrific picture of the malignant consequences of a single transgression. And the intellectual organization, the immortal soul, with all its divine and exalted moral endowments, consigned to everlasting destruction from the presence of God, and from the glory of his power, by one act of rebellion, and thus a whole innumerable race of immortal intelligents totally extinguished in their first progenitors, gives a thousand times more clear, adequate, and consistent illustration of the final consequences of sin, than all the theories of original sin, imputed guilt, and transferred moral character ever invented. Adam and Eve were, on the very day they eat thereof, immediately struck with death, or, began actually to die. To die, morally or spiritually, by suffering the penal sanctions of the higher law in the torments of their guilty consciences; and physical death, in the nervous shock and animal pains of their bodies. But, physical death is the only death that may be suffered in a single day, and was therefore the only death that could have been meant, or that Adam could have understood as being meant, in the phrase, "In the day thou eatest thereof, thou shalt surely die."

But no death was consummated on that day. The moment death threw his dart, grace interposed; and the whole process of moral depravation and physical dissolution was arrested. A new administration of moral government, adapted to the present condition of the subjects, was introduced. The whole human race was rescued; and saved from all penal consequences of Adam's fall. And the condition of all human agents who should ever live to form a moral character in the flesh, was changed to a probation under grace, administered by a divine Mediator, even by God himself, manifested in the flesh, in the person of Jesus Christ. The guilty agents in that catastrophe were indeed arrested, were convicted by the light of truth, and were melted to repentance by the revelations of grace. They believed the revelation; and in heart and purpose, returned to their allegiance. They were justified freely by grace, through the redemption that is in Christ Jesus. They were, by the law of the spirit of life in Christ Jesus, made free from the law of sin and death. All the sin of the human agents in that transaction was pardoned. All the guilt they had incurred on that day was absolved. All liability to penal suffering by any sensitive being for that sin was totally and forever extinguished. The subsequent sentence of sorrow, labor, and pain pronounced on the culprits, was merely a declaration of the physical consequences of their sin, which infinite wisdom, power, and goodness could not wholly remove during their probation in the flesh. But this sentence could bear no penal relation to past sins and guilt, which were all pardoned, absolved, and removed, with their threatened penalty, and the subjects introduced into a totally new and different dispensation of moral government, administered on totally different principles and conditions. When, by their subsequent transgression, these physical pains were multiplied, the increased suffering might seem to bear some kind of penal relation to such offences, under the new dispensation. But they are more truly and properly regarded, and generally described in the Bible, as paternal chastisements, or disciplinary exercises, rather than penal inflictions. Penal inflictions belong truly and appropriately, only in a state of retribution. In a state of probation, they are entirely out of their proper position; and can be called penal, only in a very limited and metaphorical sense, especially in a probation under grace. Hence the Saviour, and his apostles, whenever they speak of the penal sanctions of the higher law, or of the penal inflictions of God's moral government over men in this world, always locate them in the future state of retribution, after the final Judgment, at the last day. When the Saviour had described the final Judgment at his second coming, he added, "And these shall go away into everlasting punishment: but the righteous into life eternal." Matt. xxv. 46. And Paul, describing the same future Judgment of God, says: "Who will render to every man according to his deeds:—In the day when God shall judge the secrets of men by Jesus Christ, according to my gospel." Rom. ii. 6-16. And in 2 Thess., he tells us that the recompense of the wicked for their persecutions of believers, the punishment of all their disobedience to the Gospel of our Lord Jesus Christ, shall take place: "When he shall come to be glorified in his saints, and to be admired in all them that believe in that day." Thus, all, of both rewards and punishments of the present administration, are placed in the future state of retribution. Indeed, the administration of grace, and the infliction of penal suffering, are as perfect antagonisms as it is possible to conceive. They must therefore as necessarily exclude each other, as do light and darkness. Hence, the inspired writers never confound them in respect to either time, place, or subject.

The sentence pronounced, on the day that Adam ate the forbidden fruit, against the tempter, was a sentence to punishment under the previous administration of penal law, pronounced and inflicted under that administration. Immediately after this sentence, the annunciation of the new administration of grace was made. "And I will put enmity between thee and the woman, and between thy seed and her seed; it shall bruise thy head, and thou shalt bruise his heel." The woman shall not die on that day. The race shall not be extinguished in the first progenitors. She shall have a numerous seed, one of which shall utterly destroy the adversary, and save the race. This was all explained to Adam and Eve, to their full understanding and belief. The dispensation of grace then and there began. The whole race were then saved from the penal consequences of the fall. The sentence afterwards addressed to Eve and then to Adam, was pronounced and executed under the new administration of grace, on very different principles. There is no mention or allusion in it to anything but the physical consequences of their transgression. And because it was impossible for infinite wisdom, power, and goodness, wholly to remove the physical consequences of their sin at once, without defeating the glorious scheme of grace, and totally subverting the laws of all animal procreation and physical change throughout the universe; or because infinite wisdom, for good and sufficient reasons, saw it best, they were left to suffer more or less physical discomfort during their probation, according to their subsequent conduct. Therefore the physical disease or viciosity of the flesh, consequent of their eating the forbidden fruit, was propagated by Adam and Eve to their immediate posterity; and by each successive generation to their posterity, through the whole race to the present time. And this physical disease is still increased and aggravated, or else mitigated by the sins or reformation of every successive generation. And every one knows, who knows anything of animal physiology, that it is a universal and unchangeable law of animal procreation, that immediate progenitors transmit to their posterity more or less of the physical condition of their animal constitution at the time of generation.

But our present inquiry relates only to the influence of this physical depravity on the moral character of Adam's posterity. There is no dispute or doubt but that the physical depravity, or the morbid, sickly, and degenerating condition of the animal constitution of the whole race is the natural consequence of their sin. "So death passed upon all men, for that all have sinned." Rom. v. 12. But how does this physical change, this disordered locomotion in the material organization affect or influence the moral character and condition of human agents?

It hath been already shown with sufficient clearness, I think, to satisfy all common sense readers and candid thinkers that all moral character, good and bad, and all moral quality, complexion, distinction, or difference among human agents, is found alone in the relation which their voluntary action sustains to the law of God: and that every individual human agent creates, originates, or causes by his own free volition or choice, exclusive of all other causality, his entire moral character, and all that pertains to it. It hath also been shown that physical change, and especially the diseased, vitiated and painful locomotion of the animal body may produce a great variety of motive influences to excite the subject to further voluntary action; and that the moral tendency of these motive influences depends entirely on the medium through which the intelligent agent contemplates them. If contemplated in the light of truth as it shines in the law of the Lord, their sole tendency must necessarily be to right moral action. But if contemplated in some false deceptive mirror, such as the serpent presented to Eve, or such as the law of sin and death furnishes to every evil doer, their moral tendency must be to sin. We may therefore infer, as an established and incontrovertible truth, that the physical consequences of Adam's sin, or of the sin of any other parent, can have no other influence on the moral character or condition of his posterity, than that of antecedent motive influence. And we have before shown that antecedent motive influence never causes, determines, or necessitates the moral character of subsequent voluntary action. Therefore the sin of Adam, and of all other antecedents is necessarily excluded from any causality in the first sin, or the commencement of a sinful character, or the contraction of moral depravity in any of their posterity. Because there is in that case no antecedently accumulated influence of habit, no law of sin and death to disguise the motive influences present. And because the motive influences of the higher law are necessarily present, whenever it is transgressed, and are always paramount, and felt to be paramount. The first transgression which commences the formation of a sinful character, or moral depravity, is always a free, voluntary action, a willful violation of known and felt obligation. The immediate antecedent emotion of the mind may have been some precocious, violent, ungovernable animal passion, or some physically destructive habit of sensual indulgence, contracted under the influence of physical depravity, and the surrounding examples, temptations, and vicious training of a sinful world. But, having never before been contemplated in the light of the higher law, this antecedent, whatever it may have been, could have had no moral quality. Because as yet it could have sustained no possible relation to the law: the agent in the case having never before known that there was any law in the universe relating to that passion, or forbidding that indulgence.

But having in another and more extended work, considered the relation of Adam's sin to the moral character and condition of his posterity, and fully described the process of moral depravation under that relation, it is not necessary here to repeat that analysis. And, perhaps, enough has been said in this essay, to show the impropriety and danger of confounding the distinction between the moral and physical, the spiritual and material systems, or of reasoning from the laws and principles of the one, to prove facts and results in the other. The inevitable consequence of such a course must be error, solecism, contradiction, and absurdity. Because the substances and their accidents, and the nature of all changes in each, are totally different from those of the other. In the moral sphere, all cause consists in intelligent moral volition, or a moral agent acting under the motive influence of the perfect law of the Lord. In the physical sphere, all cause consists in locomotion. In the moral sphere, motive influence is an essential circumstance antecedent to all causality, or to the action of cause in the production of changes; because no intelligent moral agent ever acts without motive. But in the physical sphere, motive influence in the moral sense is a solecism, an impossibility, for all physical force, influence, power, or causality is immediately resolvable into locomotion. In the moral sphere, all change, as far as we know, consists in change of moral character, by the voluntary action of the subject, and the consequent change of the condition of the subject. In the physical sphere, all change, on the very first analysis, is resolved into change of local position in relation to space. Things as diverse in every respect, as it is possible to conceive. But confound these different things together, and then undertake to inquire after the causes and consequents of change in either sphere, or after the truth and duties of different relations in either, and you are at once, and necessarily involved in mysticism, absurdity, and contradiction. On the one hand, the infinite and holy God is made the propounder and author of all the sin and misery in the universe; an almighty tyrant! consigning to penal suffering myriads of poor helpless innocents, created with sinful guilty natures, utterly incapable of anything but sinning and suffering. On the other hand are millions of free agents, accountable subjects of moral government, totally destitute of ability to do anything but transgress and suffer punishment. In another category we have moral character created by physical power, consisting of material substance, transferable, like bills of exchange, from one person to another: and an endless series of like incomprehensible mysticisms. But when we look at the moral system, in the pure unmingled light of Divine truth, as it shines in the higher law, and regard it as totally distinct from the material, we at once behold Christianity in all its divine beauty, harmony, and simplicity; and all these inexplicable mysticisms vanish into limbo, where they belong.

CHAPTER VIII.

LIMITATION OF THE LAW OF SIN AND DEATH.

But there is another section of the law of sin and death, yet to be considered. It is the last closing section, or statute of limitation, pronounced by the supreme Legislator, on the day that sin entered the human family. "Till thou return unto the ground; for out of it wast thou taken: for dust thou art, and unto dust shalt thou return," Gen. iii. 19. As this law of sin and death has its location exclusively in the flesh, or in the members of the animal organization, and as its only medium of influence, through which it can affect the moral action of the subject, consists of the vitiated instincts, appetites, and passions of the animal nature; as soon as the animal organization is dissolved, this law ceases to exist, by the limitation of its own nature. "Sin when it is finished bringeth forth death." James, i. 15. Like all finite temporal incidents, when its mission is finished, it ceases to exist. When the body dissolves, the law in its members is necessarily extinct. The intellectual moral agent stands out then a pure spiritual being, in the clear unclouded light of eternal truth, as it shines in the higher law, the perfect law of the Lord. His probation is ended. His character is perfected. His account is made up for the final judgment. His retribution must now begin. The true believer of the Gospel of Christ, who has voluntarily renounced the law of sin, and chosen the law of the Spirit of life in Christ Jesus, as the rule of his action, enters on the full fruition of that eternal life, which is the gift of God through Jesus Christ our Lord. And the impenitent sinner, who has perfected his character, in voluntary subjection to the law of sin and death, goes away into everlasting punishment. The human agent, who has transgressed the higher law, during his probation under grace in the flesh, and died impenitent, immediately finds himself in the condition in which the divine Mediator found Adam and Eve, (their physical pains excepted). They were perfectly alive in the consciousness of their guilt, but stricken with death, through their entire being, soul and body; hating the light, and striving in vain to escape or evade it; but only exposing their own shame, deformity and increasing guilt; constrained to abhor their own character, and detest themselves for contracting it, and thus to become their own tormenters.

The higher law, which carries its penal sanction in its own absolute perfection, and executes the same by its own motive influence independent of all other power, influence, or causality, being nothing else but the eternal truth and light of the divine will or mind of the infinite God, who is light, and in him is no darkness at all, which therefore shines constantly and everywhere, penetrating every susceptibility of the pure spiritual finite being, and compelling him to see and contemplate his own sinful character just as it is, and as it appears in the light of truth, perfectly odious. But the impenitent sinner, even after his whole probation has been wasted in sin, being still in his entire nature, that noble intellectual being, which God created and endowed with those rational and moral susceptibilities, which constitute the image and likeness of God, in which Adam was created, must necessarily regard his own vile character, according to his finite capacity, with the same emotions, with which God regards it. He must detest, abhor, and despise such character, and hate himself for so foolishly contracting it, when the opposite character, was equally attainable by him. The law of sin and death having ceased to exist, he will have no power, ability, medium or means, of evading the light of the higher law, or of the presence of God, but must forever sink under its scathing, withering, and scorching motive influence. While in the flesh, and acting in obedience to the law of sin and death, he could, perhaps, most of the time of his probation, manage as Paul did, to keep himself alive without the law, (that is, in his own estimation, though actually dead in trespasses and sins). But the commandment came, sin revived and he died, not as Paul did, unto sin, but passed out of the flesh and out of probation, an impenitent in his sin. Immediately after that he began to die that death which is the wages of sin, the penalty of the higher law in the future state of retribution. A death which is never fully consummated, but the pangs of which are ever new and ever excruciating. Such is the final result of yielding obedience to the law of sin in the members.

But the penitent believing sinner, who is persuaded by the light of truth, to change the generic volition of his will, or governing purposes of his life, from doing evil to doing right, from the law of sin to the law of God, is immediately, as Paul was, freed from the law of sin and death, by the law of the Spirit of life in Christ Jesus. Yet while he continues in the flesh, he must continue the conflict with the sinful habits, propensities and inclinations, which he has contracted by actual transgression of the law of God. But as soon as death dissolves the body, he is delivered from the bondage of corruption into the glorious liberty of the children of God; having attained to the adoption, to wit, the redemption of the body.

CHAPTER IX.

CONCLUSION.—A SUMMARY OF RESULTS.

THE results of this discussion of the law of sin and death, may now be expressed in the following propositions.

1st. Every created finite intelligent, is in his own limited sphere, a cause, a primary cause and an efficient cause, as truly as God is cause in the infinite sphere. For every human agent is conscious of originating action, change and motion. And we constantly see all other intelligent creatures doing the same

2nd. Every created agent, who is endowed with a moral sense, or with a capacity of distinguishing right and wrong in relation to the law of a Supreme Being, is a moral agent, an accountable agent, and a subject of God's moral government. For consciousness of obligation, and desert of retribution are invariable and inseparable consequents of the perception of right and wrong.

3d. It is proper and essential to the nature of a moral agent, that he should create or contract his own moral character, and thus determine his own destiny. For without this the conception, or idea of a moral government is impossible.

4th. No subject of moral government can be divested of adequate ability to perform his whole duty, or be placed in circumstances, in which he is unable to discharge every obligation that may be imposed on him. Because the moment an agent ceases to have ability to perform duty, he ceases to be a moral agent, or a subject of moral government at all. Ability to perform is the only basis of obligation. Where ability is wanting, obligation can not attach. Accountability is impossible.

5th. All moral character both good and bad, is created by the voluntary action of the subject of it, acting under the motive influence of the perfect law of the Lord. "For sin is the transgression of the law." And "He that doeth righteousness is righteous, even as he is righteous." But "Where no law is there is no transgression."

6th. The emotions, passions, volitions and actions of human animals antecedent to their knowledge of law, and voluntary action under its motive influence, are mere physical locomotion, or mere animal phenomena; and as destitute of moral quality, or moral character, as the actions of the birds of the air, or the beasts of the field. Because they sustain no direct relation to the higher law, in which all moral quality exclusively consists.

7th. The law of sin and death fully accounts for all the wickedness, depravity, crime, and misery of this apostate world, were they a thousand times greater than they are, without implicating the purpose, will, counsel, decree, or agency of God, in any way, shape, or manner whatever. Because a holy and righteous God can sustain but one single relation to sin, or moral evil, and that is the relation of infinite, unchangeable antagonism, or opposition.

In view of these incontrovertible facts, we are compelled to abandon, renounce, and repudiate all the inexplicable dogmas relating to the moral character and condition of human animals, antecedent to their voluntary action under the motive influence of the law of God. As the romantic discoveries of Gulliver, or Sinbad the sailor, vanish in the light of true history, so in the light of common sense and the word of God, the incomprehensible mysteries of the covenant made before the parties existed—of sinning by proxy thousands of years before the principal was born; of the transfer of guilt and punishment through a thousand generations; and of the righteous punishment of myriads of innocent subjects;—all vanish into theological romance. And that other class of mysteries relating to innate moral depravity, the sinfulness of human nature, the total depravity of human agents as soon as they are born, and the total inability of sinners to perform any right moral action, and their tremendous obligation, at the same time, to repent, believe, be converted, obey the law of God, and fulfill all righteousness, all vanish in the light of truth, shining in the word of God. And another category of mysticisms, though not particularly alluded to, we think must be repudiated in the light of this discussion. They are often exhibited in public religious teaching, and in books, under the phrases of the special influences of the Holy Ghost, the supernatural influences of the Spirit, supernatural conversion and supernatural renovation, and the supernatural power of God, and like superlative expletives. Without this super-omnipotence, the authors of these mysticisms say, that all moral change for the better, in human character, or human nature, is impossible; and the whole system of Divine truth totally inefficient for any human improvement. But they all vanish in the light of the knowledge of the glory of God in the face of Jesus Christ. As these fictitious mysteries contradict the plain and positive declarations of revealed truth, and all the intuitions of common sense, their only influence ever has been, and ever must be, to mystify and obscure the whole subject of man's fall and recovery. The sooner, therefore, the Christian system of doctrine is divested of all such fictions, the sooner it will exhibit its legitimate influence in meliorating human society, and saving sinners. When these theological fictions are set aside, Christianity becomes a plain, common sense, matter-of-fact business between God, and the subject of his moral government; perfectly understandable and practicable by every human intellect which is sufficiently developed to contract a moral character, or appreciate or suffer moral retribution.

Only those who transgress, and incur guilt, can suffer punishment under the righteous government of the holy and just God. The progenitors of the human race, when they transgressed, incurred guilt in their own persons. That guilt constituted the distinctive moral quality of their personal identity. It was not possible, therefore, under a righteous administration of moral government, that any other person should ever suffer penal inflictions for their sin. When they transgressed, they did not incur guilt and punishment for the whole race; but they did incur, as an essential part of their own personal punishment, the total extinction of the entire race, as a succession of intellectual moral beings, sustaining relation to a common parentage. The great crowning privilege and blessing of their normal condition, was the privilege of replenishing the earth with a numerous posterity of immortal intelligents, all acknowledging them as progenitors and antecedents. But this glorious privilege they forfeited. Had no interposition of grace occurred, on the very day they ate the forbidden fruit, not a soul of Adam's posterity could ever have existed. The race had ended with the first progenitors.

But grace did interpose. The God of infinite wisdom, power, and goodness, in the person of the divine Mediator, presented himself to the guilty progenitors, and revealed to them the gracious remedial provision of the higher law; and placed them on probation, under a dispensation of grace, providing for their perfect absolution from guilt, and from all penal infliction, and their entire moral renovation. They accepted and complied with the terms of salvation. The race was saved. The moral consequences and penal retributions, incurred by the sin of eating the forbidden fruit, were all removed, extinguished, and forever blotted out of existence. But they were still in the flesh, they had a physical, an animal organization; and it was necessary that they should continue in the flesh during their probation of grace, in order to secure the peculiar benefits of the same. Therefore, the physical consequences of their sin were not fully removed during their probation. And the same are transmitted to their posterity, by natural generation; that is, by a physical medium.

In consequence of this physical viciosity of the whole race, myriads of Adam's posterity never live to develop manhood: never become moral agents in the flesh: are never accountable subjects of moral government in this world: and never begin any probation, or the formation of moral character in the body. They die in infancy. But, they are fully provided for in the dispensation of grace, through the redemption that is in Christ Jesus, and constitute a numerous and important part of the kingdom of Heaven, or the Church of the redeemed in glory. But this topic has been discussed elsewhere, and can not be introduced here, consistently. But every human being, who lives to develop a moral agent in the flesh, commences his probation, when he begins to act voluntarily, under the light and motive influence of the law of God. And by his own free voluntary action he creates his own moral character, and every thing that pertains to it. And always, during his probation, acts with perfect liberty and ability to change his character, and comply with the terms of salvation, according to his own choice or pleasure. And if ever a change of character does take place, always so acts.

All that infinite wisdom, power, and goodness could do, to save the whole race, and every individual sinner of the human family, has been done, from the day Adam ate the forbidden fruit, to the present moment; and will continue to be done, to the end of time. For the infinite God swears by his own life, "That he hath no pleasure in the death of the wicked;

but that the wicked turn from his way, and live." Ezek. xxxiii. 11. He is of one mind, unchangeable, and will do all his pleasure. Therefore, we may be assured that nothing which may be done by the infinite God, for the salvation of sinners, will ever be omitted. But the change of moral character in human agents, which constitutes their salvation, is not the immediate consequent of Divine agency. The Divine agency is not the proximate cause of such change, but the agency of the human subject. Hence, the ultimate appeal of God himself is to the sinner. "Turn ye, turn ye from your evil ways; for why will ye die?" Ezek. xxxiii. 11. And again, "Cast away from you all your transgressions, whereby ye have transgressed; and make you a new heart, and a new spirit: for why will ye die?" Ezek. xviii. 31. And hence, the apostle affirms: "Seeing ye have purified your souls, in obeying the truth, through the Spirit, unto unfeigned love of the brethren." 1 Pet. i. 22. The sinner alone can change his character and destiny, by ceasing to do evil, and learning to do well; that is, by repenting, and forsaking his sins. The Almighty can no more change the character of a human agent, than the human agent can create a world. Because all moral character, and moral change are necessarily, and invariably the work of the subject. The change of regeneration, which is the work of the Holy Spirit exclusively, is always antecedent to the change of character, and consists in persuading, or making willing the subject to change the generic volition, or governing purpose of his will, from transgression to obedience. This change is effected solely by the motive influence of truth, as shining in the gospel of Christ, the power of God unto salvation, or in that perfect law of the Lord, which converts the soul. But all motive influence may be evaded or resisted, under the influence of the law of sin and death. The sinner may wilfully persist, and die in his sins. "Why will ye die?"

But such is the infinite perfection of the higher law, that is. of the moral government of God, that every subject of that government, from the first moment that he becomes an accountable subject, has always before him, and within reach of his perception and conscience, paramount motive influence to right moral action. And such is the absolute perfection of the provisions of grace, and the administration of the same, that every sinner, under the gospel, till the last moment of his probation, is always surrounded and pervaded with paramount motive influences to repent, and be converted. These motive influences are found in the light of eternal truth, shining in the higher law. And God himself is this light of truth; and in him is no darkness at all. But God is everywhere, and always present with all his creatures, pervading their entire being, "For in him we live, and move, and have our being."

Hence, nothing in the universe can hinder, prevent, or postpone a single hour, the conversion of the sinner, who has once heard the gospel, but his own voluntary action in hating and evading the light of truth. Of this, the sinner may be wholly unconscious, as Paul was, when he thought himself alive without the law once, though actually dead in trespasses and sins. This condition of insensibility the sinner acquires and maintains, by occupying his whole time, his whole mind or thoughts, his entire ability, in the pursuits, pleasures, and indulgences of the material system, and the animal nature. He constantly hastens from one selfish pursuit to another, or from one sensual indulgence to another, without seriously considering his relations, his obligations or duty to God, or his interests in the retributions of God's moral government. But let God, in his providence, by a monetary collapse, a commercial failure, a pestilence, a famine, an earthquake, or any other means, separate between the sinner and the objects of his sensual pursuits and indulgences, so as to let in the light of truth upon his moral vision, or let the sinner himself become satiated to loathing with sensual indulgence, as sometimes happens, and turn to the light of truth for a new variety of diversion, and we presently hear the earnest inquiry, "What must I do to be saved?" If he is directly pointed to the cross of Calvary, and told to bow instant and perfect submission to the higher law, which was honored and magnified by that sacrifice, we may soon expect to hear him exulting, with Paul, in his freedom from the law of sin and death, by the law of the Spirit of life in Christ Jesus, and his determination of mind to serve the law of God, through life and death.

But, suggest to his mind, what has, perhaps, been reiterated in his ears a thousand times, the dogma of original sin, a sinful nature, innate moral depravity, total inability, the necessity of supernatural omnipotence, or some special communication of new power or ability, he is probably distressed about his condition, and very anxious to get religion, or be made a christian. Perhaps he resolves to wait on God, in the use of means; means, as he is told, as perfectly inefficient as himself, without putting forth the least direct effort, or positive volition to change his own character, or obey the higher law. And he may thus continue to wait on God, till the present special excitement is past, or till the cause of the alarm is removed, or the commercial harvest returns, or the pleasure season commences, and then the whole story is told in a single phrase, " All as you were."

Thus the word of God, which is able to save the soul, is mystified, emasculated, and divested of its saving influence, and that common sense, which ought to direct the sinner into the path of peace and safety, is befogged in the romances of theological mysticism. And as long as these romances are reiterated as Christian doctrines, the moral influence and saving effect of the gospel of Christ, the moral power of Christianity, of the Church, and the Bible, in meliorating the condition of human society, will diminish. And dishonesty, violence, crime, barbarism, and all manner of vice will increase. Revivals of religion, and moral reforms will become shorter in duration, and less productive in saving and permanent fruits, and more material, mechanical, and superficial in their forms and agencies. And the Church will continue to assimilate more and more to the world, and degenerate into mere outward formality, and physical display.

But God will still carry on his work of grace triumphantly, saving thousands, and tens of thousands of the fallen race, from every nation, kindred, and tongue under heaven. His presence which is the light of truth, is in every place, with all finite intelligence. All events are under his providential control, and he can dispel every cloud of mysticism, and pervade any intellect or conscience with the light of truth, whenever he will. And sinners also will continue to reject the light of truth, to die impenitent, and perish forever, as long as the Prince of the power of the air can invent a theological fiction, or eject a cloud of mysticism. Because, it is the prerogative of every moral agent, absolutely essential to his nature and condition as a subject of moral government, to create his own moral character, and determine his own final destiny.

Now, fellow sinner, if you are conscious that you are unregenerate, unreconciled to God, and his perfect law, your condition is perfectly simple and easy to be understood. And your duty, your interest, and your only method of escape from the penalty of the law of God, everlasting punishment, and the attainment of future happiness, is a plain, common sense, matter-of-fact business for yourself to do, and perfectly within your ability to accomplish with certainty, now, during your probation. You have transgressed the perfect law of the Lord, you have thus contracted guilt, and incurred the penalty of that law. That penalty, though now suspended by grace, cleaves to your person with the guilt of your sins, and must continue so to cleave, till you are absolved by the blood of the cross. As no person in the universe, but yourself alone, ever had any direct agency in making you a sinner, in making you guilty or liable to punishment, so, no agent in the universe can save you from the penalty of God's law, but yourself: not even the omnipotent Creator. A change of moral character is the only remedy. And you, yourself alone, can have direct agency in forming or changing your own character.

Because moral character consists exclusively in the relation which your voluntary actions sustain to the law of God. Your business therefore is immediately to change the generic volition of your will, or governing purpose of your mind, from transgression to obedience, from doing evil to doing good, from hating and evading the light of truth, to loving and seeking it. Or in other words, immediately comply with the terms of salvation proposed in the Gospel; "Repentance towards God, and faith towards our Lord Jesus Christ." Acts, xx. 21. This change of the generic purpose of your mind, and the consequent change of conduct, are perfectly within your power or ability to make now. There is not the least obstacle or hinderance to your making the change immediately, but your own will and the voluntary accumulated strength of habit, which you have freely contracted under the law of sin and death. But all force of habit yields instantly before a direct positive decision of the will to change. The influence of habit may indeed return and occasionally prevail, as long as you continue in the flesh. But the generic volition of the will always triumphs, and governs the general conduct of the agent. And you are in the habit of making just such changes of purpose and conduct, in relation to other interests, pursuits or business, whenever adequate motives for such a change are presented.

On the part of God every thing that infinite wisdom, power and goodness could do, by way of motive influence, to persuade or induce you to turn and live, has been done. On the very day that sin entered into the world, God by his grace, through the redemption that is in Christ Jesus, saved you with the rest of the race from non-existence, the dreadful forfeiture of Adam's sin. He has brought you into being in favorable circumstances, at a propitious period, under very great privileges and advantages. He has put you on probation under the perfect dispensation of grace. He has made full provision for your perfect absolution from guilt and punishment, the moment you repent and turn. He has provided every thing necessary that you may insure your own perfect moral renovation and everlasting happiness. He has sustained you in this condition for a time more or less, nothwithstanding your transgressions. Ever since you were capable of perception, you have been surrounded by the providential goodness of God in rich profusion, leading you to repentance. In the higher law, the Gospel of Christ, the whole power of God unto salvation has been put forth addressed to you, and you have felt its motive influences, and been conscious that these influences were sufficient, and ought to persuade you to repent, turn and live. But you have turned away from the light of truth, and perhaps looked at these motive influences, in the dark mirror of the law of sin and death; and thus deceived yourself into neglect and procrastination. But you are still, if yet in probation, surrounded with the light of truth, and an array of motive influences infinitely adequate to persuade a reasonable being. Now at once look at them in the perfect mirror of eternal truth, repent, believe, and be saved forever. Or turn away if you will, and forever hate, abhor and despise yourself, as a foolish, guilty man, and contemptible wretch, fit only for the deepest degradation and misery. This is your only alternative. May God yet constrain you by the love of Christ.

IV.

THE LAW OF THE SPIRIT OF LIFE IN CHRIST JESUS:

OR,

THE TRUE THEORY OF MORAL RENOVATION.

INTRODUCTION.

To understand the nature, necessity, and method of acquiring that permanent change in which the salvation of the sinner consists, is to every man the most important acquisition that can occupy his attention or awaken desire. It is the theme which occupies the most prominent place in the inspired volume. This topic was often on the lips of the divine Saviour, while here in the flesh. It is the principal burden of the message with which all his apostles are sent to the children of men. The prophets of olden time, when sent to fallen men, were commanded to say unto them, "Turn ye, turn ye, for why will ye die?" "Cast away from you all your transgressions whereby ye have transgressed: and make you a new heart and a new spirit: for why will ye die, O house of Israel?" The Messiah's advent was announced by the command to "Repent, for the kingdom of heaven is at hand." The Saviour began his own public ministry with the same proclamation. And when Nicodemus came to him by night, an anxious inquiring sinner, to know what he should do to be saved, he answered him, "Verily, verily, I say unto thee, except a man be born again he can not see the kingdom of God." There must be a great, an important, and a permanent change. Therefore, no subject in this world can be more important to a man who has sinned than this saving change.

My object in introducing the subject in this place and in this connection, is to give it a full and clear discussion, but condensed into as short a compass as the nature and importance of the topic will permit: and to present it in as plain common sense language as may be practicable. My belief is that the subject, when divested of a little human invention and mysticism, is capable of being understood by all persons of common sense, common intellectual endowments, and common education. As it is a subject of vast importance, which deeply affects the character and interests of every human agent who ever sinned in the flesh, I, therefore, infer that we ought not to doubt but that the moral Governor of the world has, in the dispensation of his grace, made the subject plain and easy to be understood by all who are interested or need the change. I do not believe that there is any incomprehensible mystery hanging over this subject, more than any other subject of revealed truth; nor that any part of the process is kept hid from the subjects of it, in the secret counsels of God; nor that any supernatural or irresistible power, influence or causality is employed by the divine Author in effecting the change. Nor do I believe that any new substance, material or immaterial, or new endowment or ability or susceptibility, is produced in, or added to, the subject of this change.

Having, in the preceding essay, discussed the cause and manner of man's depravity and ruin, under the title of the Law of Sin and Death, I propose now to discuss his recovery under the title of the Law of the Spirit of Life in Christ Jesus. I apprehend that a correct analysis of the law of the Spirit of life, and a true description of the progressive change which it produces in all willing subjects to its motive influences, will give the true and adequate illustration of our subject, and render it intelligible and comprehensible to all interested who wish to know and are willing to bestow the necessary thought and reflection.

My only desire and sole endeavor, in the discussion of the subject, will be to set the testimony of God's word, respecting this change, before the mind in a connected, continuous, plain and perspicuous method. The prominent points of the subject, on which I propose to throw the light of divine truth, are the following:

1st. The nature of the change, or of that moral renovation which constitutes the salvation of the sinner.

2d. The necessity of this very change in the case of every sinful human agent in the flesh.

3d. The Author of this change, or the primary moving agent.

4th. The instrument, cause or influence, that produces the change.

5th. A summary of results.

CHAPTER I.

THE NATURE OF THE CHANGE.—WHAT IS CHANGED?—IN WHAT DOES IT CONSIST?—WHERE IS IT LOCATED?

THE change in which the salvation of the sinner consists, as far as effected in this life, is a change of moral character and its consequents. Moral character is the only thing changed during present probation in the flesh. Moral character consists in the relation which the voluntary actions, emotions and volitions of the moral agent sustain towards the law of God. If the desires, volitions and actions of the agent sustain the relation of obedience to the law of God, his character is good, right and holy, and he needs no change. If his desires and actions sustain the relation of disobedience, or transgression of the law of God, his character is bad and must be changed, or he must remain miserable. What is truly called moral character includes all the voluntary emotions or states of the mind that may be referred to, or which bear any relation to the law of God. Voluntary action, indeed, includes all those states of the mind, or those feelings and emotions, which the agent chooses or willingly indulges. Even declining to act, either physically or mentally, necessarily involves an act of the will, which may be an act of obedience or of transgression of the law: and therefore must go to help constitute the character. Character also includes those states of mind, or habitual actions, which are called inclination, disposition, propensity, bias and proclivity. These are all results of antecedent voluntary action. They are all created by continuous repetition of the same emotions and actions of the agent; and necessarily belong to his character, because he created them by his own action exclusively. By frequent indulgence they acquire a kind of permanence, or continuous repetition, which is sometimes mistaken for something innate or pertaining to nature. But every thing of the kind, whether good or bad, holy or sinful, is, in all human agents, nothing but acquired habit. In the case of unregenerate sinners, their whole character is made up of transgressions, and all their moral habits and proclivities are thus constituted by continuous transgression. This is their entire moral character. "For whosoever shall keep the whole law, and yet offend in one point, he is guilty of all." Jas. ii. 10. He has contracted the entire character of a sinner. Compare with this Ezek. xviii. 24.

We conclude, therefore, that a radical and entire change of moral character is the great desideratum and indispensable requisite, without which no sinner can ever enter the kingdom of heaven, or enjoy perfect happiness. But when this change is perfected, all is attained that can be desired or needed or effected in this life. The sinner will then be made meet, to be a partaker of the inheritance of the saints in light. When this change shall be entirely perfected, the saint will be actually enjoying that eternal life which is the gift of God through Jesus Christ our Lord. As sin is the cause of all the misery in God's moral kingdom, the perfecting of this change of character from sin to righteousness must constitute complete salvation. This is the very kind of salvation for which Jesus suffered on the cross, and by which he derived his name. As all sin and sinfulness, and moral depravity, pertain to moral character exclusively, this entire change must include the whole of salvation. As perfect rectitude of moral character constitute the highest honor, dignity and blessedness of moral beings, even all the glory and blessedness of the Deity, the perfecting of this change will leave no higher honor, glory or felicity, to which the created intelligent can aspire.

This change of moral character, when reference is had to the radical commencement of it in the soul, is called regeneration. It always involves a generic act of the will of the subject, turning from sin to righteousness. By the Saviour it is described by the metaphor of a second birth. "Except a man be born again he cannot see the kingdom of God." John iii. 3. Paul calls it a new creation, a work of God. Eph. ii. 10. "For we are his workmanship, created in Christ Jesus." And the regenerated person he calls a new creature. "Therefore if any man be in Christ, he is a new creature." 2 Cor. v. 17. The Apostle James calls it a being begotten of God, with the word of truth, that we should be a kind of first-fruits of his creatures. James i. 18. When the agency of the subject of this change is the more prominent idea to be expressed, it is generally called conversion, or a turning of the agent from sin unto righteousness. "Repent and turn yourselves from all your transgressions, so iniquity shall not be your ruin. Cast away from you all your transgressions, whereby ye have transgressed, and make you a new heart and a new spirit; for why will ye die, O house of Israel?" Ezek. xviii. 30, 31.

Whenever the change, which constitutes the sinner's salvation, is mentioned in the Bible, in connection with the author of it, or with the cause of it, or with its final results, a change of moral character is always expressed or implied, or necessarily understood in the language used. "Seeing ye have purified your souls in obeying the truth through the Spirit unto unfeigned love of the brethren, see that ye love one another with a pure heart fervently. Being born again, not of corruptible seed, but of incorruptible, by the word of God which liveth and abideth for ever." 1 Pet. i. 22, 23.

In the phrase, "Except a man be born of water and of the Spirit, he cannot enter into the kingdom of God," the language used plainly shows that a change of moral character, and nothing else can be meant. For a man to be created by God unto good works in Christ Jesus, can mean nothing else, more or less, than a change of moral character. To be sanctified through the word of truth, means nothing but a radical change of character in relation to the Law of God. To be begotten with the word of truth, necessarily implies a change of moral character. For the word of truth is the perfect Law of the Lord, the only rule of moral action: whatever, therefore, is begotten or produced by that word of truth, must go to constitute right moral character. The whole change and the only change which fallen man are ever exhorted or commanded to seek and secure at all events, on peril of future misery, is merely a change of moral character. It is to cease to do evil and learn to do well. To cast away all their transgressions, and make themselves a new heart and a new spirit, that they may not die. It is to repent, that they may be saved from their sins by the washing of regeneration and renewing of the Holy Ghost; and to believe, with that faith which works by love and purifies the heart, that they may be made the righteousness of God in Christ. The whole that is required, or mentioned in the Bible as necessary to salvation, in the case of redeemed sinners, is included in a complete change of moral character. This is the only change for the better that is possible in the case of rebellious subjects of moral government. And this is also the only change that can meliorate their condition, or confer any permanent benefit on them, or save them from any evil consequent of their rebellion, either felt or feared, present or future. I therefore conclude, without hesitation or a shadow of doubt, that the change without which the Saviour declares a man can not enter into the kingdom of God, the change which God by his grace effects in sinful men for their salvation, consists exclusively in a change of moral character, and nothing else. This agrees with the uniform experience of all persons who give any evidence of a saving change, or indulge a rational hope of salvation. They never exhibit any change or acquisition, but a change of moral character. When they describe the bestowments of grace, and all the emotions and affections that constitute their religious experience, they tell us of nothing but what is necessarily included in a change of moral character for the better. The new heart, which God gives, and the new spirit which he puts within them, are the voluntary emotions of love, submission, and obedience, produced by the motive influences of the truth, and constituting right moral character. And all the new powers, abilities, or moral strength ever bestowed upon, or found, or felt, or exhibited by any regenerated person, are nothing more nor less than the decided resolution and generic volitions of his own will, in view of the truth, renouncing and forsaking his former vicious habits, and commencing a new and right course of life and action. The change is, therefore, always a change of the voluntary actions and emotions of the subject, from wrong to right. It is always a relative change, a change in the relations which the voluntary emotions and actions of the subject sustain toward the higher law. The voluntary act or emotion of the soul, immediately preceding the change, was an act of disobedience to the law of God, or of rejection of the light of truth, or a voluntary emotion of hatred or aversion toward his law or providence. It was a sinful act of the subject. The very next successive act of the soul, in which the change of regeneration, or the commencement of moral renovation consists, is an act of obedience to the higher law, or an emotion of love or complacency toward God, concurring with the divine Spirit, yielding to the motive influence of truth, and complying with the terms of salvation. It is always a right emotion or volition of the soul, and the outward expression will be an act of obedience to the law of the Lord.

Another fact in relation to the nature of this change is, that it cannot consist in supplying or increasing any power or ability to perform right moral action. Because the subject of regeneration always and necessarily possesses, and acts in the exercise of all the power or ability to perform right moral action before the change, that he ever possesses after it. Power or ability to all right action, within the sphere of his duty and accountability, is absolutely essential to the being of a moral agent. It is of his nature. Deprived of it he must cease to be a moral agent, cease to be a man or human agent, cease to be an accountable creature, or a sinner. And of course he must cease to be a subject of moral government, or of regeneration, or of any moral change or quality whatever. A sinner without ability, both physical and moral, for all right action within the sphere of his duty and accountability, is a solecism, an absurdity, a moral impossibility. With the same identical and personal powers, abilities, or faculties, both physical, intellectual and moral, the unregenerated sinner hated God, resisted his Spirit, and transgressed his law yesterday, with which the converted believer to-day loves, obeys, and worships him. And no regenerated person, since the fall, has ever been enabled to exhibit any new endowment, or faculty, or ability, after regeneration, which he did not possess and employ in sinning antecedent to that change. The opinion, therefore, which some have entertained, that man by sinning lost or forfeited, and was judiciously deprived of his powers, or ability for right moral action; and the opinion that propensity to sin, however strong it may be, which they affirm is innate or natural to all men since the fall, renders him unable to do right, are both very pernicious errors. Each of them, if it were true, would exclude all obligation, accountability, retribution, and moral government from this world and the human race. For every man's conscience and the word of God, absolve him perfectly from all obligation, accountability, and guilt, beyond the sphere of his ability for right action. And every man of common sense knows intuitively by his own consciousness, that whenever he committed sin or did wrong, he possessed the ability to have refrained or to have done right. And this consciousness is the only thing by which the conviction of sin or guilt can ever be awakened in his soul. Every man on the earth, who has lived to begin the development of his moral endowments, and the formation of moral character by transgression, believes this last position stated, whatever his profession or creed may say, just as firmly and as undoubtingly as he believes his own existence, and constantly confesses and acts on this truth, in all the relations of human beings in this state of probation, except his own relation to the higher law. There he would rather be excused if possible. If he cannot invent an excuse himself, he will accept his helplessness, as described by his religious teacher, though he does not believe a word of it. There can, however, be no lack of ability in the case of any sinner. And no communication, or increase of power or ability, can be included in the change of regeneration or sanctification. It must, therefore, be simply and exclusively a change of moral character.

There is one more fact necessary to be considered, in order to set the change, which constitutes the sinner's salvation, beyond all controversy and doubt. In distributing the retributions of his moral kingdom, God never takes into account any thing but moral character. He never mentions any thing as a ground or reason for penal infliction or gracious reward, except what belongs to moral character. Nothing is ever mentioned in the word of God as the procuring cause of future happiness or misery in the state of retribution, but the voluntary actions of the agent, during his probation in the flesh, the relations of which to the higher law constitute his moral character. Paul declaring the principles of the administration of God over the sinful race of men, says, "Who will render to every man according to his deeds:—In the day when God shall judge the secrets of men, by Jesus Christ according to my gospel." Rom. ii. 6, etc. "We must all appear before the judgment seat of Christ; that every one may receive the things done in his body, according to that he hath done, whether it be good or bad." 2 Cor. v. 10. "And behold I come quickly; and my reward is with me, to give every man according as his work shall be." Rev. xxii. 12. "Also unto thee, O Lord, belongeth mercy; for thou renderest to every man according to his work." Ps. lxiii. 12. "I the Lord search the heart, I try the reins, even to give every man according to his ways, and according to the fruit of his doings." Jer. xvii. 10. Such is the uniform testimony of the Bible on this point, without an exception, that I remember. As the moral character of a man includes all the relations of his doings to the law of God, and as that law inflicts its rewards and penalties by its own motive influence, independent of all other influences: it seems impossible, therefore, to conceive how any sinner should be saved in any other way or method than by bringing his moral character into perfect conformity to the requirements of that law. When this conformity of moral character is effected, it will be impossible for him to suffer penal infliction. And as soon as he is delivered from the law of sin and death, by the dissolution of the body, he must be perfectly blessed and happy under the influence of that perfect law. But no other conceivable change of any kind whatever can save him from liability to penal suffering for sin. Hence we conclude with the utmost confidence, that the sinner's salvation, from beginning to the end, consists in a change of his moral character from evil to good, from sin to holiness, by ceasing to do evil and learning to do well, and in nothing else.

CHAPTER II.

NECESSITY OF THIS CHANGE.

WITH respect to the necessity of this change, the testimony of the Saviour of sinners is clear, full, and conclusive. "Verily, verily, I say unto thee, except a man be born of water, and of the Spirit, he can not enter into the kingdom of God." Jno. iii. 5. This testimony to the necessity of an entire change of moral character, in order to enter the kingdom of God, or enjoy future happiness, is constantly reiterated in all the revelations of grace to man, from the day of his fall to the present time. It is exhibited and illustrated in all the ordinances and forms of religious worship appointed by God. It is taught in so many different forms of language, and illustrated by so many types and symbols, that no student of the Bible, or frequenter of Christian worship can be ignorant of it. It is also constantly suggested by the intuitions of natural conscience, whenever the sinner deliberately transgresses the higher law. And yet it is no easy task to make sinners feel its necessity.

And no influence in the universe, but that of the sight, of the absolute perfection of the law of the Lord, can ever make any sinner realize his own personal need of such a change. Hence the importance of setting forth the necessity of this change, in the clear and perfect light of divine truth. For though the acknowledgement of the necessity of some kind of moral change, is very common throughout christendom, and indeed throughout heathendom, too, as far as any religious sense is manifested, still the real cause and nature of this necessity is apprehended by few, even among the subjects of the change.

1st. This change is necessary, not merely because God hath made it a condition of reconciliation between himself and the rebellious transgressors of his law, but because without it no man can enter the kingdom of God, or see his face, but as an enemy; or be happy, or escape punishment out of God's kingdom. Should God pronounce the pardon of all sin in the world, or even proclaim a universal indulgence to men, still the sinner, retaining his sinful character, must remain a miserable outcast, suffering the penal consequences of his sins. Though it is perfectly suitable and becoming the divine Sovereign of the universe, out of respect to his own official character, to make a perfect moral reformation of conduct, a condition indispensable to a reconciliation, still it is not an arbitrary condition. Nor is it an act of sovereignty merely, which might be dispensed with, but for the dignity of the Sovereign, and the integrity of the law. Reconciliation to God and his moral government, on the part of the sinner, necessarily involves a total change of moral character, and is absolutely impossible without it. Sin is enmity against God. Rom. viii. 7. God is perfect in holiness. Therefore, reconciliation of the sinner to God must include a total renunciation of sin, and rectification of the moral character. Were no condition at all demanded on the part of God, still, without this change, no salvation of the sinner can exist. The enjoyment of heaven is as impossible to an intelligent being, retaining the least defilement of sin, as the enjoyment of health would be, while the body was infected with the virus of the plague. Because it is in keeping the judgments of the Lord, or obedience to his law, that the great reward and bliss of the redeemed consists. The eternal life, which is the gift of God, through Jesus Christ, is a life of perfect righteousness. The vital breath of the redeemed soul is obedience to the higher law. Hence the necessity of this change is absolutely imperious on the part of the subject. Not all the grace and glory of heaven could make him happy, or give him peace and rest without it. The omnipresent God would still be to the guilty sinner, in every place, and in any place conceivable in the universe, a consuming fire.

2d. This necessity of a perfect change of moral character in order to salvation is constantly illustrated and confirmed in the relations of sin and misery, as cause and effect in the present condition of men. For though the present is not a state of retribution, but of gracious probation; and though the natural consequences of sin are mercifully postponed and mitigated, as far as possible, by the providential arrangements of this world; and though the sin and violence, and consequent misery of mankind are greatly restrained and prevented by the influence of the gospel; yet we see in thousands of relations and events, the indissoluble connection of sin and misery, as cause and effect. Every sinner, therefore, by his own experience and observation may, if he will, know his need of a total renovation of moral character. And no sinner can avoid feeling his need of this change, but by turning away from, and closing his mental vision against the light of truth, as it shines in the higher law. This may be done for a time, more or less, by engrossing the whole mind with physical interests and sensual enjoyments. This is the cause our Saviour assigned for the stupidity and hesitancy of Nicodemus in not understanding the nature and necessity of this change, when he had described them to him. "For every one that doeth evil hateth the light, neither cometh to the light, lest his deeds should be reproved." This universal law of moral delinquency, or law of sin and death, as Paul calls it, is the only thing that hinders any sinner, and every sinner, who hears the proclamation of grace, from feeling his need of the change, and immediately complying with the terms of salvation. The necessity of a perfect moral change is nevertheless absolute, and perfectly obvious to the reason and common sense of every transgressor, who will receive the light, or even listen to the intuitions of his own intellect on the subject. If any one, therefore, remains ignorant of the nature of the change, or insensible to its necessity, his ignorance is voluntary, and his insensibility wilful; because the light of truth is in the world and always shining from the book of nature and the book of revelation, and often forcing conviction on the human intellect and conscience.

3d. Another ground of necessity for this moral change of character in the salvation of sinners is, the consideration that it would be a very unjust procedure toward all obedient subjects of moral government to restore rebellious subjects to the same privileges and enjoyments, without a total reformation of character. It would be a confounding of all distinction between right and wrong, between merit and demerit, between sin and holiness. It cannot, therefore, be under the government of a holy and just Sovereign. It is impossible under the perfect and unchangeable law of the Lord. The law is unchangeable. It can not be altered, abated or set aside. It must have its course, and produce its legitimate results. Men have sinned, and under that law, which unites sin and misery as antecedent and consequent, they must be wretched till they are perfectly freed from sin.

4th. Men are social beings. Intelligence necessarily involves sociability. Society is essential to the well-being and happiness of human intelligents. But sinful associations necessarily result in misery. God's moral kingdom is a system of social duties and social enjoyments. But sinful and holy beings can not sympathize and unite in the performance of social duties, or in the enjoyment of social pleasures. The pure intellectual and spiritual employments and enjoyments of the heavenly state, are totally incompatible with, and absolutely impossible to sinners, continuing such. Saving sinful men and advancing them to these employments and enjoyments is, therefore, nothing different, and nothing, more nor less, than the identical moral change which God requires of sinners. God and his law are unchangeable. The sinful subject must change. Omnipotence can save him from everlasting misery, in no other way, than by persuading him to change his entire moral character.

5th. But the perfect adaptation of the higher law to the nature of man, confirms the impossibility of salvation to the sinner, but in the perfect renovation of his moral character. Man was created in the image of God. This image of God, in which man was created, consisted in his moral endowments. Among these endowments is the susceptibility of distinguishing between right and wrong, good and evil, sin and holiness, and of appreciating, rejoicing in, and finding pleasure and happiness in the excellence and beauty of moral good, and of hating, abhoring, and despising the deformity and odiousness of moral evil. This image of God in man is indestructible and unchangeable. It necessarily includes immortality, or a susceptibility of continuous being. It is essential to man's existence. Without it he can not exist at all. Divested of it, he would instantly cease to exist, cease to be a man, cease to be a moral agent, and cease to be a subject of moral government at all. Hence, there is in the nature of every man, whatever his moral character may be, a basis or susceptibility of perfect felicity, in the consciousness of moral excellence and beauty, and a basis also of perfect misery in the consciousness of moral evil, pollution, and deformity. This truth is constantly illustrated in human society by the respect, awe, reverence and fear which moral rectitude and virtue inspire in wicked men, even in the most vile and criminal. The same is illustrated and confirmed by the eloquent, sublime and beautiful descriptions of moral virtue, composed by men of very vile, immoral, licentious and criminal characters. This proves to demonstration the existence of the image of God unimpaired, in the wickedest man on the earth. Though, for the present, it may be hid from all created vision, and even from the consciousness of the possessor, by the clouds of falsehood and mysticism, constantly generated by the law of sin and death, still it exists in perfection, ready to act as soon as the light of truth is permitted to shine upon it. This may continue as long as the sinner continues impenitent in the flesh. But when the impenitent sinner passes out of the flesh, he stands a naked, disembodied spirit, in the perfect light of eternal truth, shining from the perfect law of the Lord. The law of sin and death has ceased to exist. All error, falsehood, self-deception, and every possible disguise will have vanished for ever. The light of truth must constantly reflect on his intellectual vision, his own vile, and odious sinful character. Look which way he will, before or behind, to the right or left, up towards his Maker, or down upon the earth, this higher law, like ten thousand perfect mirrors, will throw back upon his sight his own depraved and hateful moral likeness.

And this indestructible image of God, which constitutes his very nature, as an accountable being, must for ever burn with shame, self-contempt, conscious degradation, and the abhorrence of all amiable and worthy intelligents in the universe. But oh! the self-torment of a guilty conscience, under the perfect light of truth, is indescribable and inconceivable. Such is "the wrath to come." Such is the unquenchable fire. And such the "everlasting destruction from the presence of the Lord, and from the glory of his power." All the atoning merit and perfect righteousness of the Son of God, were it transferred to the impenitent sinner, could not save him, or mitigate his self-abhorence a moment. The richer the grace and merit of the Mediator proffered to him, and the more glorious the power of truth revealed for his salvation, the deeper his degradation, and the keener the self-torment. The sinner's character must be totally renovated.

CHAPTER III.

THE AUTHORSHIP OF THE CHANGE.

ALL who believe in a complete radical change of moral character ascribe the authorship to God, the infinite and eternal Spirit, the moral Governor of the universe, and first cause of all things. The testimony of the Bible to this truth is copious, uniform, full and explicit. Says the Saviour, "Except a man be born of water, that is, of the Spirit, he can not enter into the kingdom of God." Water is here mentioned only as a symbol of the truth. Washing or sprinkling with water has constituted a part of all divinely instituted worship in all ages. It has always been used as a symbol of moral purification or reformation of moral character. It can in this connection only symbolize the truth, the means by which moral renovation is produced. Being born of water, and of the Spirit, must, therefore, mean a change of moral character, of which the Holy Spirit is the author and the word of truth the cause. Hence the entire change of moral character in which the salvation of the sinner consists, from the first enlightenment of the soul, or awakening of the subject, to the perfect sanctification of the believer, is all ascribed to the Holy Spirit as the author and prime agent of the whole. Other agents are employed in the work of moral renovation only as armor-bearers of the Spirit, in multiplying and distributing the weapons, and applying the means of conversion and sanctification. But the authorship of the change belongs exclusively to God the Spirit, the third person of the Godhead. The change originates in the gracious purpose of his will. The only means, instrumentality, cause or influence, by which the change is effected exclusively of the subject, is the same will of God contained in his law. It is, therefore, his work peculiarly and appropriately, as he is not only the author of it, but the means are all of him immediately, the subject is his erring and lost creature, who lives and moves and has his being in him. He, therefore, claims all the glory and praise of the whole work, from beginning to end. "Not by might, nor by power, but by my Spirit, saith the Lord of hosts." Zech. iv. 6. Paul says, "For the law of the Spirit of life in Christ Jesus hath made me free from the law of sin and death." Rom. viii. 2. To Titus he says, "Not by works of righteousness which we have done, but according to his mercy he saved us, by the washing of regeneration and renewing of the Holy Ghost; which he shed on us abundantly through Jesus Christ our Saviour." Tit. iii. 5, 6.

But in order to understand the process by which this salvation is effected, and to know definitely what the subject may and ought to do in relation to it, it will be necessary to describe the person of the Sanctifier, and the law of the Spirit of life, or the method by which moral change is produced.

Personality of the Sanctifier.

Person and personality are variations in the forms and use of words and the construction of language, to express the varieties of the relations which moral agents sustain to each other, and to things in general, from which duty and obligation result. All personality, therefore, pertains exclusively to these relations, and to nothing else. Whether predicated of God, men, angels or devils, personality can only qualify or express any meaning in reference to the relations they sustain to other beings. When, therefore, personality is ascribed to God in human language, it has respect alone to the relations which God sustains towards men in their present fallen state, under a gracious probation. Personality can have no reference to the substantive being or essence of the Deity; and, therefore, whenever predicated of the divine essence, (as it often is both by unitarians and trinitarians,) it involves the party in the most profound absurdity, contradiction, and mysticism. In this error doubtless originated most of the subjects of controversy about the trinity and incarnation of the Deity, and the inexplicable dogmas of the one party, and absurd infidelity of the other.

But when personality is applied to the relations of God to fallen men, in its appropriate and true signification, it removes the whole category of mysticism by which the subject has been befogged for ages. Godhead is a word constructed to express, in the concrete, all the different relations which God sustains to men since the fall. These relations are distinguished into three personal varieties; or they are designated by three varieties of personality, very properly called the three persons of the Godhead. The first person, designated as the Father, includes all the natural relations of God to man antecedent to the fall; as Creator, Preserver, Benefactor, etc. The second person, called the Son, includes those relations which he sustains to men subsequent to the fall and antecedent to the commencement of their moral renovation, such as the relations of Mediator, Redeemer, etc. The third, called the Holy Ghost, includes those relations to men which he sustains as their Sanctifier and Saviour from sin. All the relations included in the second and third personalities were constituted or brought into existence by the transgression of man. They had no existence antecedent to that event.

But God, in the exercise of his infinite goodness, has constituted the second and third personalities of the Godhead for the purpose of accomplishing the beneficent works of mercy and grace which these new relations had imposed on infinite goodness. The second person he constituted by taking into personal unity with himself the man Jesus of Nazareth; and thus prepared a person qualified to fill the office of Mediator, and a person able to perform the work of redemption. No such person ever existed in the universe till the incarnation of Deity in the person of Jesus Christ. The third person he constituted by embodying in human language his own will, that is, his perfect law, that converts the soul, and which marks the line of distinction between right and wrong, as it runs through all the relations of moral agents, from the humblest accountable being on earth up to the throne of Jehovah. This is the will of God which Christ the Mediator reveals to us for our salvation, and which is now recorded in the Bible. "By the which will we are sanctified through the offering of the body of Christ once for all." Heb. x. 10.

The necessity of constituting these new and unique personalities results from the absolute perfection of the law of God, and the contrary opposing influence of the law of sin and death. Antecedent to the fall this perfect law of the Lord was intuitive in every human intellect. That is, as soon as the human intellect perceived any relation which involved duty and obligation, the duty of that relation was instantly and intuitively understood, and the obligation was felt and concurred with. But such is the law of sin and death, that the first voluntary act of transgression closes the intellectual vision of the transgressor against the law of God. "For every one that doeth evil hateth the light, neither cometh to the light, lest his deeds should be reproved." The immediate influence of the first act of transgression on the intellect and conscience of the transgressor, according to the law of sin and death, amounts to perfect nullification of the law in his case. It is not a loss of ability, but a voluntary averting from the hated light of truth. As long as he continues in the flesh impenitent, he continues under the law of sin and death. Some new medium of access to his moral susceptibilities, without destroying life and sending him to perdition, must be devised, or the sinner is irretrievably lost. For if God should abandon him, or withdraw his favor the moment after his first transgression, (as Dr. Hodge says He treats all men the first moment of their existence,) the law of the Lord would reach his moral susceptibilities in a moment, and begin the execution of its horrid and irresistible penalty, dissolving his physical nature and ending his probation at once, as in the case of Adam. "For the word of God (this light of truth) is quick and powerful, and sharper than any two-edged sword, piercing even to the dividing asunder of soul and spirit, and of the joints and marrow, and is a discerner of the thoughts and intents of the heart." Heb. vi. 12.

But God does not abandon, nor regard, nor treat as out of his favor, a single soul of the human race, till that soul has enjoyed a gracious probation in the flesh, or has been removed beyond the reach of falsehood, temptation, and sin. On the contrary, he did interpose immediately on the occurrence of the first evil deed committed by a human agent; not to execute a judicial sentence of eternal punishment on myriads of innocent subjects, but by a gracious providence to shield the sinner from the light of his perfect law, and preserve his physical and probationary existence till he might reach his moral susceptibilities with a healing ray of that same light of truth reflected from the cross of calvary, tinged with the mild and cheering hues of infinite goodness and redeeming love. "For our God is a consuming fire." Heb. xii. 27. "God is light, and in him is no darkness at all." 1 Jno. i. 5. "His presence is every where." Ps. cxxxix. But reflected from the cross of Christ, this consuming fire becomes the light of life to the penitent believer. Thus God regards and treats every transgressor of the human race. This he does in the third person of the Godhead, the Holy Ghost, the Comforter, whose office it is to reprove the world of sin, of righteousness, and of judgment; and to show the things of Christ to all who repent and believe in him, and thus to perfect their moral renovation.

When Adam had sinned and brought death upon himself, God assumed the human form, walked in the garden as a human person, called the culprits in a human voice. They came trembling from the bush. They could not endure the light a single day, and hid themselves to eke out their animal life a few short hours. The Judge, in the second person of the Godhead, pronounced sentence upon the tempter. In uttering that sentence, there is mentioned a seed of the woman; a ray of mercy from the Son of righteousness, beaming through that fiery law; a seed that will be an adversary of the tempter. How the gracious light brightens! A seed that shall bruise his head, crush him, destroy him. Glorious salvation! They were melted into penitence. They believed. They were pardoned. Their guilt was for ever removed. Not a word of penal infliction for that sin has ever been heard from God or his word, and not a pang of penal suffering has been felt or can be for that sin, while God reigns.

Thus the perfect law of the Lord, which was by a single evil deed converted into a flaming sword turning every way to keep the way of the tree of life, is graciously changed into the law of the Spirit of life in Christ Jesus, freeing the penitent sinner from the law of sin and death. This law, as now magnified and made honorable by the cross of Christ, has become the power of God unto salvation to every one that believeth, whether Jew or Greek, Christian or pagan. But without an atonement this perfect law has no such saving power, but to every transgressor carries a sentence of death on the day of transgression. "For to be carnally minded is death." That is, a sight of the horrid evil, degradation and tendency of sin, in the clear, full, and perfect light of the higher law, must produce death, dissolution of the sensitive organization, and continuous torment of the immortal soul.

The Law of the Spirit of Life.—How constituted.

"But God sending his own Son in the likeness of sinful flesh, and for sin, (or by a sacrifice for sin,) condemned sin in the flesh: That the righteousness of the law might be fulfilled in us, who walk not after the flesh, but after the Spirit." That is, that those who believe and obey might be perfectly renovated in moral character, and conformed to the law. Thus the law of the Spirit of life is constituted by embodying, in human language, the Law of the Lord, as illustrated by the cross of Christ, and thus made perceptible by the depraved physical senses of sinful men. The word law, as used by Paul, Rom. viii. 2, is an antithetical parallel to the law of sin, used in Rom. vii. 23, and expresses the method which God uses to deliver the sinner from the law of sin and death. Hence the Law of the Spirit of life in Christ Jesus, and the third person of the Godhead, is each of them the same agent, who, in the beginning, created the heaven and the earth, and moved on the face of the waters, putting the physical laws of matter into operation for the reduction of chaos into organic and useful forms. The same divine agent spake during his incarnation, in the second person of the Godhead, in personal unity with the man Jesus Christ. The same identical agent that freed Paul from the law of sin and death, and now reproves the world of sin, and shows the penitent believer the things of Christ, in the beginning of the physical creation, said, "Let there be light, and there was light." And this identical agent, in another subsequent beginning, in the person of the Word, that is, of the Son, "was with God, and was God." "In him was life; and the life was the light of men." Jno. i. 4. And this same identical agent is the Almighty Creator of the heaven and the earth, and all that in them is: the Father of the spirits of all flesh, and the only Saviour of sinners, acting in a variety of persons, according to the various personal relations from which the duties and obligations he discharges are derived.

The first transgression of each sinning human agent produces a new and peculiar relation between that agent and his Maker, his moral Sovereign. It is the relation between a guilty rebel and his infinitely wise, good, and gracious moral Governor. The obligation resulting from this relation, on the part of the Sovereign, is to do all that can rightfully, equitably, and justly be done, for the salvation of the miserable, deluded sinner; and, on the part of the sinner, to comply immediately with such terms as the infinitely wise, good and gracious Sovereign may prescribe. Now, the higher law, the law of eternal truth and equity, "The law of the Lord (which) is perfect, converting the soul," contains a gracious proviso, a remedial clause, a provision of mercy, perfectly adapted, by infinite wisdom, to this very contingency. If the sinner will consent to be saved by grace, if he will accept life by a Mediator, he may yet live. In the second person of the Godhead the divine Mediator immediately undertakes the fulfilment of the terms of this proviso. On the very day the contingency occurred, he was present in the appropriate personality, with every thing necessary arranged, prepared, and ready for the salvation of the whole race, and every individual of the race, from sin and its consequences. But who will communicate the knowledge of this gracious proviso to the sinner? By the law of sin and death, under which the sinner acts, and tries to shield himself and find life and happiness, the light of truth is excluded from his moral susceptibilities. Should God, who is light, and in whom is no darkness at all, even a consuming fire to the wicked, in the person of the Father, present himself to the apprehension of the sinner, he would be destroyed in a moment by the brightness of his presence and the glory of his power. For the everlasting destruction of the damned is from his presence and the glory of his power. 1 Thess. i. 9. Or should he withhold from any human transgressor the influences of his Spirit, the law would reach his soul immediately, by the death of the body, and commence his everlasting punishment.

And yet this terrible Law, this light of eternal truth, this consuming fire to the wicked, is the only power, influence, cause or causality in the universe, external to the agent, for the production of right moral action, or any moral change for the better. It includes the entire moral omnipotence of the Deity. God produces right moral change in agents finite only by the motive influence of truth. This light of truth must, therefore, be brought into contact with the moral endowments of the sinner, or he must perish under the law of sin and death. For "how shall they believe in him of whom they have not heard?" Rom. x. 14. But how and by whom shall this saving contact be effected? Infinite wisdom is always competent to any possible emergency in the finite. God embodies his moral omnipotence, that is, his will, his perfect law, his benevolent and gracious provisions, designs and purposes, in human language; and in the third person of the Godhead begins his work of renovating grace by communicating of this will thus revealed to the moral perception of the sinner, through his viciated animal organs of sensation, in such manner and measure that he may be able to receive, to feel, and to improve the motive influence of the same. This will of God thus revealed, thus modified by reflection from the cross of Calvary, and thus brought into contact with the carnal mind, is the law of the Spirit of life in Christ Jesus. By this law the sinner is awakened, convicted, and melted into penitence. "For I was alive without the law once: but when the commandment came, sin revived, and I died." Rom. vii. 9. By the motive influence of this same law of light and truth, the humbled penitent is quickened, persuaded or induced, to put forth a new, a generic or controlling act of volition, or, in other words, to resolve unconditionally and without reserve that he will henceforth cease to do evil, and learn to do well; that he will cast away from him all his transgressions, and make him a new heart and a new spirit (that is, a new character); or that he will submit to the perfect law of the Lord, and henceforth endeavor to serve God with all his ability. Thus the change of regeneration, or the beginning of that entire change of moral character which constitutes the salvation of a sinner, is effected. "For the law of the Spirit of life in Christ Jesus hath made me free from the law of sin and death." Rom. viii. 2.

Whatever variety of antecedent or accompanying circumstances may be associated with, or whatever emotions, desires, or affections may be felt in the process, or whatever physical agencies or instrumentalities may be employed, or in whatever variety of language the subject may describe the change, or though he may have made no record of memory at the time, and may, therefore, be unable to tell anything about it; still the commencement of the change or regeneration must consist in a generic volition of the subject, or in an entire change of the action of his will in relation to the law of God. For the whole change, from beginning to end, is a change of moral character, and nothing else. And all moral character, good and bad, sin and holiness, lies in the relations of the volitions of the subject to the law of God. If his volitions are conformity to the law, they are right, good, holy, and his moral character is good; he is a holy man. If his volitions are opposition to the law, they are wrong, evil, sin, and his moral character bad; he is a sinful man. The change must, therefore, commence in a right voluntary act of the will. It must be a generic volition; that is, it must include an unreserved, unconditional resolve, that the whole genus and course of his voluntary conduct henceforth, shall be conformity to the law of God. Till this generic purpose of the soul is formed, no saving change is commenced. The sinner is yet unregenerate. "Now if any man have not the Spirit of Christ, he is none of his." Rom. viii. 9.

The only motive antecedent or causative influence, exterior to the subject, that can sustain causal relations to this change, is the moral omnipotence of Jehovah, or the word of truth, or the perfect law of the Lord converting the soul, or the gospel of Christ, or in other words, the personal influence of the Holy Ghost, the third person of the Godhead, which is nothing else or different from the will of God, revealed to us in the Bible for our salvation. And each of these causalities, and all of them together, is nothing else but the eternal, omnipresent, and unchangeable God, the Father of light, putting forth, exercising, and employing his infinite wisdom, power, and goodness in saving sinful men. This he began to do on the very day that sin entered into this world, and has never ceased a moment to employ these infinite perfections in this benevolent enterprise; and I hope and believe never will till the last sinner that infinite wisdom, power, and goodness can save, has attained to the adoption, to wit, the redemption of his body.

The Subject of the Change not Passive.

Though the change, whenever it takes place, is the effect of divine agency, yet the subject is not passive, either in relation to the change or at the time of the change. As the change is a change of moral character, and as all moral character consists in the relation of the voluntary action of the subject to the law of the Lord, it is impossible that any such change should take place while the subject remains passive. Because there is no subject of moral change, but the voluntary action of the agent which constitutes his character. But the divine agent never interferes, or has anything to do with the voluntary action of the human agent, who is the subject of regeneration. His voluntary actions are all his own. He is the sole author of them. His own personal agency is the only cause of them. He only is accountable for them. It, therefore, becomes necessary, in the ultimate analysis of this subject, to make a distinction between the change of regeneration, and the subsequent change of moral character. The first is exclusively the work of God. The sole cause of it is the motive influence of the light of truth, which is the direct and immediate action of the will of God on the soul. "God is light, and in him is no darkness at all." 1 Jno. i. 5. "In thy light shall we see light." Ps. xxxvi. 9. "For God, who commanded the light to shine out of darkness, hath shined in our hearts, to give the light of the knowledge of the glory of God, in the face of Jesus Christ."—2 Cor. iv. 6. The second is exclusively the work of man, the subject of regeneration. "Repent ye, for the kingdom of heaven is at hand." Matt. iii. 2. "Repent and turn yourselves from all your transgressions, so iniquity shall not be your ruin. And make you a new heart and a new spirit." Ezek. xviii. 30, 31. "Turn ye, turn ye, from your evil ways: for why will ye die?" Ezek. xxxiii. 11. "Seeing ye have purified your souls in obeying the truth, through the Spirit, unto unfeigned love of the brethren." 1 Pet. i. 22, compared etc.

The last voluntary act of the subject, antecedent to regeneration, must have been put forth under the law of sin and death, or at least it was not obedience to the law of God, and was therefore not right, not holy. It might have been an emotion of sorrow for sin, as a cause of pain. It might have been a volition of the mind, or resolution to amend his conduct, in order to escape punishment, or to secure some temporal selfish interest. Or, it might have been an emotion of delight or complacency in contemplating the beauty, excellence, or utility of moral rectitude. But whatever it might have been, it was wrong in some way. There was some selfish reserve about it; or it was associated with some wicked purpose of the will not yet renounced, or with some vicious habits not condemned. Or, it was put forth or felt, subject to the controlling influence of some antecedent generic volition of the will, not yet yielded to the influence of truth. It was, therefore, in direct opposition to the motive influence of the light of truth, which God the Spirit is urging upon the sinner, to induce or persuade him to turn and put forth that generic act of the will, which commences the radical change of his moral character. The agency of God the Spirit and of man the subject of regeneration, are perfectly distinct from each other, and in reference to this change are perfectly opposed to each other; and the human agency never concurs with the divine, in effecting the change, till after the change is wrought. The human agent concurs with the divine agent, that is, submits to his authority and obeys his will, in putting forth a new and generic act of will, extending in purpose, to his whole future course of action, without exception or limitation.

The human agent has perfect ability to put forth this right moral act of will, and always had since he commenced moral agency, and always must have. This ability is essential to his existence; without it he would not exist at all as a subject of moral government. The divine agency ceases or ends, in relation to this change, the moment this change is secured or effected. But it never ceases to be put forth, continuously in all places, at all times and in relation to all creatures, who have moral susceptibilities or endowments. "God is light, and in him is no darkness at all." But God is everywhere present. And his law is where he is, for his law is his will, his infinite light of truth, pervading all space and time, and shining on all creatures. With respect to this sinning human agent, since his first transgression, it has been weak through the flesh, not able to effect this moral renovation, because the sinning human subject is in the flesh, under the law of sin and death, and has been able through the motive influences of the viciated instincts, appetites and passions of the flesh, and contracted vicious habits, to exclude the light from his mind, or resist it, whenever it reached his conscience. There is, therefore, no confounding of the divine and human agency in this change. The change, which the divine Agent produces, is as exclusively his, as the original creation of the heaven and the earth, and as far beyond all human agency or ability, as extra to the subject. And the first right voluntary act of the subject, in which the change of character commences, is as exclusively the act of the human agents as any of his previous sinful acts, and as impossible for God to have any agency in producing it as it is for God to lie; though the moral quality of that act was a consequence in the second degree, or sequence, of the change which God had wrought in the human agent. The merit of that act was a consequence of God's agency in the same manner and degree that Cain's sin was a consequence of Adam's agency in eating the forbidden fruit. There was no causal relation in either case, because, in both cases, another adequate, free and responsible cause intervened. For every moral agent is an adequate, a free, an original and efficient cause in himself, for any moral change or act, within the

10

sphere of his duty and obligation. And that makes him an accountable agent and subject of moral government. Herein the relation of cause and effect in the moral sphere differs totally from that relation in the physical sphere. In the physical sphere all changes, and all causes of change, consist in locomotion, and nothing else. Hence, the most remote antecedent of any chain of sequences, is a cause of the ultimate change, as truly as the proximate cause, only at a more remote distance. But when a moral agent acts, he is the sole cause of the change produced as far as its moral quality is concerned. Because he is perfectly free to give it what moral character he will, and actually does give it moral character, and is solely accountable for it. There is nothing special or supernatural in relation to the agency or influence of God in the production of this change of regeneration. The putting forth of this influence or power is not a favor or distinction which he confers on a few, or on a select number, few or many, and withholds from the rest, or which he bestows at one time or place, and not at another and at all others. The power or influence which the Holy Ghost puts forth to regenerate a soul, is nothing more, and nothing else, but the natural, moral omnipotence of "The Father of lights, in whom is no variableness, neither shadow of turning. Of his own will begat he us, with the word of truth. But specialty and supernaturalness both necessarily imply variableness and change. Therefore, all specialty and supernaturalness that pertain to the whole concern of salvation, lie in the effects and results among sinful subjects. And the cause must be sought in the past sins or present character and condition of the subjects. The unchangeable God was present when Eve ate the forbidden fruit. His power unto salvation was then put forth. The Holy Ghost was then present with all his converting influences, and regenerated the human offenders. The perfect law of the Lord, which converts the soul, was then revealed, with all its remedial provisions of grace, through an atoning Mediator. And not an individual of the human race has ever sinned and died impenitent without knowing, feeling, and resisting this power of God, and this influence of the Holy Ghost, which converts the soul. Because such an event is a moral impossibility; it involves a contradiction in itself, and a flat contradiction of God in the Bible.

The change of regeneration or conversion in several relations is unique. There is nothing exactly like it, as far as we know, in all the phenomena of the universe beside. It is a radical and universal change in the voluntary actions of a moral agent, in relation to the perfect law of the Lord, which extends to every relation that involves moral obligation. The subject always acts with perfect freedom, and perfect ability, to do just as he chooses; that is to concur with and obey either class of motives, that may be present at the time, the right or the wrong. The change is always in direct opposition to the previous volition, purposes and voluntary habits of the subject. And yet the change must be effected without the least violation of his freedom of will at the time. He must be persuaded freely to cease his opposition of will, and freely to concur with the motive influences of truth, which tend to the saving change. I know that awakened, anxious sinners are often called seekers, and are exhorted to seek conversion, to pray for conversion, and to wait upon God for a change of heart, etc. But the change of regeneration is the farthest thing in the universe, from all the conceptions, desires and wishes of the unconverted sinner. Awakened sinners may, indeed, be called seekers with the utmost propriety. But they are always seekers of deliverance from the consequences of sin, the torments of a guilty conscience, and the terrors of the wrath to come, and not from sin itself. And they can never be too anxious in seeking, nor too importunate in praying, nor too submissive and self-abased in waiting upon God, nor too persevering in the strife. Nay, they should be determined never to cease striving, but to attain deliverance, or die in the strife. For such is their position, and such the nature of the change required, as to exclude all finite agency and physical causation, except their own moral agency, and that is still under the law of sin and death, and therefore can not bear the relation of causal antecedent to this saving change. The law of the Spirit of life in Christ Jesus is the only immediate and invariable antecedent to this moral change for the better. Hence, the command and exhortation to follow the Spirit, to walk in the Spirit, and to mind the things of the Spirit. "The last Adam was made a quickening spirit." 1 Cor. xv. 45. "For the letter killeth, but the spirit giveth life." 2 Cor. iii. 6.

But although the Spirit, the Holy Ghost, the third person of the Godhead, is the author, and his motive influence the sole cause of the saving change of regeneration and sanctification, still the renovated moral character, which is the result, and in which the salvation of the subject consists, is entirely the work of the human agent. He is the sole author of it all. Every emotion, volition, or action, which goes to constitute that renovated moral character, are the results of his agency alone. He himself is the only, the immediate, and the invariable antecedent and sole cause of all. The divine agency, the power of God unto salvation, the sanctifying and saving influences of the Holy Ghost, end, are exhausted, and cease in the moral endowments or susceptibilities of the sinning subject All right emotions, volitions, and actions that follow are exclusively of the human agency of the converted sinner. And all the merit of them is his personal merit; and the deficiency of them is his demerit. He is accountable for all. All goes into the deeds done in the body, which will measure and determine his future destiny. It is, therefore, of the greatest importance that every person, and especially every regenerate believer, should know, remember, and feel the motive influence of this truth at all times. For though we are God's workmanship, created in Christ Jesus unto good works, which God hath before ordained that we should walk in them, yet God's working is never the cause of a single good work, or a single step in the right course to heaven. But we are commanded to "Work out your own salvation with fear and trembling;" and it is added, by way of motive influence, to persuade and excite us, "for it is God which worketh in you, both to will and to do of his good pleasure." Phil. ii. 12, 13. God, indeed, works in us, to will and to do; but he works only with the motive influence of truth. And his omnipotence in the moral sphere, extends no further than to keep always paramount motive influence to right moral action, before the mind and conscience of every subject of his government. The believer has all the ability that any saint in glory ever had to perform his whole duty, and must work out his own salvation or never be saved. His own free will must give moral quality to every emotion and action, that goes to constitute his meetness for the inheritance of the saints in light. Though the right emotions of the believer are, with truth and propriety, called the fruit of the Spirit, it is never to be forgotten that the believer is the sole author and proximate cause of the whole, as truly as before conversion he was the author and cause of his own sins.

If the regenerated person again freely and voluntarily transgresses the law of God, he is again under the law of sin and death, and the same process must be renewed. The law of the Spirit of Life, the third person of the Godhead, must again reach his moral susceptibilities, with the motive influences of the higher law, and persuade him to renew that generic volition or resolve, which began the formation of his new and right moral character. And through the whole progress of the believer's sanctification, he is excited, induced, and persuaded to all right emotion and action, by the same divine motive influence of the light of truth, which is always the same in all places and at all times, and which always produces the same right and saving effect, except when evaded or resisted by actual trangression, or the force of vicious habits voluntarily contracted and indulged under the law of sin and death. The only difference in the subsequent process of this moral renovation, is that it is not wholly new to the converted sinner. It has become a part of his past experience. He has commenced the formation of habits of right thought and right action. When his conscience begins to reprove and convict him of recently contracted sin and guilt, he knows what the needed remedy is, where it is to be found, and what he must do to obtain relief. He must turn his eyes again to the God of truth, who is light, and in whom is no darkness, must fall on his knees, confess his faults, and renew the generic resolve with which he began the reformation. Every renewal of a right purpose or a right act is a victory won; because the enemy is again foiled, the right habit is strengthened, and the knowledge and skill in the use of the right weapon increased. And thus the law of sin and the force of evil habits is continually awakened. But the conflict must, in every case, continue as long as the subject continues in the flesh. For the law of sin is there, with all its false and delusive motive influences, exciting, enticing, and persuading to moral evil. It cannot be ejected but by the dissolution of the body. The believer can not escape its motive influence till he is seperated from depraved mortal flesh. He has perfect ability to resist and overcome with the sword of the Spirit. But the ultimate victory and final triumph of the saved sinner, will be when he attains to the adoption, to wit, the redemption of the body. And the true believer only, who is conscious of walking, not in the flesh, but in the Spirit, may now rejoice in hope of this final victory.

CHAPTER IV.

THE INSTRUMENT, CAUSE, OR INFLUENCE THAT PRODUCES THE CHANGE.

Though I have, in the preceding chapters, affirmed that moral suasion, or the motive influence of the light of truth, is the sole cause of the change of regeneration and entire moral renovation, and have identified the cause with the author of the change, yet I deem it important to mark the distinction, and further illustrate this important truth. The identification which I have made is a personal identification, plainly taught in the Bible. "By the which will we are sanctified through the offering of the body of Jesus Christ, once for all." Heb. x. 10, compared with Rom. viii. 3, 4.—"For what the law could not do, in that it was weak through the flesh, God sending his own Son in the likeness of sinful flesh, and for sin, condemned sin in the flesh: That the righteousness of the law might be fulfilled in us, who walk not after the flesh but after the Spirit." This sword of the Spirit, which is the word of God, which is identical with the will of God embodied in human language, and also identical with the law of the Lord, which is perfect, converting the soul, and with the gospel of Christ, the power of God unto salvation, is the only instrument, cause, or influence which God, the Almighty Spirit, the third person of the Godhead, ever uses, employs, or puts forth to free the sinner from the law of sin and death, and save him from all its malignant influences and consequents. This law of the Lord, which is the light of eternal truth, includes all the means, power, influence, or causality in the universe, which is applicable for the production of right moral effect. God has no other means, causality, or power, whereby to accomplish any moral purpose among his creatures, or to produce in man any right moral purpose or change for the better that we know of or can conceive of, than this perfect law, which converts the soul. No man was ever yet conscious of any other influence exciting him to right emotion, volition, or action. Falsehood always excites or moves the subject to wrong or sinful volition and action, as it did in the case of Eve. These two, truth and falsehood, are the only moral influences of the universe. When, therefore, Jesus Christ, to set us an example, prayed the Almighty Father to sanctify all his redeemed followers, he said, "Sanctify them through thy truth, thy word is truth." Jno. xvii. 17. And the old serpent, when he invaded the moral kingdom of God, had only the other alternative, to arm himself with falsehood. These words of the Saviour of sinners himself, uttered with the most solemn and awful crisis of the work of redemption immediately before him, addressed to the Omnipotent, the Author of all power, if they have any meaning at all, do connect, in the intimate relation of cause and effect, the word of God and the entire moral renovation of all the redeemed, and identify this cause with the person of the Sanctifier, the Author of the change. Now, we may defy all the professors of

Biblical criticism on the earth, to show any other or different meaning of these words, without stultifying the Saviour, and converting his language into nonsense. And whenever the instrument, cause, or means of this saving change is mentioned or alluded to in the Bible, nothing but moral suasion, or the motive influence of the light of truth can be made out of it, or found in that relation.

When the Apostle Paul affirms—Rom. i. 16—that the gospel of Christ is the power of God unto salvation, the plain, obvious meaning of his affirmation is, that the motive influence of the truth which he taught, was the sole cause of the salvation of all believers. So he explains it himself. "For therein is the righteousness of God revealed from faith to faith: as it is written, The just shall live by faith." He repeats the same truth to the Corinthians. "For the preaching of the cross is to them that perish foolishness; but unto us, which are saved, it is the power of God." 1 Cor. i. 18. And again he reiterates the same important fact, chapter xv. 1, 2.—"Moreover, brethren, I declare unto you the gospel which I preached unto you, which also ye received and wherein ye stand; by which also ye are saved, if ye keep in memory what I preached unto you, unless ye have believed in vain." Paul told the Elders of the church at Ephesus, that he had not shunned to declare to his hearers all the counsel of God. And certainly no preacher, before or since him, ever presented the perfect mirror of God's law more distinctly, plainly, and fully before men than he did. But the gospel of Christ, which he preached is the power of God unto salvation,—the very thing by which his hearers were saved, and the only thing intervening between God the Saviour and the salvation, as seen in the renovated character of the converted man. Nay, this gospel of Christ, which is the power of God unto salvation, he perfectly identified with the will of God, embodied in human language and recorded in the Bible, Heb. x. 10.—"By the which will we are sanctified," etc. And this sanctifying, saving influence it derives by being reflected from the cross of Calvary. Rom. viii. 2-4. Again the Apostle affirms, Heb. iv. 12, "For the word of God is quick and powerful, and sharper than any two-edged sword, piercing even to the dividing asunder of soul and spirit, and of the joints and marrow, and is a discerner of the thoughts and intents of the heart." If this language does not ascribe to the word of God infinite moral power or efficiency, I know not what language can. The effects here ascribed to the word are certainly divine prerogatives, pertaining exclusively to the infinite Spirit. But the word of God produces these effects. Can it not regenerate the sinner? Does it not convert the soul? Is it not the very power of God that saves?

The Apostle James testifies of God, the Father of lights, "Of his own will begat he us, with the word of truth, that we should be a kind of first fruits of his creatures." And immediately after, in the same connection, affirms respecting this word of truth, "Which is able to save your souls." The power or ability to save is here perfectly identified with the word of truth, the word of God, or his revealed will in human language. The Saviour himself makes the same identification in Jno. xv. 13: "Now ye are clean through the word which I have spoken unto you." And all his apostles do the same, not only in the passages already quoted, but in many more, too numerous to be quoted in a short compass. See Eph. v. 26; Acts xv. 9; 2 Tim. iii. 15; Acts xiii. 26; 1 Pet. i. 22.

I thus multiply quotations because I wish to state the testimony of the Bible on this subject fully and plainly; in simple language which can not be misunderstood by any person of common sense who wishes to know and is willing to read and think on the subject. This I desire, because I believe there is in the minds of very many persons in this Christian land, under the light of the gospel, including professors of religion, preachers of the gospel, and even not a few professors and teachers of theology, a great deal of error, confusion of thought and mysticism, in relation to this subject; a subject the most important, the most practical and most necessary to be understood, of all subjects in this world. And I believe it is a subject most plainly revealed, and capable of being understood by all who are interested. But a great part of the public teaching on this subject I regard as "darkening counsel,

10*

by words without knowledge," and furnishing sinners a valid excuse for not trying to do any thing to attain their own moral renovation. The general course of teaching on this subject, which we hear from the pulpit and read in books, represents the conversion of the sinner as some mysterious change of human nature, by infusing into it some substance, quality or attribute, which has never been found in it before since the fall. This change, or addition to the nature of the subject, is effected only by the supernatural power of God. Omnipotence being a natural attribute of Deity, the influence or causality that produces this change must be somewhat more than mere omnipotence. We are not told exactly what that power is which is supernatural to the omnipotent agent, but the necessity of it, for the conversion or recovery of the sinner, we hear reiterated again and again, in various forms, by different sects. The natural inference is, that all finite agency and instrumentality are necessarily excluded. The language generally used to express the cause of the regeneration of the sinner is, that it is wrought by the special influence of the Holy Ghost, or by the supernatural power of God. But sometimes it is affirmed that nothing but the irresistible power of God can effect the change. At the same time we are told that the word of God is totally inefficient, and can have no influence at all on the sinner, to produce the change, till his nature is changed by this special divine power. Such language and such affirmations generally convey to the mind of the unlettered hearer or reader the idea that the only cause of the change is some mysterious, inconceivable, incomprehensible, but tremendous effort of physical power, such as we may suppose was put forth when the matter of this world was created out of nothing; and, therefore, the subject can have no manner of agency about it, either helping or hindering it. Perhaps the learned and venerable teacher himself makes the necessary inference, and affirms the total inability of the sinner for any right emotion, volition or action. And under such tuition from grave and learned divines and pious parents, in venerable creeds and catechisms, and elegant volumes by D.D's, the sinner generally feels very unconcerned and perfectly innocent in relation to any moral change necessary in his case. If the premises be true, if it be a fact that he labors under any inability to repent, believe, to cease to do evil and learn to do well, till some act of supernatural, divine power changes his nature or gives him new power or ability, his excuse is a good one, and he will be able to justify himself, for aught I can see, before any righteous tribunal in the universe.

But it is not fact that he labors under the least inability, moral or physical. This whole representation of the case is erroneous, false, and contradictory to the word of God and common sense. No physical power is ever put forth in the case. No special, or supernatural, or mysterious, or incomprehensible, or irresistible power, influence or agency, is ever used, or can be used in the case, or bear any causal relation to the regeneration or moral renovation of a sinner, or to any moral change whatever. But the change under consideration here is a purely moral change throughout. The subject is a moral agent. The thing to be changed is his moral character: consisting in the moral relation which his voluntary action, that is, his moral conduct, sustains to the moral law of the universe. The author of the change is the moral Sovereign of the universe. The final results to be attained are all moral and spiritual, to be enjoyed principally in the future spirit world. The whole subject pertains exclusively to the administration of God's moral government over the human race, and, therefore, lies entirely within the moral sphere, and not in the physical. To talk about physical, supernatural, special or irresistible power, influence or agency, in relation to such a change, is preposterous. No influence, power or agency can have any relation to such an event, but the moral influence with which God governs his moral kingdom; and that is the motive influence of truth only. In its causal relation to change of character it is properly called moral suasion. And, as far as the character and interests of human agents may be affected during the present probation, this truth is recorded in the Bible, and properly called the higher law.

It may not be improper, but may perhaps be useful to some

reader, to mention some of the causes of the errors and absurd mysticisms which have wrapt up this subject in profound obscurity for ages. The first I would mention is the ignoring, forgetting or disregarding, the distinction between things physical and things moral, or between the relation of cause and effect, in the physical and moral spheres. This distinction was described in the preceding essay on the law of sin and death. I would only here observe that this is a distinction which is never ignored or disregarded through ignorance; because God has taught every moral intelligent on the earth to know the nature, necessity, and use of this distinction from the earliest dawn of intellect. The knowledge is acquired by direct intuition, on the first occasion that occurs for the use of it. Your child of seven or five years old understands the nature, necessity, and use of this distinction, as well as the learned divine or philosopher who fills a professor's chair in the seminary or university. If he wishes you to change the generic purpose of your will, on any subject whatever, if it is only to give a cent, an orange, a new book or a new garment, he presents to your intellectual perception some truth or consideration which he thinks may have motive influence to persuade you to change your purpose. If he should frequently mistake and seek to produce the moral change by physical force, would you not soon be seen consulting the physician, or mental physiologist, to know whether your child was really becoming an idiot? But some very learned men either forget or mistake, and carry the axioms of physical causality into the moral sphere, and thus fall into great errors and gross contradiction. For example, "The antecedent and consequent are always of the same nature or quality," is an axiom in the physical sphere, but not in the moral. When, therefore, the learned theologian infers from the fact that this man has committed sin, therefore he was a sinner before he committed sin, he commits an error, and contradicts all the intuitions of common sense, and the whole testimony of the word of God on that subject.

Another source of error, deception, and mysticism, is the habit of speaking and reasoning about the mere relations of things, and the qualities and circumstances of relations, as though they were real substantive existences in themselves. Hence we have the two varieties of moral character, the good and bad, holiness and sin, which consist exclusively of the relations, or rather of the qualities of the relations, which the voluntary actions of moral agents sustain to the law of God, converted into substantive existences, endowed with the essential attributes of real existences, transferable from one subject to another, transmissible from one generation to another, created by proxy or representation, thousands of years before the principals or constituents came into existence. The righteousness and true holiness which constituted the perfect character of Adam antecedent to the fall, we are told, were produced by the direct agency of God in the creative act, by which man was brought into existence and constituted an essential part of his being. And again, that all the sin, which constitutes the total moral depravity of all the human race, was brought into existence by the single act of Adam in eating the forbidden fruit; and is distributed to each individual of the race, even to the innocent babes, making them guilty, and deserving of a punishment which "is of all evils the essence and the sum."—(Hodge, Rom. v. 13, 14.) Of course, involving everlasting punishment. Also, all the righteousness which constitutes the perfect character of the redeemed, and meetens them for heaven, is often represented as a substantive existence, created by divine agency, and transferred and distributed to individuals, like bills of exchange, or rations to an army.

The relation of antecedent and consequent, or of cause and effect, is often represented as a real substance possessed by the antecedent previous to the existence of the consequent, and therefore something existing separate from, or independently of both cause and effect. Hence the generic term power, which means nothing but this relation in the abstract, is often used in a very vague manner, without any definite meaning, or as though it meant something entirely different from this relation. Thus it has been often used, when the idea intended to be expressed was the ability of a particular agent to put himself into the relation of antecedent to a certain voluntary act, change, or consequent. One person, on the authority of antiquity, the church, or the General Assembly, and under the conventional influence of a creed, a denominational connection, or other social relations, affirms that a sinning unregenerate human agent is totally destitute of power or ability to repent, believe, or obey any requirement of the perfect law of the Lord. Another person, taught by the intuitions of that common sense with which God has endowed him, affirms that every moral agent has necessarily all power and ability, to fulfil all obligation and perform all duty, which Law, or Omnipotence, or divine Sovereignty can impose. Here is a contradiction arising out of this vague confounding of the meaning of two generic terms, signifying nothing but relations, viz., power and ability. Neither of these affirmations is true, in the vague, indefinite manner that I have expressed them. But both are or may be perfectly true, if expressed in the definite and proper terms, without confounding words of different and opposite meaning in describing the same thing. A sinful human agent may sustain no causal relation to any right moral action, having never yet performed any such action under motive influence of law. And the same agent, and every moral agent, must necessarily possess, at all times, the ability to perform all duty and fulfil all obligation. Because no law, authority, or sovereignty can impose obligations in any case, beyond the present ability of the subject to perform. Where ability is wanting obligation can not attach. But this unmeaning and foolish contradiction, thus originated, has produced a controversy to convulse the church for ages, and already to consume more time, waste more labor, thought and effort, and sacrifice more lives than sufficient to put a Bible in every human habitation on earth, and teach every human agent to read the same.

Several other generic terms, expressive of pure relations, such as grace, righteousness, depravity, etc., are used in such a manner and in such connections, as to carry to the mind of the unlearned hearer or reader, the idea of a substance existing independently of the subjects, which sustain these relations. Thus the grace of God to men is often so described, and such things predicated of it, as to give the conception of a real substance, imponderable, but actually existing in some form, material or immaterial, and actually conveyed from the divine person to the regenerate human person, making a real addition to his nature and essential endowments; without which the unregenerate person is totally destitute of ability to repent, believe, love God, or do anything morally right. A very gross absurdity; a profound mysticism.

Another prolific source of error, absurdity, and mysticism is the making of distinctions in things which are identical, or in transferring distinctions belonging to one relation to other relations or substances, where unity and identity are alone predicable. Thus, when the three distinctions of personality in the Godhead, which belong exclusively to the various relations which God sustains to fallen men, are transferred to his mode of existence, they involve the absurdity, the contradiction and profound mysticism, of three existing in one, and of one being in three, and a whole category of like mysticisms. And all the mysticisms of super-omnipotence, special influences of the Spirit, total inability and the like, have grown out of these and like vague, indefinite, and improper uses of language, and confounding distinctions, or using them where there is no difference.

But we never find the phrases, special influence, supernatural influence, irresistible influence; or supernatural power, special power, or irresistible power; or special, supernatural, or irresistible agency, or any other phrases implying or involving change in the Supreme Being, in the Bible, or used by an inspired teacher. All such phrases are the invention of human dogmatizers, to express their own false assumptions, which can not be expressed in the language of the Bible or of common sense. If these phrases convey any ideas or conceptions to the minds of common hearers or readers, they must be erroneous or false conceptions, contradicting the uniform testimony of the Bible, and totally incongruous with the moral nature of the whole subject. I would here ask the common sense reader, what he understands by the phrase,

'Supernatural power of God'? How much greater is it than God's natural omnipotence? Wherein does it differ, either in adaptation or efficiency, from mere omnipotence? Or what is the specific difference in the operation, between the supernatural influences of the Holy Ghost, and the motive influences of the light of truth? The Bible and common sense perfectly identify the influence of the Holy Ghost, and the motive influence of the word of truth. Compare Rom. i. 16, with James i. 18.

But in opposition to these incongruities and absurdities, I have ventured to affirm that the whole efficiency, or causality, or influence, which produces the moral change of regeneration and the entire moral renovation of the redeemed sinner, is found alone in that system of truth which is revealed to us in the Bible, and which constitutes the perfect law of the Lord. This I believe to be the plain, common sense, and true meaning of the language of our Saviour and his Apostles already quoted; and the very meaning which they intended to convey to their hearers when they ascribed the regeneration, the sanctification and salvation of believers to the word of truth, to the gospel of Christ, and to the will of God. I believe this is the true meaning of the Psalmist, when he affirms "The law of the Lord is perfect, converting the soul." And that he intended to assert the fact, that the law of the Lord was the immediate and invariable antecedent, the only efficient cause of the conversion of the soul. The fact that the law converts the soul is affirmed as the evidence or illustration of its absolute perfection. But if it has no efficiency in itself to produce this effect, David certainly offered a very stupid illustration for an inspired poet. But the Psalmist affirms that the law is actually doing what the mystifiers ascribe to the supernatural power of God. If it is not in itself adequate to the conversion of the soul, for what conceivable purpose was it ever revealed in the language of fallen man?

But with respect to the efficiency of the word of God, to produce moral changes in the character of fallen men, we have the direct and positive testimony of the holy Spirit, the Sanctifier and Author of regeneration himself, in plain unequivocal language. He assures us that it is able to save our souls. Jas. i. 21.—That it is able to make us wise unto salvation. 2 Tim. iii. 15.—That it is the very seed or moral influence by which we are born again. The seed, which God puts in our minds, to reproduce right affections, volitions and actions. Not a corruptible seed, or physical influence, but an incorruptible, that is a moral influence, which liveth and abideth for ever. "Being born again, not of corruptible seed, but of incorruptible, by the word of God, which liveth and abideth for ever." "And this is the word, which by the gospel is preached unto you." 1 Pet. i. 23–25. It is also called the sword of the Spirit; that sharp two-edged sword, that goeth out of the mouth of Him, who hath the keys of hell and death. It is also represented as the infinite, exhaustless armory of moral and spiritual weapons, whence the Captain of salvation himself, and the innumerable host of his redeemed soldiery are equipped for the conflict, with the powers of darkness: "weapons that are mighty, through God, to the pulling down of strong holds; casting down imaginations, and every high thing, that exalteth itself against the knowledge of God, and bringing into captivity, every thought to the obedience of Christ." 2 Cor. x. 4, 5.

Does any person object to this view of the subject, and accuse me of detracting from the honor of God the Holy Ghost, by ascribing his peculiar and gracious work to the moral influence of his word? In answer to such objector, I ask, who is this Holy Ghost, the Author of regeneration and Sanctifier of believers? Is he a different agent, from that infinite and almighty Spirit, who spake the world into existence, and gave laws to all the works of his hands? Whose gospel was it which Paul called the power of God unto salvation? And by what Agent was he, and the other writers of the Bible, inspired and directed? I know of but one God, one infinite Being, one divine Agent, the Creator, the Saviour, and the Sanctifier of men. When this divine Agent speaks to me as my Saviour, I think that I recognize the same identical God, of infinite wisdom, power and goodness, who created me and all the world around me: though he now sustains toward me a different relation than that of Creator. He is my Redeemer. And when he speaks to me as my Sanctifier, I think that I recognize the same divine Agent, who gave himself a ransom for the salvation of my soul: though he now sustains toward me a third different relation. In these three divine, personal relationships, I have been able to find but one divine Agent, the one living and true God. And I have always supposed that the word of God, the word of truth, the gospel of Christ, the higher law and the law of the Lord, which is perfect, converting the soul, were each and all of them the identical word of the Holy Ghost, the Sanctifier, and Author of regeneration. I believe, and have endeavored to show, in the preceding discussion, that the word of God is the very expression of his will, his purpose, and the whole desire of his soul. And that the higher law, the gospel of Christ is the very emanation of the whole desire and purpose of the divine mind on the subject of salvation. And that embodied in human language, accompanied by the historical facts and examples, necessary to illustrate the nature and perfection of the same, it constitutes the third personal distinction of the Godhead, and is the actual goings-forth of the moral omnipotence of Jehovah for the salvation of the sinner, in the entire renovation of his moral character.

I ask the mystical objector now, which is the most dishonorable to the infinite Spirit, to ascribe the salvation of a world, to the moral influence of his word, or to represent that word as totally inefficient for the moral renovation of the sinner? Is it a fact that the eternal purpose of God, according to the counsel of his will, is so perfectly inefficient, that not the least moral change for the better can be produced by it, till some special, some supernatural, some profoundly mystical, some inexplicable, some inconceivable—I do not know what to call it—is introduced, to clear the way, or begin the work, or add power or ability to begin with? If the goings-forth of all the efficient will of the Deity in the third person of the Godhead, which was constituted for that very purpose, is not an adequate cause of the moral change which saves the soul, where shall we find an adequate cause?

When I affirm, that the motive influence of truth is the sole efficient cause of the moral change of regeneration, and of the entire sanctification of the redeemed sinner, I intend, and I think that I do actually ascribe this saving change to the immediate agency and sole efficiency of God my Creator, Redeemer and Sanctifier, to the exclusion of all created, finite agency, and of all physical or material instrumentality. But the mystical objector, who affirms, that nothing but the supernatural power of God, or the special influence of the Spirit, can effect this change, does, in fact, ascribe the change to a mere mythical, inexplicable and inconceivable nonentity, implying real change of purpose or attribute in the Deity, and annihilating in the human subject, free agency, moral obligation, accountability, and all moral retribution in relation to the whole subject. For what is more than natural, must be a real addition to natural endowments. And whatever is special, must be a change from what is common, and imply both partiality and imperfection. It is, therefore, the imputation of mysticism to his word and works of grace that dishonors God, and destroys the saving influence of the gospel of Christ, and not the ascription of saving influence to the word of truth. To perfectly divest a human agent of all ability to perform any right moral act, can not be a very powerful persuasive to the performance of duty.

But God did not think it any dishonor to himself, to take into the most perfect, personal union with himself, a human agent, made in the likeness of sinful flesh, to become a servant, and suffer as a malefactor, in order to bring this will of God, expressed in the higher law, and recorded in the Bible, to bear on the case of depraved, sinful men. He said, "A body hast thou prepared me. Then said I, Lo, I come do thy will, O God." This will he did in the flesh, and finished when he bowed his head on the cross, and gave up the ghost. He magnified this law of the Lord, and made it honorable. He has embodied it in the language of men, and thus made it capable of being brought into contact with the carnal mind of the sinner, for his moral renovation. Therefore, the Apostle thought it no disparagement of the Holy Ghost to ascribe the moral renovation of the whole Church to the will of God, which Christ obeyed and magnified. "By the which will we are sanctified, through the offering of the body of Jesus Christ once for all." Heb. x. 10. By perfectly obeying this law of the Lord in the relations of human society, and suffering, (not the punishment for our sins, nor the penalty of the law, both of which were impossible) but a voluntary sacrifice, for the honor of the law, and the love of perishing souls, he magnified it, or put that divine, motive efficiency and adaptation into it, by which it is able to reach and penetrate the heart of the evil doer, and save his soul; and not destroy him, as it must have done without this atonement. And whenever it is rightly presented, by those who undertake to be armor-bearers of the holy Spirit, it will reach the moral susceptibilities of the sinner, and effectually persuade and constrain him to come to Christ, submit to God, to embrace the Saviour on the terms proposed. Or, rather it will constrain the sinner to look at his own character and condition, in this perfect mirror of divine truth, and he will instantly find power, ability, and strength, both moral and physical, and a right good will to come to Christ, to cast away all his transgressions, to make him a new heart, and a new spirit. The endowments and abilities he before employed in resisting and evading the light of truth, and obeying the law of sin and death, he now finds perfectly adequate, and all-sufficient for all right doing.

Another fact which confirms the truth of this position is, that without the higher law, the perfect law of the Lord, or the system of truth called the gospel of Christ, no sinner ever is, ever was, or ever can be converted. This is the fact on which alone the whole utility and necessity of the dispensation of the gospel depends. The command of Christ is, "Go ye into all the world and preach the gospel to every creature." Mark xvi. 15. But why do this? Because, "Whosoever shall call upon the name of the Lord shall be saved." But, "How then shall they call on him in whom they have not believed? and how shall they believe in him of whom they have not heard? and how shall they hear without a preacher? And how shall they preach except they be sent? as it is written, How beautiful are the feet of them that preach the gospel of peace, and bring glad tidings of good things!" Rom. x. 13, 14, 15. But if the word of God have no efficiency in it to produce the great and necessary moral change, why all this urgency and importance of preaching the gospel to every creature? If a direct omission of divine supernatural power be necessary in the case of every individual sinner, why all this array and expense and delay of external machinery, totally destitute of any efficiency in relation to the end to be attained? Away with such scandalous imputations against the wisdom of God and the efficiency of his truth! A mere child, of common sense, must necessarily and intuitively know, on the first conception of the subject, that nothing in the universe can have causal relation to such a change but the motive influence of truth. "The law of the Lord is perfect, converting the soul: the testimony of the Lord is sure, making wise the simple." It is the very power of God which causes the saving change in the mind of the sinful agent.

Again, if we analyze the whole process of moral renovation by which the sinner is saved from the bondage of corruption and the wrath to come, not a single item can be found but what is an immediate effect of the motive influence of the truth contained in the law of the Lord and in the Bible, ascribed to the influence of the truth. And not a single step can be taken, in the whole process, even by the Almighty author of the change, without the instrumentality of the truth.

Is it necessary, in the commencement of the process, that the sinner should be enlightened sufficiently to have some just or right conceptions of the law of God, of the nature of sin, of accountability, or of his own character and condition as an accountable subject of moral government? Not a single right suggestion on one of these topics can be put in his mind but by the light of truth. "By the law is the knowledge of sin." Rom. iii. 20. "Nay, I had not known sin but by the law: for I had not known lust except the law had said, Thou shalt not covet." Rom. vii. 7. If any objector reply to this, That the heathen have a knowledge of sin, though they never saw or heard the written law of the Lord, that is very true. "They are a law unto themselves: which show the works of the law written in their hearts." The identical truths which constitute the first principles of the written law of God, were, at the beginning, made intuitive in every human intellect. They are intuitive still in the intellect of every human agent, and can never be obliterated. They may be, and are, obscured, hidden, buried deep under accumulated vicious passions, habits and propensities, contracted by continuous evil doing, according to the law of sin and death. But these first principles of moral rectitude must be disentombed, in order to bring their life-giving energies to bear on the great fact of God's revealed will, viz: Christ, the Son of God, given as a ransom for sinful men. And, as a general thing, the written word in the hand of the living teacher is as necessary to effect this as the artificial magnet in the hand of the mineralogist is to discover the precious ore hid in the bowels of the earth. But the moment any sinner sees his own character and condition in the light of the higher law, as reflected from the cross of Calvary, that moment he is more effectually awakened and convicted than all the thunders and terrors of the material universe could awaken or convict him. If, therefore, we may suppose that God may, or does, convert and save some, or many, among the heathen, pagan, and savage tribes of men, (and I know of no reason why we may not suppose this to be so,) yet we can conceive of no possible method by which he can convert and save them but by bringing this light of evangelical truth into contact with their moral susceptibilities, either by intuition, oral tradition or direct revelation; because every other conceivable method must necessarily involve a contradiction: there being but the one kind of antecedent to any right moral change conceivable, and that is the motive influence of truth. If conviction of sin, or conscious desert of punishment, be a necessary antecedent or accompaniment of the saving change, it can not be produced but by the knowledge and motive influence of the higher law. Saith Paul, "I was alive without the law once:

but when the commandment came sin revived, and I died." "For without the law sin was dead."

Does the saving change include believing in Christ, coming to Christ, or accepting of Christ, as he is freely offered to us in the gospel? "The law was our schoolmaster to bring us unto Christ, that we might be justified by faith." Gal. iii. 24. It is not possible that any knowledge or conception of Christ, as a Mediator, or of his offices or work, or of the necessity of a Mediator or atonement, should reach the subject at all but by the word of truth contained in the Bible.

Is regeneration a ceasing to do evil and a learning to do well? is it a change from evil affections, volitions and actions, to right feeling and action? The law of the Lord is the only rule which marks the distinction between right and wrong, good and evil, in any and in every relation that can exist among intelligent agents. It is impossible for finite intelligents to recognize or perceive any moral difference in actions or emotions but in the light of the higher law. Is repentance involved in this moral renovation as a necessary condition of pardon? Transgression of the law is the only thing to be repented of, and the love of God to a sinful world, manifested in giving his Son to die for every man, is the only motive influence that ever did, or ever can melt the carnal mind into true repentance. Neither of these can be seen, or known or conceived of, by a human transgressor, but by the light of truth revealed in the gospel of Christ. You may threaten wrath upon the sinner, or you may inflict physical suffering ever so long, and it will only harden him in sin, but never melt him to evangelical repentance. Nothing but the love of God in Christ can effect that.

Is faith an essential product of the saving change, and a necessary condition of justification? The word of God is the only subject of saving faith; and his testimony in that word the only sure and safe warrant to believe. "But the testimony of the Lord is sure, making wise the simple." And, "The works of his hands are verity and judgment; all his commandments are sure." Ps. cxi. 7. Is love to God and men the legitimate fruit of moral renovation? Only by the light of truth is any amiable or lovely trait of character discoverable in either. Does the believer need a light to guide him through this dark world of sin and ignorance? "Thy word is a lamp unto my feet, and a light unto my path. The commandment of the Lord is pure, enlightening the eyes." And this is the only light that can guide him a single step in the right course to heaven. Does the believer often need consolation, comfort and support, during the process of sanctification and the conflicts of probation in the flesh? "Thy testimonies have I taken for a heritage for ever: for they are the rejoicing of my heart." "And in keeping of them there is great reward." "Thy statutes have been my song in the house of my pilgrimage." And what humble, afflicted or suffering believer on the earth, does not know by experience that the word of God gives the strongest and best consolation that can be desired or conceived in this world?

And whatever else can be named or conceived, as desirable, or necessary, or useful to a sin-sick soul returning to God and seeking heaven, "through the redemption that is in Christ," that also is promised in the word of God, secured to him in the covenant of grace, confirmed by the testimony of God, and conferred upon him, at the proper time, by the influence of the higher law.

Now, if any person, in the light of all this divine testimony, feels doubtful, or hesitates about receiving this view of the efficiency of divine truth; or if any person objects to this view of the subject, That the word of God often fails to produce the effects I ascribe to it: that many who hear the gospel and read the Bible, and are instructed in the knowledge of the truth, remain impenitent, unconverted, and their moral character unaltered for the better, and finally die in unbelief: that often very learned, pious and faithful ministers preach the gospel for years, and little or no visible effect is produced, no sinner is converted, no person reformed, but multitudes hardened in sin. But when the Spirit is poured out, sinners are converted by scores and hundreds, under the same preaching, with the same word of God in their hands.

To remove every objection of the kind, and resolve every

doubt of the sincere inquirer after truth, it will be necessary to call his attention again to the character and position of the subject of regeneration, to the peculiar nature of the desired change, and to the circumstances of the cause, when the change does take place, or the assigned cause fails to produce the effect. The subject of regeneration is an intelligent being, a free moral agent, capable in himself of originating moral change, either good or bad, and of forming a moral character. This is his nature, and these attributes are essential to his nature. And in the exercise of these attributes he must act, if he acts at all. Perfect freedom of choice is so absolutely essential an attribute of his nature, that to deprive him of it, or to necessitate his volition or action, would be to deprive him of existence as a moral agent. He would instantly cease to be a moral agent, or an accountable being. He would be as totally incapable of moral character as a block of wood, and therefore a totally impracticable subject of regeneration, sanctification, or any moral change or quality whatever. Continuous consciousness, or immortality of being, is also another essential attribute of a moral agent. Deprived of it, man would instantly cease to be an accountable agent. When, therefore, a change of moral character is proposed to a human agent, or when the means or motive influences for the production of such a change, are presented to his consideration, he must exercise perfect liberty to receive or reject them, to choose or refuse the proposed change, to yield to the motives presented, or to reject them totally, and to refuse to consider them at all.

In the case of the sinner and this proposed moral change, the subject has already formed a moral character. And every emotion, volition, and action which went to constitute that character, was of his own voluntary agency. He is the accountable author of it. It is his chosen character, which he had voluntarily contracted for himself, and which he still cherishes and cultivates, because he chooses it and because it is of himself. It is a sinful character, and he still prefers and chooses to commit sin. But the proposed change is from this sinful character to a character the very reverse of it; to one

11

that necessarily condemns all his past conduct, all contracted habits, propensities, inclinations, and dispositions. One that involves the most profound self-abasement and condemnation, and totally destroys all past hopes and anticipations. It must, therefore, be perfectly obvious to common sense, that all the habits of moral feeling and action, the inclinations, propensities, desires, and volitions of the unconverted sinner, antecedent to regeneration, must be directly opposed to that change. Now, suppose that nine hundred and ninety of every thousand, who hear the gospel or read the Bible, reject the truth, refuse to submit to its teachings, or resist its motive influence and die impenitent, does that argue the least deficiency in the word of God as a means, or cause of regeneration, or the least limitation of its efficiency to produce a perfect renovation of moral character? Suppose a thousand persons are dying daily in the city by the cholera, and that an infallible remedy is offered at every door to every patient, as soon as he is taken with the first symptom. Ten of the thousand take the medicine and recover immediately. The nine hundred and ninety refuse to take it and die. Does their death prove anything against the excellence and efficiency of the remedy? Does not the immediate cure of all who took it sufficiently establish its perfect efficacy? So also the conversion and salvation of every sinner who ever received the word of God into his mind, and suffered its actual contact with the moral susceptibilities of his soul, proves its perfect infallibility, as God's instrument of moral renovation. "He that believeth on the Son, hath everlasting life." That is, every one who receives the truth as such, is regenerated, sanctified, and saved by its purifying and saving moral influence.

But in order to know and understand the relation of any cause to its effect, in any case whatever, it is necessary to take into consideration all those circumstances which are essential or without which the consequent cannot follow. For instance, a spark of fire is sufficient to produce the conflagration of a house or a city. This we know, because a single spark has often been the cause of the destruction of much property and of many lives. But several circumstances were essential to the cause, without which the effect never could have followed. The spark must have been in actual contact with some combustible part of the house or city, or of their contents. And the atmosphere, at the time and place of the contact, must have been in a certain state favourable to combustion. These circumstances, though necessary to make out the relation, and, therefore, essential to the cause of that particular event, yet not being of the substance and essence of the cause, are not usually mentioned in assigning the cause of that event. These circumstances are often varying in particular cases, and, therefore, can not always be seen and particularized in describing the cause of a class or series of events. A quart of water may, if applied at the moment when the combustion begins to kindle, be sufficient to prevent the conflagration, and save the city. But if the application be delayed a few moments only, tons of water may be totally insufficient. The city may burn to ashes, while the ocean flows all around it. So also the light of truth may shine around the sinner with perfect brilliancy, but can never improve his character while his mind is closed against it. The circumstance of contact with the moral susceptibilities of the subject, is always essential to moral change; and the circumstance of time may render the application totally inefficient. Habits, by long indulgence, often become inveterate, which, if taken in time, might have been easily subdued. Till the truth comes in contact with those moral susceptibilities which originate character, no change of character can be effected by it. The habit of rejecting and resisting the light of truth, if long continued, may become so inveterate as to exclude it for ever. "Can the Ethiopian change his skin, or the leopard his spots? then may ye also do good that are accustomed to do evil." Jer. xiii. 23. The light of truth in the law of the Lord, which now, during probation, is able to save the soul, must, after the period of probation is closed, only serve to kindle the everlasting burnings which constitute the future punishment of the finally impenitent. We are not always competent to decide who are subjects of moral renovation, and when the word of God has produced or failed to produce a saving change of character. External circumstances may be very fair and promising while the generic volition of the will, the controlling purpose of the soul, and the true character of the agent may remain unchanged, perfectly selfish and carnal still. Nicodemus was a member in good standing of the only true and orthodox Church on earth at the time, a ruler, a magistrate, and teacher in that Church, and at the same time an unregenerate person. The thief that was converted on the cross but a few hours before he entered Paradise, was, to say the least, a very unpromising subject. A man may also at the present day be a fashionable Christian in good standing in an orthodox Church, may contribute a few thousands of his millions for the support and promulgation of Christianity in the world. He may occupy a very comfortable seat in a very splendid church every pleasant Sabbath morning. He may commend very highly the eloquent sermon, as a splendid production of learning and talent. He may be an officer in the church and society, a teacher, or preacher of the gospel, or a manager of a missionary or benevolent society. He may read a chapter in the Bible occasionally on the Sabbath morning, and make or read a prayer with his family, if business be not too urgent. Nay, more; he may even attend a daily prayer meeting, make very fervent and eloquent prayers, and tell very affecting stories about conversions. And still the generic, controlling purpose of his soul, the prevailing thought of his mind, and all the warmest affections of his heart, may all the time be in his counting room, at the stock market, the theatre, the opera, or some other place of profit or pleasure. And he may remain unconverted, and die impenitent. While, on the other hand, it may not be impossible that thousands of poor, ignorant, despised persons, slaves, pagans and savages, whose characters and conditions have never been regarded or valued by their fellow-men in the world as the least remove above the brute animal, either in physical or moral worth, guided by a single ray of light from the cross of Christ, may be winging their glorious flight from caves of the earth, from cabins, wigwams, garrets and altars of squalid misery, to the mansions of eternal bliss. A credible professor of religion may be a very convenient, cheap and profitable accompaniment of almost any decent worldly profession, pursuit or business, for the accumulation of wealth. And a ray of the light of life, reflected from the cross of Christ, may penetrate the deepest, darkest cavern of human wretchedness and degradation, and free a broken-hearted soul from the law of sin and death.

The word of God has never yet failed to convert the soul, and save the sinner, in any case, where it has really come in contact with the moral susceptibilities of the carnal mind, during probation. Till such a failure is produced and proven, its absolute infallibility, as the cause of moral renovation, can not be successfully controverted. Because every human agent is at all times a perfectly free, voluntary agent, with perfect ability to exclude from his serious consideration any subject which he regards as undesirable. But in accounting for the supposed failures of the word of God to convert the soul, we must not forget, that first principle of the law of sin and death, which Christ taught Nicodemus. "For every one that doeth evil, hateth the light, neither cometh to the light, lest his deeds should be reproved." Every sinner, who evades the light of truth, and dies impenitent, has of course been an evil doer, and has passed through that process of moral depravation described in the preceding essay on the law of sin and death. He has so long and so often evaded the light of truth, that it has become a fixed habit, a permanent and uniform state of the mind, a continuous desire, or a generic volition of his will. He has long since forgotten the first evil deed by which the process was commenced. He has, probably, from his childhood, heard it often affirmed, that he was born into the world with a sinful nature, a child of wrath, exposed to eternal punishment, with a natural disposition or propensity to sin, and totally destitute of any ability to do right, or help himself out of this condition. He has also been taught, that all this was inflicted upon him by God his Creator, in punishment for Adam's sin committed long before he existed. That this and all the sin that is committed in the world, was agreeable to the eternal purpose of God, and according to the counsel of his will, foreordained and brought to pass by his agency in the works of creation and providence. He has heard reiterated from the pulpit, and read in books, that nothing but the supernatural power of God can change his sinful nature, and save him from this helpless state of inability to all good. These dogmas of orthodoxy have very much relieved him of the compunctions of a guilty conscience. For he intuitively infers, and can not avoid feeling, that he can not be very much to blame for that which is natural. If he is only what God and nature made him, he can not be very far out of the right way. He feels that he can not be very guilty for being just what God foreordained he should be, and just what God, in his most holy, wise and powerful work of providence had caused him to be. If nothing but supernatural power of God can help him, or change his condition, it must certainly be useless to make any efforts of his own. And if the word of God has no efficiency in itself, there can be no use in perplexing his mind, or wasting his time about it.

This reasoning from the doctrine of original sin is perfectly natural, legitimate, logical, and conclusive. And as perfectly scriptural, as it is logical and conclusive. Admit the premises, and the conclusion can not be avoided. No intelligent of common sense can evade or deny it. But the premises are false. Human agents are not sinners by nature, but only by transgression. They are not helpless imbeciles, but possess ability to do right and fulfil all duty. The moral influence of truth is the omnipotence of God, for all right moral change. In the case of the finally impenitent sinner, the habit of hating the light and evading the influence of truth, has long since become a permanent or continuous state of the mind. He has made no record of the process by which this state of mind was acquired, and has entirely forgotten the commencement. He, therefore, readily assents to the declaration, that it is natural, inflicted on him, or transmitted to him, without his knowledge or consent; and of course it is impossible that he should feel any blame for it, or conviction of sin, thus imposed upon him without his concurrence. Is it a strange thing, that such an evil doer, after such a process of moral depravation, under the influence of such habits, established on such premises, confirmed by the teaching of pious parents, and grave divines, should finally evade the light of truth, and die impenitent? Is the infidelity and the final impenitence of such a sinner, any disparagement of the efficiency of divine truth for the renovation of human character? And is not the preaching of the false doctrine of original sin, and its kindred dogmas, casting a stumbling block in the way of sinners? Our Saviour, while on earth, setting an example to all future preachers of the gospel, did not thus deal with inquiring sinners.

CHAPTER V.

THE CONVERSION OF NICODEMUS.

NICODEMUS was a ruler of the Jews, a master or teacher in Israel, a speculative believer in revealed religion, a member of the only true Church on earth, and of the strictest sect, or most orthodox denomination of that Church. Yet it appears that he was still an unregenerate sinner. At least the Saviour dealt with him as such. From his office and standing in the community, he must have been well acquainted with the letter of the higher law, and with all the instituted rites of religious worship, by which the law was illustrated, under the Mosaic dispensation. He had been an evil doer, and his conscience troubled him. He had hated the light, and had succeeded hitherto in excluding its moral influence from governing his voluntary conduct. Under a spurious outward deportment, he had been prosecuting that course of moral depravation, which is the natural and necessary consequence of continuous evil doing, according to the law of sin and death. He had acquired, by evil doing, those habits of hating, evading, or resisting the motive influence of truth, which, in the language of modern orthodoxy, are falsely called innate moral depravity, or natural propensity, inclination or disposition to sin, a sinful nature, or original sin. He had confirmed and strengthened these habits by a course of many years of impenitence, under the clear light of the higher law, and a fair external profession. But he seems to have been awakened in some degree by the miracles or preaching of the Saviour, or some other cause; and came to Jesus by night, an anxious inquiring sinner. The time and manner of his coming shows that he sustained a fair character before the public, and highly valued the good opinion of his countrymen. Nicodemus, therefore, presented to the Saviour a perfect specimen of a human agent, having contracted a sinful character, under the light and motive influences of the perfect law of the Lord. He needed that moral change, without which no man can see the kingdom of God. To insure his conversion the Saviour directed to his moral susceptibilities; first, the fact of his own voluntary transgression and guilt; and second, the great crowning fact of the higher law, or the remedial provisions of grace, which the perfect law of the Lord alone provides in the otherwise remediless case of the transgressor. These two important, but simple truths, are something more than the carnal mind of the transgressor can quietly bear. The essential point is to bring them both, at the same time, into contact with his moral sense.

Jesus began by declaring to him the absolute necessity of being born again. But Nicodemus was so wholly engrossed by the things of the flesh, and his mind so effectually closed against the light of moral truth, that he could think of nothing but a physical change. He, therefore, made the stupid inquiry, "How can a man be born when he is old?" Jesus explained to him the metaphor of the new birth. He meant by it that entire, radical change of moral character, symbolized by the typical sprinklings and washings with water, in their religious services. Nicodemus understood the meaning of all these symbols of moral purification. "Jesus answered, verily, verily, I say unto thee, Except a man be born of water, that is of the Spirit, he can not enter into the kingdom of God. That which is born of the flesh is flesh; and that which is born of the Spirit is spirit." Here is no mention of original sin, of innate moral depravity, or of inability of any kind. No necessity of supernatural divine power, or special influence is suggested, in relation to this important and necessary change. The thing meant, by being born of the Spirit, was a plain common sense matter of practical duty, as easily understood as the course of the wind. Nothing is required, or included, or involved in it, but to "Cease to do evil and learn to do well." "Turn ye, turn ye, from your evil ways, for why will ye die, O house of Israel?" "Cast away from you all your transgressions, whereby ye have transgressed; and make you a new heart and a new spirit: for why will ye die, O house of Israel?" It is all a practical duty, done by the subject of the change, within his personal ability, and depending exclusively on his own volition. "Cease to do evil, Turn ye,—Cast away your transgressions,—for why will ye die?" It is all done by willing and obeying. Nicodemus understood the whole subject, and had, doubtless, often enjoined the duty on other evil doers. Being a member of the Sanhedrim, a magistrate, and a master of Israel, it is impossible that he should have been ignorant of the nature of the change, or wholly unconscious of his own obligation to perform the duty.

Jesus, therefore, tells him, "Marvel not that I said unto thee, Ye must be born again. The wind bloweth where it listeth, and thou hearest the sound thereof, but canst not tell whence it cometh, and whither it goeth: so is every one that is born of the Spirit." Of all the perversions of language ever attempted, the effort to force, out of this plain similitude of the wind, the profound and inexplicable mysticisms of supernatural omnipotence, and total human inability, rather exceeds in bold presumption, and stupid absurdity. Every person of common sense knows that the motion of the wind is the most common, the most frequent, the most obvious and changeable phenomenon in nature; that it is the most easily perceived by the senses, and its uses and inconveniences the quickest understood of all natural phenomena; that it is most easily adapted to the use and convenience of men, though the whence it came and the whither it goeth are not perceivable by the senses. This phenomenon of the wind is used by the Saviour to illustrate the obvious necessity of the transgressor's turning from his evil way, ceasing to do evil, and learning to do well, or changing his moral character, in order to attain peace and happiness, and escape punishment. As if he had said to Nicodemus, You have no cause to marvel or inquire about the methods of this change: it is a plain matter of obvious duty, as easily understood as the phenomenon of the wind. You can hear the sound of the wind, you can perceive its motions and force, you can adjust your position, attitude and motions, either to avoid or improve its force, without knowing whence it came, or whither it goes. You do not think, or stop to ask so stupid a question as, Where did the wind come from, or where will it go to? So with respect to this moral or spiritual change, all inquiries about the whence and the wherefore, the how and the why, are perfectly useless and impertinent. You Nicodemus know, as well as you know your own existence, that you have sinned, are guilty, and that is the cause of your present sufferings and fears of the future. And you know too, as well as you know your own existence, that you must repent or perish, turn or die, cease to do evil, or suffer the consequences. Your presence here, at this time of night, on this business, is demonstrative proof that you are perfectly conscious of the whole disease, the cause and remedy.

A little thought and reflection will discover to any person the force and point of this beautiful comparison. All the observations, the science and experiments of the world, have never enabled any man to tell, with respect to any current of wind, at any particular location, from what point of compass, or what location it came, or at what place the motion commenced. The result of all inquiry and observation on the subject, as far as they tend to confirm any theory is, that the motion of the atmosphere, which we call wind, is never in a direct line, but always in a curvilinear or circular direction. This is caused by the globular shape of the earth, and the curvilinear or circular direction of all its motions; and also by several other influences, which tend constantly to vary the course and velocity of the wind: as the varying aspect of the sun to different parts of the earth, and the various relative heights of different parts of its surface, etc. It is supposed, also, according to this theory, that all the considerable changes of wind and weather, or storms and hurricanes move in a complete circle; and that as their velocity is increased, the radius of the circle is diminished, and the concentricity of the course increased. And when the velocity is increased to the extreme the wind is condensed into an irresistible tornado, mingling every thing movable or frangible, in its course, in utter confusion, destruction, and ruin. "So is every one that is born of the Spirit," or that needs this change. The sinner, who has formed a moral character by transgression, and contracted permanent habits of hating and evading truth, and indulging depraved instincts, appetites and passions, cannot, while under the law of sin and death, or impenitent, conceive how these things can be. The reason is, he has never made any record of this course of sin and moral depravation, but has always justified himself, and endeavored to believe that his conduct had been a direct course of right moral action. But, instead of this, his first evil deed was a deviation from the straight course of truth and moral rectitude. And every step of the process since, has been a further deviation, increasing the velocity of his progress and the concentricity of his character towards total depravity; which, if not changed by conversion, before probation ends, must concentrate in a burning tornado of depraved passions, guilt, wrath, and final perdition.

Nicodemus was probably a man of liberal education, a man of wealth, high in office, and of most respectable standing in society; to secure his favorable attention, and indelibly fasten conviction, Jesus, in this striking comparison, set before him a mirror, in which he might see his entire moral character and depravity of heart, perfectly separate from all causal influence but his own free, unconstrained volition and choice. Though he could not remember or tell what false motive influences had first induced him to turn aside from the path of truth and rectitude, or what delusive influences had led him, as it were, a voluntary captive, so far along the way of sin and death, no more than he could tell whence came the wind and whither it went; yet he could not avoid seeing and feeling that his present, habitual and voluntary course of action and feeling was in direct transgression of the perfect law of the Lord, and no conceivable cause for it but his own will.

And as the least cultivated human intellect on the earth, though he can not tell whence the wind cometh and whither it goeth, is nevertheless capable of understanding the phenomenon of the wind, if he will, at least as far as his own senses perceive the sound and course of it, and of adjusting his own position and course of action, to avoid its force, or turn it to some useful purpose. And as even the brute animals, when they suffer by the cutting blast, understand the cause of their suffering, and have wit enough to turn tail to, or take the lee side of the barn, to avoid the force of the wind. Even so, every transgressor of the law of God, on the face of the earth, knows or may know, if he will, just as well as he knows his own existence, when his guilty conscience disturbs his peace, what the cause of his misery is, and what he must do to avoid the consequences. If he is ignorant, his ignorance is wilful. If he professes inability, his inability is feigned and false. But the hardened impenitent, under the light of the gospel, has been so long in the habit of doing evil, and evading or resisting the light of truth, that he will not turn or change his purpose or action as long as he can taste a drop of sensual pleasure in his wonted course, or form the shadow of an excuse for delaying the change. And yet we hear grave divines in the pulpit quoting this illustration, to prove that the transgressor never does, and never can turn, or change the character of his moral conduct, but that he labors under a total inability, or rather impossibility of turning, or of doing any thing morally right, or conformable to the higher law. An inability or impossibility, which no power or influence in the universe, but the supernatural power of God, can remove or remedy.

But Nicodemus was so full of original sin, or some other kindred dogma of mysticism, that he still doubts and makes another effort to justify delay. "How can these things be?" A question as destitute of any object, subject, point or meaning, as the inquiry, How can a man and himself occupy the same space at the same time? And, therefore, Jesus paid no attention to it, but to reiterate the truth he had affirmed. "Art thou a master of Israel, and knowest not these things?" Now, if there had been any such thing as original sin, or innate moral depravity, or a natural propensity to sin, or any inability, or other obstacle, in the case of Nicodemus, or of any sinner, to hinder him from changing his moral conduct, or from being born again, or from making to himself a new heart, and a new spirit, or to hinder him from complying with the terms of the gospel, or from being regenerated, at any time: or if there had been any incomprehensible mystery about the subject, which Nicodemus could not understand, or which was above the comprehension of mankind in general; this was certainly the time for Jesus to have mentioned it, and explained it to the mind of this inquiring, anxious sinner. If any such thing existed, or might materially affect the condition or the recovery of the sinner, we must think it ought to have been mentioned in this discourse, which was to be recorded, and stand as a pattern and example of the means and method of converting sinners in all future time. But not a word suggesting any such thing is found in this discourse, or in all the Bible beside, except merely what obstacles lie in the free voluntary action of his own will at the time. I know, and have not forgotten, that the Saviour said, "No man can come to me, except the Father which hath sent me draw him." And to the same gospel-hardened Jews he said also: "And ye will not come to me, that ye might have life." But both in the case of Nicodemus, and these untoward Jews, the Father had for years been drawing, with all the motive influence, and moral omnipotence, which infinite wisdom, power and goodness could contrive, or bring to bear on their case.

Jesus answered him just as if Nicodemus understood the whole subject, and knew perfectly well that there was no mystery about the subject of this moral change, and not the least obstacle in the way to prevent his making the change at any moment during his probation; and that it was just as easy for him to make the change, symbolized by being born of water, that is of the Spirit, as it was to turn his back to the wind when it blew too hard in his face. Nicodemus undoubtedly did know, and was perfectly conscious, that he had sinned and was guilty, and must turn or die, repent or perish. He had just confessed that he knew Jesus was a teacher come from God, "For no man can do these miracles that thou dost, except God be with him." Of course, then, he knew that what Jesus said unto him was true as God himself is true; and he now understood, perfectly, what was meant by being born again. When, therefore, Jesus added, "We speak that we do know, and testify that we have seen; and ye receive not our witness," he was convicted out of his own mouth, and perfectly confounded at his own duplicity, self-deception, perverseness and stupidity, and did not answer another syllable during the interview. And that common sense, or gift of intuition, which God has implanted in every created moral intelligent, making it an essential part of his nature, renders it impossible that Nicodemus, or any other gospel sinner, should have been ignorant of these things, or unconscious of his obligation and ability to cease to do evil, and learn to do well, or to change the generic purpose of his will, in relation to the law of the Lord.

But if there was, at that time any sin, or sinfulness, or moral obliquity, in the nature, the character or disposition of Nicodemus, which he had not contracted by his own voluntary agency, or which had been inflicted on him by any other agency, or which had come upon him by any other influence whatever, without his knowledge, previous consent and volition, or which he had not ability to turn away from, avoid or cease to practice, or if he labored under any inability to change the relation of his moral conduct, then this discourse of Jesus, addressed to him, was deceitful, delusive; and the close of it implied a false accusation against Nicodemus. And if sinners, at the present time, come into existence, full of innate moral depravity, or original sin, or have a depraved, sinful and guilty nature inflicted on them, in punishment of Adam's sin, antecedent to their knowledge volition or action; and if no influence, but the supernatural power of God, can change this polluted nature, then the pretended offer of a free salvation in the gospel, the invitation to come and take of the water of life freely, and the exhortations to turn and live, believe and be saved, repent and receive remission of sins, are all solemn mockery, false pretences, and abusive insults of human misery. As if a cold-hearted, unfeeling tyrant should cast an innocent victim of his hatred into the dungeon, load him with chains and fetters, and rivet them down to the floor, and then invite him to walk up into his splendid palace and dine with him, and after make the range of his pleasure grounds, and regale himself on the rich fruits of his gardens, and then take a seat in the privy council, and assist in the administration of his government. Who can avoid feeling that this conduct would be the utmost refinement of malice, hatred and malignant cruelty. But the God of the Bible and Saviour of men is an infinitely different character. And his method of dealing, even with sinful men, is exactly and totally the reverse of this. He reproves for nothing but voluntary transgression. He commands nothing, but on the basis of entire ability of the subject, both moral and physical, to obey. He invites only when ready and willing to bestow at the moment. He never tantalizes; but always exercises his infinite wisdom, power and goodness, to save the sinner, as long as there is a single ray of hope, or the least possibility of salvation in his case.

He, therefore, proceeded with Nicodemus : "If I have told you of earthly things, and ye believe not, how shall ye believe if I tell you of heavenly things." Jesus had stated to him a plain matter of obvious duty, absolutely necessary to his salvation, which must be performed during his earthly probation in the flesh. He must change his moral conduct, by ceasing to do evil and learning to do well. The Holy Ghost had been striving, with the word of truth, to persuade him to make this change, ever since he committed his first evil deed. The Spirit was still striving with him, and he was resisting the Spirit by rejecting the truth, which he knew and acknowledged had come from God. And there was not the least obstacle in the universe to hinder his turning that very moment, but in his own will. His whole case, disease, trouble, and distress of mind, which brought him to Jesus by night, is told in a single sentence, "Ye will not come unto me, that ye might have life."

How did Jesus farther proceed with this convicted sinner? Did he tell him to wait till some supernatural power of the Almighty was put forth to change his nature? Did he tell him that he had no ability to believe or obey the truth? Or did he tell him there was no efficiency in the word of truth to effect a saving change of character? Or did he tell him to wait for or expect any special, or different, or greater influence of the Spirit, than the plain, simple influence of the truth? —He told him nothing of the kind, nor uttered a syllable from which he might infer any thing of the kind. But he gave him another thrust with the sword of the spirit, which is the word of God, the higher law. And at the last saving thrust, he pointed it with the great crowning fact by which the perfect law of the Lord was magnified and made honorable, and its moral omnipotence brought to bear on perverted human intellect. "As Moses lifted up the serpent in the wilderness, even so must the Son of Man be lifted up." "For God so loved the world that he gave his only begotten Son, that whosoever believeth in him might not perish, but have everlasting life."

Having thus set before Nicodemus the true character of God, and the nature and perfection of his higher law, as illustrated in the atonement made for all men on the cross of Calvary, he again reiterated the humbling fact, that his own hatred of the light of truth, contracted by his own evil doing, was the sole obstacle in the way of his conversion; and that his own voluntary action was the sole cause of all his blindness or want of understanding, of all his inability and insensibility. "And this is the condemnation, that light is come into the world, and men loved darkness rather than light, because their deeds were evil. For every one that doeth evil hateth the light, neither cometh to the light, lest his deeds should be reproved. Such was the character of Nicodemus when he left Jesus, or when the conference closed. And such is the character and condition of every gospel sinner, whether awakened and anxious, or ever so stupid, careless, and indifferent. And no human agent was ever condemned or guilty, or felt compunction of conscience, or fear of punishment, or is ever capable of suffering penal infliction under moral government, till he has actually seen the light of the higher law, felt the obligations it imposes, and transgressed its requirements.

When, exactly, Nicodemus submitted, and found peace in believing, we are not told. But it could not have been long; probably it was before he slept again. The next we hear of him, like a bold Christian confessor, he is pleading the higher law, in defence of Christ, before the assembly of the chief Priests and Pharisees. This conversion of Nicodemus is a true specimen of the conversion of an enlightened or gospel-hardened sinner, with the word of truth. This conference with Jesus is recorded in the third chapter of John, to be an example and pattern, through all future time, to all teachers of Christianity, of the true method of dealing with enlightened, unregenerate sinners. It first shows us the propriety and utility of private social conference, with one or a few individuals on this important subject. It shows how few, and how plain and simple are the proper topics of such conference. Jesus was very careful to suggest only two plain, simple, personal topics to Nicodemus. First, his own exclusive and personal authorship of everything that constituted his sinful, guilty, wretched condition, as a subject of God's moral kingdom, including all his pretended ignorance and inability. His second topic, or object of discourse, was to present to the apprehension of Nicodemus a just conception of the true character of God and his perfect law, as illustrated on the cross of calvary. By placing these two plain but important topics in antithetical contrast, in the mind of Nicodemus, he kindled in his conscience a temporary hell, with which he could neither eat, drink, nor sleep, nor taste a drop of sensual pleasure, rest, or peace, till his independence, pride, self-complacency, and self-righteousness were broken down and crushed out, and the second glorious topic had absorbed his whole soul. Jesus treated the ignorance, doubt, marvel, and pretended inability of Nicodemus, as entirely out of character, absurd, and false, and sent him away perfectly convicted, out of his own mouth, of their falsehood. Therefore, in the account of this conference, there is not the least intimation of any mystery, obscurity, or inexplicability in relation to this change, or any inability of the subject, outside of his own will or voluntary action. Nor is there the least intimation of any power, influence, or instrumentality in causal relation to this saving change, except the motive influence of the light of truth. And the same is true in respect to the conversion of Saul of Tarsus, of Cornelius the centurion, of the Philippian jailer, and of the three thousand on the day of Pentecost, and with respect to every conversion mentioned in the Bible.

Though most of these conversions were preceded or followed by miraculous circumstances, yet not one of these miracles is ever represented as the causal antecedent of any conversion, or moral change for the better. But in every case the circumstances prove that the miracles could have had no possible influence on the subjects of conversion, but by way of motive influence, to awaken their attention, or bring the light of truth to bear on their moral susceptibilities. And in every case, the truths of the higher law are set forth as the obvious and sole cause of the moral changes, or the conversions that took place at the time. In the case of Saul, he says of his conversion, "When the commandment came, sin revived and I died." "For the law of the Spirit of life in Christ Jesus hath made me free from the law of sin and death." In the case of Cornelius it is written, "While Peter yet spake these words, the Holy Ghost fell on all them which heard the word." Remember, the person of the Holy Ghost is constituted by God acting through and with the motive influence of his will, embodied or expressed in human language. In the case of the jailer, it is said that "They spake unto him the word of the Lord, and to all that were in his house." And the three thousand were pricked in heart only when they saw their own sin and guilt in crucifying the Lord of glory; but they did not believe till the love of God and his gracious promise to the fathers, was set in contrast before their minds. And so of every conversion mentioned in the Bible; the light of truth was the sole efficient cause of it.

CHAPTER VI.

SUMMARY OF RESULTS.

1st. WE learn from the discussion of the subject what the guilty sinner, under the light of the gospel, may and ought to do. When he feels the first painful twinge of conscious guilt, he may and ought to look to Jesus Christ, the one living and true God manifested in the flesh, giving himself a ransom for all, and illustrating the infinite perfection of his law on the cross of Calvary, and to receive a ray of the light of truth reflected from thence. A single ray will, in a moment, bleach out of his character every tinge of sinful pride, self-righteousness, self-complacency, and every high thing that exalteth itself against the knowledge of God, and will give him sweet and delightful peace of conscience. This is perfectly within the compass of his ability to perform, and just as easily performed as turning his back to the wind when too keen for his face. It is a perfectly plain and obvious duty, of which the sinner himself is conscious, and often resolves to perform at some future indefinite period. When he is persuaded and freely wills to do this, it is the easiest and pleasantest thing to do that ever was done by human agent in the flesh.

But the sinner long accustomed to evade or resist the light of truth will not do this as long as he can occupy his mind with sensual pleasures, or contrive an excuse for delay. The reason why he will not is seen in the law of sin and death, described in a preceding essay. That law having been once chosen, must govern, till the subject forms a new generic purpose of will to obey the law of the Spirit of life in Christ Jesus, or the perfect law of the Lord.

2d. We infer what the object of the Christian teacher of such sinners should be, how it must be effected, and with what instrumentality. His ultimate object should be, as soon as possible, to persuade, that is, morally constrain them by motive influence, to make this generic purpose of will, or this unconditional resolve of soul, to change their whole course of moral conduct, in obedience to the command of their Maker and Saviour. He will then perfectly concur in object and motive with the Holy Ghost, and become a co-worker with God for the salvation of sinners.

The method, and the only method of effecting this, is the one which Jesus pursued with Nicodemus and with Saul. The same that Paul and Silas took with the jailer, and Peter with the thousands on the day of Pentecost. They brought the great leading facts, or pervading truths of the sinner's condition, and of God's holy and gracious administration, into contact with the intellectual and moral endowments of their hearers. First, of the sinner's condition, the fact that all his sin, his guilt, his moral depravity, and every shade of moral deformity that darkens his character, including all his inability, physical, intellectual and moral, with all his ignorance and stupidity, are of his own contracting. He is the sole agent and accountable author of it all. His own voluntary agency brought it into existence, and was the sole, proximate, primary and efficient cause of its existence. He himself, with evil heart and wicked hands, has perpetrated the whole. Second, of God's administration, the fact of his infinite love, benevolence, pity and compassion, embodied in the provisions of his perfect law, illustrated on and reflected from the cross of Calvary. These two important facts, brought into contrast and presented to the carnal mind of the sinner, constitute the necessary and only efficient instrumentality in the case of such sinners. These are the two divine, motive factors which the Holy Ghost always employs to effect the saving change of regeneration. When these two facts, in connection, come in contact with the moral susceptibilities of any sinner in the flesh, he must quail, he will kneel, and pray, and submit, and become a sinner saved by grace.

3d. In this whole change, which constitutes the salvation of the sinner, there is no change of nature, no impartation of power, no conferring or increase of ability, no giving of new propensities, dispositions, inclinations, etc., *ab extra*, and no transference of character, of habits, or any moral qualities. These are all created, contracted or formed, by the subject to which they belong. But it is a change of moral character; and the change, and the character of the agent which is changed, are two distinct things, and must be conceived of as distinct things, if we would either think or speak intelligibly on the subject. The character changed is wholly and exclusively the creation of the human agent, both antecedent and subsequent to the change. The change is exclusively in the relation which the character sustains to the law of God. But the change is the creation of God, acting in the third person of the Godhead, the Holy Ghost. The motive influence of the light of truth, or of his holy will embodied in human language, is the sole cause of the change. This Holy Ghost and light of truth, this Author and instrument, are a perfect personal identity. There is no confounding or mingling of divine and human agencies; but a perfect opposition of action between them, antecedent to the commencement of the change in regeneration. A concurrence commences then, and increases as sanctification progresses, but the agencies continue perfectly distinct through the whole process of moral renovation, or as long as the subject continues in the flesh. There is nothing in this change, or in the whole process by which it is effected, of the nature of physical agency, physical power or force, causation or instrumentality. It is all in the moral sphere, a purely spiritual change. It is perfectly unique, without a parallel: because the only radical and entire change of the character of a free subject of moral government within the compass of our knowledge.

4th. No human being can be the subject of conversion, regeneration or sanctification, but a subject of moral government, who has actually transgressed the law and incurred guilt, and thus commenced the formation of a sinful character. This will exclude the millions of infants, idiots, etc., who pass out of the flesh before their intellectual and moral susceptibilities are sufficiently developed to give moral character to their actions. They need no moral renovation, because they have no moral character to be renovated or changed. Their physical organization has not animal life and strength or vitality sufficient for the development of manhood, of a moral agent, or a subject of moral government. They are, therefore, by the divine Redeemer, who gave himself a ransom for all, graciously removed out of this world of sin and misery, into another sphere of purer atmosphere, where they may develop their endowments out of the reach of temptation to sin. There they contract their moral character, meet for the inheritance of the saints in light. "For of such is the kingdom of God." Luke xviii. 16.

5th. No human agent, during his probation in the flesh, ever labors under any inability, either physical, intellectual or moral, to perform all duty, and fulfil all obligation, that can be imposed upon him; because no authority, power or sovereignty in the universe, can impose duty or obligation, in the least degree, beyond the ability of the subject to perform; for it is a natural impossibility for a human agent to feel obligation or discern duty beyond his ability to perform. Therefore, secondly, duty and obligation can not attach where ability of any kind is wanting. And, thirdly, because, whenever a human agent in the flesh does act, either in obeying or transgressing the law, he acts in possession and in exercise of, and employs all the ability that can be employed in fulfilment of all obligation. If he obeys, all duty and obligation are fulfilled, and all needful ability employed. If he disobeys, all the motive influences of the law of God, which are always present, paramount and greater than any possible motive influence to the contrary, are resisted, evaded and overcome: and, therefore, much more ability, physical, intellectual and moral, are necessarily put forth than was sufficient to have fulfilled all the duty and obligation the law could impose. "The way of transgressors is hard," because every trangression they commit costs them vastly more expenditure of ability, of every kind, than was necessary to have fulfilled all the law required. As the drunkard's first debauch of a single day costs him more wear and tear, of all his animal organs, than a whole year of temperate, healthful and useful living. And every repetition of the debauch requires a still greater expenditure of animal vitality and strength to work it off. So every transgression of the law of God, even the most secret sin of the soul, which is never developed into overt action, requires more expenditure of ability than to have obeyed the law. And all this strength of ability, which ought to have been employed in obedience, is converted into strength of sinful habit, by free, voluntary transgression against the paramount motive influence of all truth. No human agent has two sets of organization or endowments or abilities. Those endowments and abilities with which he does right, are identically the same with which he must do wrong if he will commit sin: and identically the same with which he must repent, believe, cease to do evil and learn to do well, and fulfil the whole righteousness of the law, in his own perfectly renovated, personal character, if he is ever saved.

Therefore, the cause of any human agent's committing sin, or of his continuing to commit sin, or of his not being converted on his first consciousness of guilt, or at any subsequent time, is never of the nature of inability, and never can be; but is always of the nature of positive agency, actual effort or efficiency put forth, in opposition to moral influence, and must necessarily be of this nature. To talk about the inability of sinners, on probation under the light of the gospel, to repent, believe, love God and perform all Christian duties, is simply preposterous. And to quote those passages of Scripture, which represent these Christian graces as the gift of God and the work of the Spirit, to prove the inability of sinners, is perverting and falsifying the word of God. God does give these graces, and every good and every perfect gift, and by his Spirit does work in all men both to will and do of his good pleasure, whenever they do any thing agreeable to his will. But he bestows these graces, and works all these good gifts, and every thing else in his moral kingdom, with the motive influence of the word of truth. This word of truth is always before the intellect of the gospel sinner.

6th. There is no incomprehensible mystery about the regeneration, conversion or sanctification of the sinner. No supernatural power, influence or agency, is ever put forth or employed in effecting the moral renovation of human character. The whole needed and saving change consists in ceasing to do evil and learning to do right. God persuades the sinner to do this, by presenting a few plain, simple facts to his intellectual and moral perception. This is effectual calling, regeneration and conversion. The necessary facts are so plain and simple that no human agent, who has ability to distinguish between right and wrong, or do either, can avoid understanding and feeling their saving motive influence, without greater effort and more expense of ability than to make a new heart and a new Spirit. Therefore, every sinner, if he will, may know and understand the whole process of moral renovation, and all the agency and instrumentality connected with it. If he is ignorant, it has cost him a continuous effort, from his first evil deed, to keep in the dark.

When the God of infinite wisdom, power and goodness, had created an innumerable race of intelligent moral agents, it was perfectly natural for him to put them under an infinitely perfect system of moral government, making adequate provision for their highest perfection and happiness. In doing this he must necessarily make adequate and perfect provision for every possible contingency incidental to such a system. The entrance of sin is such a contingency. Having made such provision, and the contingency having occurred, it was perfectly natural for this God, on the very day that sin by one man entered the world, to put in requisition his perfect provision of grace. It was perfectly natural for him, on that day, to assume the necessary personal relations towards the fallen race, and to commence the work of converting and saving sinners. This he did, on that very day, presenting himself, in the personal relations of Redeemer and Sanctifier, to the two first evil-doers of the human family. They were converted, repented, believed, were pardoned, were absolved, received into divine protection and instruction, for their complete moral renovation. And the very same truths were used on that day, in the conversion of our progenitors, which the same divine Agent addressed to Nicodemus in their night conference. The same that Peter preached to the thousands on the day of Pentecost: the same that slew Saul in the road to Damascus: the same that converted Cornelius and his friends; the jailer, and every other sinner that ever was converted. The seed of the woman should bruise the serpent's head. God so loved the world that he gave his only begotten Son. Addressed to guilty, convicted sinners. And this work and method of salvation is so perfectly natural and agreeable to the will of God, that he has never ceased, to this day, to pervade with the omnipresent light of his higher law every corner of his footstool where human intellect was ever developed to know the difference between right and wrong, or to commit sin. And he has never withdrawn his Spirit, or withheld the light of his truth, from any guilty sinner, till that sinner had enjoyed and ended a sufficient day of probation under his administration of grace. Nor has he ever ceased to do all that a God of infinite wisdom, power and goodness, can justly, equitably and consistently do, to convert and save the whole human race, and every individual of the human race. It is his declared will and pleasure that all men should be saved, and come to the knowledge of the truth. "Say unto them, As I live, saith the Lord God, I have no pleasure in the death of the wicked; but that the wicked turn from his way and live." Ezek. xxxiii. 11. "But he is in one mind, and who can turn him? and what his soul desireth, even that he doeth." Job xxiii. 13.

Therefore, no man on the earth having committed sin, ever did, or ever can die in his sins, or end his probation unconverted, with God's consent or by his direct agency, or by his neglecting to do any thing for him that God can justly or consistently do for his salvation. Every man that commits an evil deed, knows, or may know, by his own intuitive consciousness, if he will suffer the light of truth to reach his conscience, that he is guilty, and must repent and cease to do evil, or suffer the penal consequences of his evil doing. And every man knows, or may know if he will reflect a moment, that it is perfectly natural and consistent for infinite goodness to forgive sin, if justice can be satisfied, and the moral influence of the law maintained. And all men, without the least exception, know and believe as firmly as they believe their own existence, that whenever sin is committed or injury perpetrated, atonement is necessary to satisfy justice and preserve the moral influence of law; and that atonement is, or may be made in some way or another. Therefore, as soon as they are conscious of guilt, they go about to find or to make atonement, as naturally and as uniformly as they seek food to satisfy hunger. Even the most learned and zealous unitarians, who totally repudiate the idea of atonement for offences against the moral government of God, always claim it in their own case when they suffer injury, and acknowledge it in all other relations, except when their own evil deeds may be implicated. They never speak or write about the relations of human society, without affirming the necessity of atonement, whenever a proper occasion occurs.

God, on the day when Adam first sinned, revealed to the whole human family the true atonement, which taketh away the sin of the world, and thus provided that every individual of the race might know and understand it, and avail himself of the benefit, unless prevented by his own or his neighbor's fault. The tradition of this has never been wholly lost, that I know of, by any tribe or family of the race to this day. But mankind have been prone to turn away from this atonement, and try to make one themselves. The reason why so many decline or refuse to accept this atonement is a simple, plain, perfectly natural, and to every evil doer, a very powerful and adequate reason. This Lamb of God that taketh away the sin of the world, is the same offering by which the law of the Lord is magnified and made honorable, and its moral influence brought to bear on the carnal mind without destroying life. The evil doer can not, therefore, look to this atonement, without seeing the glorious light and infinite perfection of the higher law, the light of truth, the light of God. And this light immediately reflects his own deformed, polluted, odious character, which torments his guilty conscience.

The sight of this glorious light of the higher law, as magnified and illustrated in the cross of Christ, is death to the impenitent sinner. A single flash of it killed Saul of Tarsus, in a moment. Says he, "I was alive without the law once, but when the commandment came sin revived, and I died." It was a moral death, a very natural death, a timely death, and, therefore, a saving death. And this light of the higher law, which slew the guilty Saul, proved to be the light of life to his soul. And he was led into Damascus a regenerated man. To him it was the power of God unto salvation: the law of the Spirit of life in Christ Jesus, freeing him from the law of sin and death. He was effectually persuaded, and found ability in himself to embrace Christ, to cease doing evil and learn to do well, by proclaiming this same Redeemer and his atoning blood to others for their salvation.

Now, there is no inexplicable mystery about this subject, except in the infinity of the love of God to sinful men. Every person of common sense may, if he will, understand the whole agency, instrumentality and process, as easily and as perfectly, as he can find the way across the street to the theatre, the museum, or the church-door. Even the child of ten years may understand the whole, if plainly stated to him. For the Holy Ghost, in this whole work of saving sinners by their moral renovation, uses the very same instrumentality, and pursues the same method, which your child of ten years, uses to change your generic purpose of will, or persuade you, to give him a ride, or get him a new garment. The Spirit just presents to the intellectual and moral sensibilities of the subject a few plain facts, involving and illustrating the condition of the subject, and the necessity and importance of the change. The child knows how intuitively, and does precisely the same thing in the same method, to produce a similar change in the generic purpose, or will of the parent. And the sinner, who becomes the subject of this saving change, goes through the very same process, and no other or different process of feeling, emotions and volitions, which the offending child passes through, in becoming reconciled to, and securing the favor of his offended parent. He believes the truths his parent presents to his perception. He is sorry for and repents of his faults; and resolves and promises to amend his ways in the future. The converted sinner can do no more. The only conceivable difference is in the magnitude and importance of the interests involved, and the consequences to follow. In the one case, they are comparatively very trifling, and very limited in extent and duration; in the other, they are to human conception of infinite importance, and unbounded both in extent and duration. Therefore, Jesus Christ, the divine Saviour, presents the case of the child and the converted sinner, as in all other respects, exact parallels. "Verily I say unto you, Except ye be converted, and become as little children, ye shall not enter into the kingdom of heaven." Matt. xviii. 3.

Where now are the inexplicable dogmas, which have, for ages, enveloped this whole subject, in profound mysticism, and filled the Church with contention, strife and bloodshed? Where are the dogmas of original sin, of guilt antecedent to moral action, of total depravity antecedent to transgression, of entire inability, of innate moral pollution, and sin judicially inflicted on innocent babes in punishment of Adam's transgression? Where is the covenant made thousands of years before the parties existed? Where are the representatives, who commit sin by proxy, and contract guilt for their principals, thousands of years before their constituents come into existence? Where are the relations, that existed and imposed duty and obligation, before the subjects of these same relations commenced existence? Where the one God that exists in three persons, and begets his Son by eternal generation? Where is the supernatural power and special influence of the almighty and unchangeable God? Or where is the sentence, the word or phrase, in the Bible, that teaches or suggests one of these absurd contradictions or mysticisms? In the light of divine, revealed truth, and common sense, all these mysticisms vanish into metaphysical romance and theological fiction. Not one of these inexplicable dogmas can be expressed, or any conception of it, presented to the human mind, by all the words in the Bible, put together in all the myriads of forms of which they are capable, without the addition of some other word, or words, of human invention, to express these fictions of depraved human imagination. It can not, therefore, be reasonably supposed, that any of these dogmas belong to, or sustain any relation, to the system of Christian doctrine, taught in the Bible.

But, divested of these mysticisms, the subject of the sinner's character, condition and destiny, becomes a plain, common sense matter, of practical duty and obligation, between him and his Maker; just as easily understood and performed, when seriously attempted, as the duties of any other relation. We have sinned and incurred guilt, or desert of penal suffering, by transgressing a perfect law. This every sinner is as conscious of as he is of his own existence. And that indestructible image of God, in which every human agent was created, consisting of those moral susceptibilities which we call conscience, or the moral sense, includes all the agency, the whole material, and the entire instrumentality and efficiency, for the production of all the misery, torment and suffering, indicated in the Bible, by everlasting punishment, the lake of fire and brimstone, the wine of the wrath of God, and all the horror-exciting metaphors of that class. And the higher law, with all the motive influences of eternal unchangeable truth, is ever ready, the moment the impenitent leaves the flesh, to excite and kindle the everlasting burnings. And the same identical image of God, which is essential to the nature and existence of every human agent, includes also the whole agency and material for the production of all the glory and felicity indicated by the kingdom of heaven, kingdom of God, love of God, fellowship of Christ, communion of the Holy Ghost, and eternal life; and by all the hope-inspiring metaphors of the Bible. And the same perfect law is ever ready, the moment you submit your will to the law of the Spirit of life in Christ Jesus, to kindle this felicity, and give you as much of heaven as you are capable of receiving, till you enter its gates of pearl.

God has done all that infinite wisdom, power and goodness

could do, to save you and every sinner of the human race. All this is implied in every invitation of the gospel. If the sinner will turn, he shall live. If he will not turn, neither omnipotence, nor super-omnipotence, nor any nor all special influences, forces and powers in the universe can save him. "Look unto me, and be ye saved, all the ends of the earth: for I am God, and there is none else." Isa. xlv. 22. "As I live, saith the Lord God, I have no pleasure in the death of the wicked: but that the wicked turn from his way and live: turn ye, turn ye from your evil ways; for why will ye die?" Ezek. xxxiii. 11.

CONCLUSION.

The result of this whole discussion may now be stated in a very small compass, and be contemplated at a single view.

1st. These primary, fundamental and essential doctrines of Christianity have, for ages, been obscured, perverted, emasculated, and often entirely divested of their natural and appropriate motive influence, in converting and saving sinners, and meliorating the condition of human society. This has been effected by adding to them, mingling up with them, and endeavoring to illustrate them, by whole categories of unmeaning, inexplicable and incomprehensible fictions, which have no foundation, ground or existence, either in the nature or relations of things, created or uncreated, and which are, therefore, necessarily absolute falsehoods.

2d. The only tendency of the motive influence of falsehood is to excite human agents to commit sin, incur guilt and increase misery. And these falsehoods have been so long iterated and reiterated, from the pulpit, the pen, the press, in creeds, in catechisms and symbols of faith, enforced by all the authority of imperial edicts, the decrees of general Councils, Popes, Bishops, Synods and Assemblies of Divines, that they have given to the public sentiment of Christendom, that is, to the manner and habits of thinking, reasoning, willing and acting, of vast multitudes, even whole communities and nations, calling themselves Christians, a very strong and predominating tendency to estimate things falsely, choose evil courses, and persist in the most sinful pursuits and habits.

3d. But these inexplicable, incomprehensible and unmeaning dogmas of mysticism, fiction and falsehood, have been invented, affirmed and taught, as being religious truths, fundamental and essential doctrines of the gospel of Jesus Christ, divine truths, revealed by God himself to the children of men, for their salvation ; and, therefore, to be believed and practically obeyed, on pain of everlasting punishment. Being thus taught and enforced, they are, of course, assented to by vast multitudes, as religious and divine truths, (though they have no conception at the time of any definite meaning to which they are assenting or professing to believe,) and, of course, these fictions bring into exercise, excite and control all the religious endowments, susceptibilities, emotions and passions of their living, immortal souls. And the religious susceptibilities of the living soul, being thus brought under the direction and control of the motive influences of falsehood, naturally and necessarily combine and concur with the depraved animal instincts, appetites and passions, in the pursuit, defence or justification of any interest, habit or practice, however wrong, unjust, sinful and destructive. Thus all the endowments of the human agent, intellectual, moral and physical, combining his entire efficiency, through the motive influence of falsehood, may be engaged sincerely, conscientiously and religiously, in the most vile, sinful and pernicious enterprise or action, while the deluded sinner thinks he is doing right, rendering God service, and conferring benefits on his fellow creatures.

4th. Such is the infatuation, or lunacy, which inspired the conspiracy, and now stimulates the suicidal rebellion and civil war against the government of this nation. Having, in the introduction, described the process by which such infatuation results, from assenting to unmeaning fictions and falsehoods as divine truth, we need not repeat it here.

5th. No person, who wishes to know or is willing to know, can avoid knowing that the institution of chattel slavery, as it exists in the southern States, and is defended and justified by the inexplicable dogmas of universal predestination, and of the transfer of moral character and desert, by natural generation or divine imputation, is the sole proximate cause, the only political cause, the entire commercial or pecuniary cause, and the only municipal or social cause, of the present causeless, inexcusable, and foolish war; and that no other interest, right, privilege or prerogative is questioned, or can be decided by the conflict. And every human agent, who has fairly begun to develop human nature, manhood, moral agency or accountability, knows intuitively and necessarily that there is a moral cause, antecedent to, or lying back of all these proximate causes, some motive influence, good or bad, truth or falsehood, some extensive, powerful and long-continued influence, so shaping and perverting public sentiment as to render such infatuation, and such destructive, fiend-like conflicts, possible in Christian communities. If the public sentiment of Christendom was shaped by the pure motive influence of revealed truth, or if every Christian nation (so called) were truly evangelized, such conflicts would not be possible among Christian people. The true moral cause, or ultimate antecedent of the present war, is, therefore, to be found only in those inexplicable and incomprehensible dogmas of mysticism, which we have endeavored to describe and repudiate in the preceding essays. The same is the true reason why the whole world has not been evangelized ages ago: and which still hinder, and must continue to hinder, the conversion of the world, till the gospel of Christ is entirely divested of such dogmas. For what greater progress can we hope that the gospel of Christ will make, while these fictions, in which it is wrapt up, corrupted and perverted, are vastly more numerous than the simple propositions necessary to teach the whole gospel of salvation, and infinitely complicated? That it has made any progress at all, in converting sinners and saving the world for fourteen centuries, is perfect demonstration that it is divine, omnipotent and saving. Let the leaders, teachers and rulers of the Church, think on these things.

www.ingramcontent.com/pod-product-compliance
Lightning Source LLC
Chambersburg PA
CBHW031952230426
43672CB00010B/2132